SOCIAL WORK

Sara Miller McCune founded SAGE Publishing in 1965 to support the dissemination of usable knowledge and educate a global community. SAGE publishes more than 1000 journals and over 800 new books each year, spanning a wide range of subject areas. Our growing selection of library products includes archives, data, case studies and video. SAGE remains majority owned by our founder and after her lifetime will become owned by a charitable trust that secures the company's continued independence.

Los Angeles | London | New Delhi | Singapore | Washington DC | Melbourne

SOCIAL WORK

From Assessment to Intervention

PHILIP HESLOP
CATHRYN MEREDITH

SAGE

Los Angeles | London | New Delhi
Singapore | Washington DC | Melbourne

Los Angeles | London | New Delhi
Singapore | Washington DC | Melbourne

SAGE Publications Ltd
1 Oliver's Yard
55 City Road
London EC1Y 1SP

SAGE Publications Inc.
2455 Teller Road
Thousand Oaks, California 91320

SAGE Publications India Pvt Ltd
B 1/I 1 Mohan Cooperative Industrial Area
Mathura Road
New Delhi 110 044

SAGE Publications Asia-Pacific Pte Ltd
3 Church Street
#10-04 Samsung Hub
Singapore 049483

First published 2019

Editor: Kate Keers
Assistant editor: Talulah Hall
Production editor: Victoria Nicholas
Marketing manager: Camille Richmond
Cover design: Wendy Scott
Typeset by: C&M Digitals (P) Ltd, Chennai, India
Printed in the UK

Library of Congress Control Number: 2018943077

British Library Cataloguing in Publication data

A catalogue record for this book is available from the British Library

ISBN 978-1-5264-2448-8
ISBN 978-1-5264-2449-5 (pbk)

At SAGE we take sustainability seriously. Most of our products are printed in the UK using responsibly sourced papers and boards. When we print overseas we ensure sustainable papers are used as measured by the PREPS grading system. We undertake an annual audit to monitor our sustainability.

TABLE OF CONTENTS

ABOUT THE AUTHORS

PHILIP HESLOP (PHIL)

I have been a social worker since 1992 and chose social work as a profession to challenge inequality and discrimination. I have worked mainly in childcare social work, and from 1995, specifically in fostering and adoption. I have worked in statutory, voluntary and independent social work and have worked in all four countries of the UK. I developed a specialism working with male carers, as well as caring for children on the autism spectrum. Having held a wide range of practice, training, reviewing and management roles, I am also a passionate educator. I am qualified to teach adults and children, have been an NVQ assessor and am a Fellow of the Higher Education Academy. I completed a PhD on foster fathers through Durham University, and joined Northumbria University's teaching team in 2013. I teach across all social work programmes, focusing particularly on social work assessments and interventions. I supervise PhD students, and I am currently principal investigator on an evaluation of simulation-based learning in social work programmes.

CATHRYN MEREDITH (CAT)

I qualified as a social worker in 2001, and went on to practise in a variety of mental health settings. I became an Approved Social Worker (ASW) and later an Approved Mental Health Professional (AMHP). I developed a specialism in working with people diagnosed with emotionally unstable personality disorder and self-harming and suicidal behaviours. I qualified as a Best Interests Assessor (BIA), and went on to become a local authority Mental Capacity Act lead. From 2013 until its closure, I was a College of Social Work accredited Expert Safeguarding Adults Practitioner. I left practice in 2013, to teach and research at Northumbria University. I teach across all qualifying and post-qualifying social work programmes, focusing particularly on social work with adults, mental capacity, adult safeguarding and mental health. I am a Fellow of the Higher Education Academy and I am currently completing a PhD, which explores how adult safeguarding is performed with people experiencing dementia.

ACKNOWLEDGEMENTS

Philip ~ For Cath and my adult children Joe, Simon and Siobhan and my granddaughter Lucy Heslop and her mam, Kayleigh. Thank you. Also in memory of Maureen Heslop, Brian and Maureen Dowling.

Cathryn ~ For my loves, Stew and Mia, and for Sarah Beer and Alan C. who taught me most about social work. Thank you.

We would both like to thank Kate Keers for getting us here!

INTRODUCTION

Social work is about making sense of complex and difficult situations so that we can understand how to navigate towards solutions. We assess to inform decisions about how to intervene with people in situations of need and risk, and the decisions that we make can have an enormous impact on their lives. We need to understand how to skilfully incorporate a range of knowledge, theories and interventions so that our practice is robust and informed, and results in credible, evidenced-based judgements. This book is an accessible, comprehensive resource that will support you develop in-depth knowledge and understanding of social work assessment and interventions. Whether you are undertaking your social work training, are in the early years of practice, or are a more experienced social worker attending to your continuing professional development (CPD), this book will equip you with the skills you need to assess and intervene effectively. We reference a range of key theories that can inform and enhance assessment and intervention, drawing particularly on contemporary knowledge about social work practice. Initiatives and innovations age, alter and change; however, a constant feature of social work is making sense of complex problems and intervening to make a positive difference. In short: assessing to intervene.

SOCIAL WORK IS EVOLVING

It is rather clichéd to say social work is in flux; our professional history has been about change. Social work exists at the crossroads where social issues and social change intersect, and whilst there is a need for the profession, it always will. Whilst there is much political debate about the extent, nature and cause of social issues, there is no doubt that they are complex and problematic. Social work takes a central role in helping society to address these issues. It has progressed from its origins as a voluntary, charitable activity, to a highly regulated profession. Our role has become increasingly focused on safeguarding vulnerable children and adults from abuse and neglect, and in situations where significant harm or fatality occur, the profession comes under intense scrutiny and criticism.

To ensure that social workers are accountable and equipped for increasingly complex practice, professional standards and guidance have rapidly expanded. The Professional Capabilities Framework (PCF), first implemented by The College of Social Work in 2012, sets out consistent expectations for social workers at every stage in their career, from initial social work training, through to continuing professional development after qualification (BASW, 2018). Since 2014, the Chief Social Workers for England have been introducing a series of Knowledge and Skills

Statements (KSS) setting out the expectations for social workers in specific roles and settings (Department for Education, 2014; Department of Health, 2015). The PCF and the KSS emphasise that in every practice setting, and at every career stage, social workers must be able to use their knowledge and skills to assess and intervene effectively in people's lives.

Social work education must provide conditions that enable students to apply knowledge and skills in practice. Until 2010, traditional university programmes consisting of teaching and practice placements presented the sole route to qualifying as a social worker; however UK social work education is evolving at a rapid pace and several models and routes are now available. *Step Up to Social Work, Frontline* and *Think Ahead* are all fast track, work-based, postgraduate routes. *Social Work Teaching Partnerships* are accredited collaborations between Higher Education Institutions (HEIs) and statutory employers, which aim to ensure teaching is informed by the contemporary demands and requirements of practice, and employers are committed to creating and sustaining learning cultures for their social work workforce. Social work apprenticeships will provide a further, undergraduate, work-based route to qualification.

The context of social work practice has never been more challenging. The political and economic climate of austerity has created an increased demand for social work interventions, and reduced public spending means that we are required to do more with less. A United Nations inquiry found that people with disabilities have been disproportionately affected by UK austerity policies (United Nations Committee on the Rights of Persons with Disabilities, 2016). Across the UK, people who are disabled are more likely to be unemployed, live in poverty, experience crime, and die than non-disabled people (EHRC, 2017a). UK citizens are living longer, requiring more support to maintain independence and quality of life; however, many local authorities have seen their adult social care budgets cut by up to 30% in real terms (ADASS, 2017). Early preventative support for children and families has been reduced, and since 2004 there has been an 18% increase in the number of looked after children (The Children's Society, 2015). During 2016/2017 an estimated 1.2 million people used food banks (Trussell Trust, 2017).

In 2017 the British Association of Social Workers (BASW) produced a Manifesto for Social Work, calling on the government to support the profession to better meet people's needs by ending austerity and ensuring that social workers have manageable workloads, effective organisational models and the right working conditions for best practice (BASW, 2017). In January 2018, the Department of Health was renamed the Department of Health and Social Care. This development has been positively received within the profession, seeming to demonstrate that central government is at last recognising the importance of social care, and its intrinsic relationship with health care (Dennis, 2018).

OUR MOTIVATION

This book has been written by two people of different genders and ages, who qualified as social workers in different decades, and practised in very different fields. We began teaching on Northumbria University's social work programmes during the same academic year, located in the same office. Like most social workers we are great talkers, and it naturally followed that we began to share our experiences and reflect together on the process of transitioning from *doing* to *teaching* social work. We found we shared many commonalities which motivated us to write this book. When reflecting on our teaching experiences, we noticed that many students approached assessment as a task to be completed as quickly as possible in order to get onto doing what they perceived as 'real social work' – intervening. We also found that when we visited students during their practice placements, although they could describe their practice in great detail, they struggled to relate theory to it. People who are drawn to a career in social work are invariably problem solvers, but we suspected that some students were attempting to resolve situations before they had made sense of them. As social work educators and the authors of this book, our strong commitment is to demonstrate that effective interventions are constructed when they are informed by analytical assessments and theoretical knowledge.

We recognise that it can feel uncomfortable to stay in that space of not knowing. Social workers never have the luxury of time, and can feel enormous pressure to fix a situation and move onto the next. However, a fix is unlikely to be effective if it is not based on evidence and tailored to the individual situation. Professional curiosity is one of a social worker's most important tools. In our practice, we reach points where we have to take decisions based on the evidence that we have, but this does not mean that we have nothing more to discover and our understanding is complete. Throughout the full duration of our involvement with a person or family, we must continue to be curious, gathering and analysing information that may challenge and cause us to change our previous understandings.

STRUCTURE OF THE TEXT

Assessments and interventions are not linear processes, they overlap and repeat. Whilst assessing we intervene, and each intervention model invariably involves assessment in some form. The structure of this book reflects its title: *From Assessment to* Intervention. Part I, *Assessments: Making Sense and Planning to Act,* builds clearly and logically through to Part II, *Interventions: Now Let's Go and Help People*. There is enormous pressure on social workers to 'get things right', but we do not develop an ability to do this simply by qualifying to practise. Social workers never stop professionally developing; our practice and our thinking evolve over time in response to our experiences. Throughout this book, we share examples from our own practice in sections called **Author's Experience**, to model how reflection supports practice. You will see that we did not always get things right; however, reflection, supervision and tapping into further sources of knowledge helped us to learn and improve.

As social work educators, we understand that learning is more effective when knowledge is contextualised, allowing consideration of how skills, theory and research are applied in practice situations. To give life and context to the learning offered, we have populated this book with case studies involving the residents of a cul-de-sac and entitled these **Residents' Experiences**. We take an *across social work* approach, exploring social issues and experiences which may bring the residents into contact with social workers within local authorities, the National Health Service and Private and Voluntary Organisations, and a *through the life course* approach, visiting residents at different points of their lives to demonstrate how their needs and responses change over time. At the beginning of each chapter, we set out how its content relates to the current professional standards frameworks for social work – the British Association of Social Workers (BASW) Professional Capabilities Framework (PCF) and the Department of Health and Social Care Knowledge and Skills Statements (KSS).

Contents

PART I Assessments: Making Sense and Planning to Act

Chapter 1: Definitions and principles of assessment

This chapter explores the expectations of our profession, and considers just what the task of assessment is. We explore key approaches, models and principles, and define key values and concepts that will be referred to throughout the book.

Chapter 2: Social work's evolving context: a brief history

This chapter offers insights into social work's contemporary identity by considering its historical evolution. We follow social work from its charitable beginnings, through to the establishment of the welfare state, regulation and professionalisation, demonstrating how assessment practice has been shaped by changing times, attitudes and social policy.

Chapter 3: Risk and professional judgement

This chapter considers how concepts of risk are constructed and recognises the circumstances that can result in defensive practice and act as a barrier to effective professional decisions. We explore features of professional judgements, notions of professional autonomy and accountability, and discuss approaches and models of decision making.

Chapter 4: Assessing children, young people and families

This chapter begins with a brief history of childcare social work practice, highlighting key legislation and exploring public debates. We consider safeguarding children, young people and their families from risk and harm, reflect on assessment perspectives, and explore notions of childhood, family and gender.

Chapter 5: Assessing adults' needs

This chapter briefly outlines the history of adult social work policy and practice and considers human rights. It sets out how adults and carers are assessed, exploring key concepts of wellbeing, autonomy, personalisation and mental capacity. We then consider critical issues when assessing people with disabilities, older people, people experiencing mental distress and safeguarding adults.

Chapter 6: Planning, reviews, flexibility and supervision

This chapter sets out the principles for planning responses, explaining how to incorporate outcomes and considering plans for children and adults. We recognise the need to be flexible, as well as process savvy, and then move on to explore integrated and concurrent elements of our practice, reviews and supervision.

Part II Interventions: Now Let's Go and Help People

Chapter 7: Intervening as a social worker

This chapter includes information on key professional skills and values for social work interventions. We recognise social work practice can be challenging as well as rewarding, and reflect on professional resilience and the need for social workers to consider their personal wellbeing.

Chapter 8: Relationships, systems and complexity

This chapter provides a practice-orientated summary of systemic approaches. We focus on relationships in professional practice, offering different theoretical perspectives including general systems theory, family therapy, ecological systems theory, attachment, complexity, chaos and intersectionality. We detail how to use practice tools, such as genograms and ecomaps.

Chapter 9: Intervening during a crisis

This chapter explores the nature and stages of crisis and considers social work responsibilities and responses. We detail knowledge and approaches that social workers can use to support people when intervening during a crisis.

Chapter 10: Task-centred interventions

In this chapter, we identify how task-centred approaches were developed. We explore the concept of recovery, and reflect on the power imbalance between social workers and people who use services to consider how we should construct our professional response. We then explore each of the interlinking stages of task-centred practice in detail.

Chapter 11: Strengths and solution-focused interventions

This chapter recognises how strengths and solution-focused approaches can present social workers with the opportunities to be catalysts of change, empowering people by encouraging hope and identifying and suggesting ways forward. We consider a wide range of different tools and techniques including Signs of Safety, Motivational Interviewing, Brief Solution-Focused Therapy, Inquiry and Three Conversations.

Chapter 12: Working with groups and group work

In this chapter, we identify how social workers operate within multiple groups and argue that awareness of the theoretical perspectives of groups is essential to contemporary practice. We provide guidance on different group work skills which can inform professional social work practice whether or not we are undertaking formal group work.

THE CUL-DE-SAC

This book is rooted in practice, and we have populated it with case studies involving the residents of an urban cul-de-sac who represent a cross section of the UK population. The cul-de-sac comprises of six ex-local authority homes in a post-industrial city, some rented, some owner-occupied. The narratives and experiences of the residents and their extended networks give life and context to the learning offered, enabling you to consider how theory, research and practice experience can be applied to their situations.

NUMBER 1

Mary lives alone.

NUMBER 2

Alfie and Suzie are a different gender couple of foster carers who offer placements for up to three children.

NUMBER 3

Maureen and Claire are a same gender couple who have a blended family made up of their children from previous relationships, Harry, Sam and Asif.

NUMBER 4

Olivia lives with her children, Matty and Georgia. Georgia has learning disabilities and Olivia is her full time carer.

NUMBER 5

Max and Samantha are a different gender couple with a daughter, Tyra

HOUSE 6

Liam, Sally and Adnan are three young adult care leavers with multiple occupant tenancy.

PART I

ASSESSMENTS: MAKING SENSE AND PLANNING TO ACT

1 DEFINITIONS AND PRINCIPLES OF ASSESSMENT

Learning in this chapter relates to

PCF	KSS Adult Services	KSS Child & Family
1. Professionalism 2. Values & Ethics 5. Knowledge 6. Critical Reflection & Analysis 8. Contexts & Organisations	3. Person-centred practice 4. Safeguarding 6. Effective assessments & outcome-based support planning 7. Direct work with individuals & families 8. Supervision, critical reflection & analysis 9. Organisational context	5. Effective direct work with children & families 6. Child & family assessment 11. Organisational context

INTRODUCTION

Assessing, or making sense of situations, is an ordinary human activity: we *all* assess situations to identify problems and find solutions. For social workers, assessment is the tool through which we make sense of a situation in order to inform professional judgements. Like social work itself, assessment can be described as a 'complex' activity (Adams et al., 2009). In this chapter, we explore the expectations of our profession, which have evolved in response to our increasing focus on safeguarding, leading to overarching standards of practice. We look at approaches to social work assessments, exploring key models and principles. Finally, we define some of the key values and concepts which inform all social work assessments.

THE EXPECTATIONS OF UK SOCIAL WORK

Social work can be an elusive concept to understand. Our roles are many and varied – they have to be, because we work with people across the life course, from babies through to older people. The British Association of Social Workers (BASW) uses the International Federation of Social Workers (IFSW) definition as the basis for UK social work practice.

> Social work is a practice-based profession and an academic discipline that promotes social change and development, social cohesion, and the empowerment and liberation of people. Principles of social justice, human rights, collective responsibility and respect for diversities are central to social work. Underpinned by theories of social work, social sciences, humanities and indigenous knowledge, social work engages people and structures to address life challenges and enhance wellbeing. (IFSW, 2017)

'Social worker' is a legally protected title, which may only be used by a person registered with an appropriate regulatory body. Regulatory bodies are responsible for setting professional standards, holding the professional register, approving initial education and training courses for social workers and operating 'fitness to practise' systems. In the UK, the social work regulators are the Scottish Social Services Council, Social Care Wales, the Northern Ireland Social Care Council, and in England the newly established Social Work England (having replaced the Health and Care Professions Council).

The social work profession's standards are set out in the Professional Capabilities Framework and the Chief Social Workers' Knowledge and Skills Statements. It is crucial that professional standards exist, to set clear and consistent expectations of social work practice. However, standards must help the profession to flourish and continually develop, rather than stifling it through narrow prescription. Social work has become increasingly concerned with anticipating and responding to situations where there is a risk of harm in order to safeguard children and adults, to the extent where safeguarding has achieved paramountcy over all other social work tasks. The consequences of '*getting it wrong*' are extremely high, and therefore the inherent pressure can engender anxiety in both individual practitioners and whole agencies. Guidance and requirements intended to ensure consistency and minimise error have imposed rigid timescales, targets and statistical performance indicators. Operationalising these requirements can result in procedural and managerial approaches reliant on pro formas, electronic record management systems and inflexible assessment tools, rather than professional judgement and discretion. In these conditions, social workers can lose their professional autonomy and feel that their knowledge and skills have been devalued (Galpin, 2016). There is much evidence that children and adults who have experienced procedural models of safeguarding have found it impersonal and excluding.

THE PROFESSIONAL CAPABILITIES FRAMEWORK (PCF)

The PCF is the underpinning framework of social work practice in England. It is a visual tool that promotes social work as one profession, setting out the capabilities expected of social

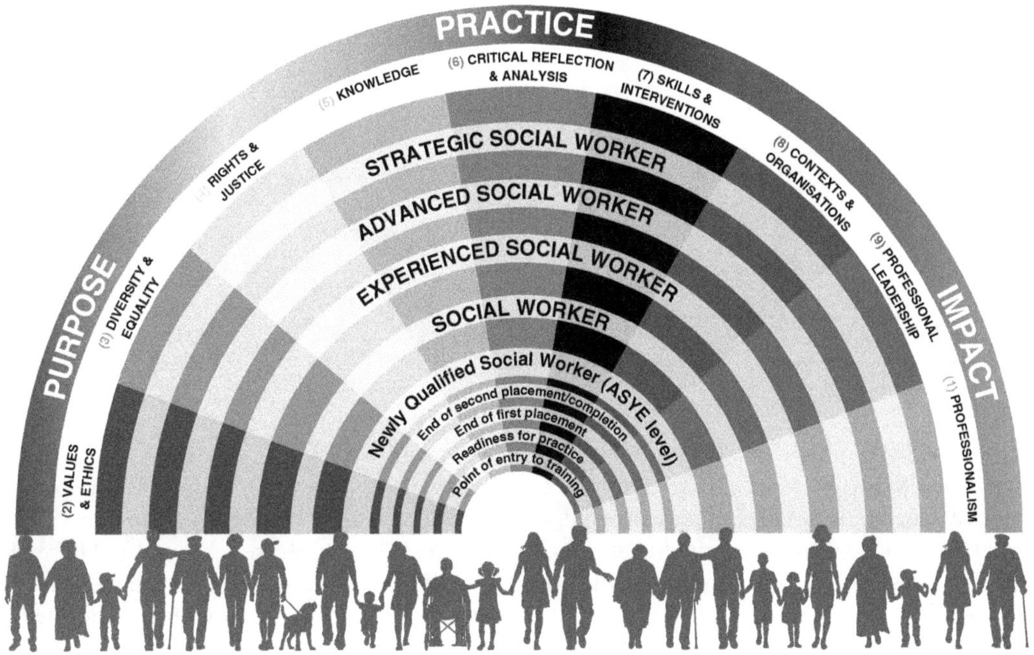

Figure 1.1 The Professional Capabilities Framework

Source: Published with kind permission of BASW – www.basw.co.uk

workers across all fields, all levels of practice and all stages of career. BASW is the custodian of the PCF, and in 2018 it launched a refreshed version of the framework (see Figure 1.1).

The refreshed PCF has three, overarching themes:

- The *purpose* of social work; its values, ethics and commitment to equalities, diversity, rights and social justice.
- The *practice* of social work with individuals, families and communities: its distinctive knowledge base, its application of reflection and critical analysis and the development of specific interventions and skills.
- The wider *impact* of social work through leadership, professionalism and influence at organisational and other contextual levels (BASW, 2018).

Each theme is subdivided into domains of capabilities, i.e. the knowledge, skills, behaviours and values required for effective social work practice. There are nine domains in total:

1. Professionalism
2. Values & Ethics
3. Diversity & Equality
4. Rights & Justice
5. Knowledge

6. Critical Reflection & Analysis
7. Skills & Interventions
8. Contexts & Organisations
9. Professional Leadership

Assessment permeates the whole PCF, but is most explicitly apparent within the *Practice* theme and the *Critical Reflection & Analysis* domain.

THE KNOWLEDGE AND SKILLS STATEMENTS (KSS)

Unlike the PCF, which takes an *across the profession* approach, the Knowledge and Skills Statements describe what a social worker should know, and be able to do, within specific practice settings and roles. The Knowledge and Skills Statements are issued by the Chief Social Workers, following consultation with the profession and those who use it. There are separate Chief Social Workers for Adults and for Children and Families, and therefore KSS are specific to practice with either children and families *or* adults. A number of Knowledge and Skills Statements have been produced, e.g. *Knowledge and Skills Statements for Practice Leaders and Practice Supervisors* (Department for Education, 2015a), *Knowledge and Skills Statement: Achieving Permanence* (Department for Education, 2016). Within this book we will focus on the two KSS with the broadest application for our readers, i.e. *Knowledge and Skills for Child and Family Social Work* (Department for Education, 2014), *Knowledge and Skills Statement for Social Workers in Adult Services* (Department of Health, 2015).

THE RELATIONSHIP BETWEEN THE PCF AND THE KSS

In early 2018, BASW's Chief Executive and the Chief Social Workers issued a joint statement clarifying that the PCF and KSS are intended to be used in conjunction with each other to guide everyday practice, with the KSS mapped onto the domains of the *Practice* theme of the PCF, *Knowledge, Critical Reflection & Analysis* and *Skills & Interventions*:

> ... the PCF is the overarching framework for social work in England, from pre-qualifying to strategic levels, across all practice areas. BASW now hosts the PCF, on behalf of the profession. The KSS have been developed by the Chief Social Workers to set out what is expected of qualified social workers in specific practice settings and roles. Both the PCF and the KSS have been developed by the profession through extensive engagement with social workers at all levels, representative bodies and the public.

> Together, the PCF and KSS provide the foundation for social work education and practice in England at qualifying and post-qualifying levels and are used to inform recruitment, workforce development, performance appraisal and career progression. (BASW et al., 2018).

APPROACHES TO, AND PRINCIPLES OF, ASSESSMENT

We all assess, all the time. It is simply an everyday human activity, crucial to decisions such as 'what will I have for breakfast?' or 'is it safe to cross the road?' Unfortunately, assessments are not always accurate or successful, and therefore we will sometimes make the wrong decision about our breakfast, or more significantly, when to cross the road! To assess is to gather and use information to form an opinion; it is synonymous with judgement, evaluation, calculation, analysis and estimation. When we enter social work education, we already have the ability to assess, but through our training, we transition from making everyday *personal* assessments, to making *professional* assessments, the objective of which is to make robust, accurate and defensible judgements, founded on analysis of evidence. This professional assessment is a completely new level.

Social work is a highly personal profession: just think about how you assessed whether or not to enter it.

EXERCISE 1.1

- When can you first remember considering becoming a social worker?
- What influenced you to think about this?
- Did you consider any other careers? If so, why did you choose social work over them?
- What do you want to achieve by being a social worker?
- Has your experience of social work education changed your views and aspirations? How?

You may have been motivated by personal experiences or events, by negative or positive interactions with social work, by the experiences or examples of people close to you. You will have an emotional or cognitive rationale for choosing this career, and it will be individual to you. This personalised approach to practice should be appreciated and valued. How much awareness social workers have of their own theoretical approaches and personal values is difficult to determine, as we often struggle to recognise how much our internalised histories, values and theoretical preferences relate to our social work practice. Hennessey (2011) recommends that students studying social work complete a visual tool called a lifeline (we will explore lifelines in Chapter 8) to identify and reflect upon the significant events of their life from birth to the start of their training. Knowledge of this context is critical because the 'theoretical approach taken by social workers and the agencies in which they work influences the assessment process in a similar way to personal values and belief systems' (Parker and Bradley, 2014: 8).

AUTHOR'S EXPERIENCE (PHIL)

As a newly qualified social worker, I was very happy to receive a thank you from a woman I had never met. She reminded me that we had spoken on the telephone a while ago, and told me how grateful she had been to talk to me at a time when something was bothering her a great deal. Although I was very pleased to hear I had helped, to be completely honest, I could not recollect the conversation. I must have said or done something right, if only by instinct. We do not always realise when our actions have impact. The telephone call had not seemed significant enough for me to remember, but it had been extremely significant to her.

SOCIAL WORK ASSESSMENTS

Social work assessments are concerned with professional judgements, risk identification, case management and decision making that are professionally and sometimes publicly accountable (Rutter and Brown, 2015). A simple reliance on the practitioner's perspective is ineffective and not tailored to the person's needs or situation. Acting instinctively, intuitively or without pause for reflection, does not enable us as social workers to make sense of and/or look for alternative problems, solutions or ways forward (note that Munro (2011) discusses professional intuition, which is grounded in practice experience and not personal intuition: we will return to this theme later in the book). The act of assessment rises to a new, professional level through the gathering of information, incorporation of theory and consideration of different views and perspectives to construct knowledge and enable the practitioner to understand what is happening. Parker (2017) argues that assessments are both subjective art and objective science; we concur that they are neither exclusively subjective nor objective, but rather a combination of the two.

The tasks of social work are very practical: we use our skills to engage and communicate with people and seek to help make a difference to their lives. However, a complex intellectual process is also at play, whereby we reflect on the information we are gathering and analyse it in conjunction with our knowledge of different theories and approaches. Even though we may never *conclusively* be able to give a fluent theoretical explanation of why people have come to be in the situations that cause us to become involved, we use our knowledge of theory so that our judgements are evidence based and robust.

The ASPIRE model was devised by Sutton (1999) as a prompt to facilitate a social work process from assessment to evaluation. The ASPIRE acronym stands for:

AS – Assessment
P – Planning
I – Intervention
RE – Review & Evaluation

(Sutton, 1999, cited in Parker, 2017)

The ASPIRE model is very useful in describing the overall process of *what* we do as social workers, but *how* we do it is a different matter. Social work assessments are contextualised within lives, relationships and situations that are complicated, evolving and often conflicted; therefore, they are not easy or straightforward. Baginsky et al. (2017), in their Department for Education evaluation of child protection social work and Signs of Safety, suggest social workers ask three questions:

- Firstly, 'What has been happening?'
- Secondly, 'What is happening now?'
- Thirdly, 'What could happen in the future?'

Despite the wealth of literature addressing the difficult task of social work assessments, and Baginsky et al.'s encapsulation of the process in three straightforward questions, there is still no single accepted definition of social work assessment. This apparent absence of a concrete definition can be seen as problematic; however, Milner and O'Byrne's five stages of assessment (Milner et al., 2015[1998]) is generally regarded as the most influential model, having influenced many of the definitions offered in other publications (Martin, 2010).

The five-stage model of assessment offered by Milner et al. (2015[1998]) consists of the following:

1. Preparing for the task.
2. Collecting data, including the person's, family's and other agencies' perspectives.
3. Applying professional knowledge, to seek understanding, analysis and interpretation of gathered data.
4. Making judgements, about needs, capacity, risk, seriousness and potential for change.
5. Deciding and/or recommending what is to be done and by who.

If we accept that assessment is a basic human interaction, then why are social work assessments so problematic, particularly when assessment or forming judgements is not unique to social work? Most, if not all, professions and occupations involve assessments at some level. A line judge in a tennis match will assess the ball's proximity on the tennis court to determine if the ball is 'in' or 'out' of play. In this activity the line judge will make a very quick decision which is then held up to scrutiny by the umpire, players and spectators, as well as having to suffer the indignity of a potential video replay and/or an electronic tracking device reversing the human-made decision. This must be stressful, and you have probably witnessed a tense player seemingly overreacting when receiving an adverse decision. These assessments are difficult, contested and problematic; however, they act to *regulate* the game and not determine the match, which depends on the tennis players' abilities to compete and perform. Each contested point and decision represents one component of the overall game, and in the end the best player on the day usually wins. In contrast, assessments are integral to social work practice and our work to support people during crisis.

Halmos (1978) identified three elements which interact to form the foundational trinity of social work practice – person, social worker and agency. De Montigny explains that 'every assessment emerges from a personal and institutional dialogue between worker and client' (De Montigny, 2016: 4).

Person

What a person is willing to share is shaped by the context of the assessment interaction. It is influenced by a number of factors, including whether or not the person wants, or perceives themself to need, the involvement of the social worker and the agency, and what outcome they are hoping to achieve. Payne (2006) cautions us to remember that assessments give us only a glimpse of the person's situation. A reported experience is not the same as a lived experience. We select the things we choose to share with others, and the way we represent ourselves. This is usually more about human nature than any intention to deceive, but it is important to realise that people are least likely to share the things of which they are most ashamed. People may over- or understate their needs, resources and abilities during assessments.

Social worker

Becoming a social worker is learning how to professionally use 'self'. We figure out ways to professionally employ our existing unique personal qualities, alongside the skills, experiences and knowledge we acquire during training. When someone is described as not engaging with an assessment, the implication is that they are at fault. As social workers, it is our responsibility to find ways to cultivate engagement. When that engagement is not successful, we must consider whether the fault lies with us, and reflect upon whether what we have tried has been sufficient.

Agency

There are boundaries to any social worker's role, which are determined by the focus of the agency employing the social worker. Social work services tend to be organised around age and type of need, even though the situations we find ourselves in as practitioners are rarely exclusively about adults *or* children, or only a single category of need. The remit of the agency and its thresholds, policies and resources will affect the social worker's assessment practice and the experience and outcomes of the person being assessed.

AT NUMBER 5

Max held a well-paid middle management job for a manufacturing company, and was responsible for a large staff team. Seven months ago, Max collapsed whilst jogging. He was taken to hospital where it was discovered that he had suffered a massive stroke. The stroke caused paralysis down one side of his body and difficulties with his speech and memory. After a long period of residential rehabilitation, his speech improved and he became able to mobilise in a wheelchair. A social worker visited Max and his wife Samantha at the residential rehabilitation unit to undertake an assessment to inform decisions about the support that he would need at home. During the assessment, the social worker felt that Max seemed to be minimising the seriousness of the stroke and describing himself as a lot more able than his medical assessments suggested he was. Although Samantha verbally agreed with what Max said during the assessment, on a number of occasions the social worker saw her raise her eyebrows and look concerned, especially when Max reported that he would not need help with aspects of personal care at home.

EXERCISE 1.2

- Why might Max's explanation about his needs and abilities differ from the medical opinions?
- Why might Samantha's facial expressions be incongruent with what she says?
- How should the social worker approach this situation to make sure that Max gets the support he needs?

As social workers, we are required to work with a raft of guidance intended to ensure that policy and legislation are adhered to and applied consistently. This can encourage a *procedural* model of assessment, where we become more caught up in the process of gathering information, rather than analysing and making sense of it. It is vital that we remain fully conscious of how important assessments are to our practice (Galpin, 2016). In our teaching, we encourage students to understand and differentiate between the 3 Ps of assessment, i.e. the purpose, process and product of social work assessments (see Table 1.1).

Table 1.1 The 3 Ps of assessment

Purpose of assessment	To develop an understanding of a situation in order to inform professional decisions about what action to take.
Process of assessment	Gathering information through a range of different methods and from a range of different sources AND
	Analysing it in using knowledge and theory in order to make sense of it AND
	Making decisions about what action to take based on the evidence of the analysis.
Product of assessment	The document that records the information gathered, the analysis undertaken and the professional decisions/conclusions reached. This may have a structure of headings and criteria that the assessor populates, or it may be a narrative report, or a visual tool such as a genogram or ecomap.

When they are first learning how to undertake social work assessments, our students often diligently populate pro forma documents with a great deal of information, providing lots of description, but no analysis of the situation. They have fallen into the trap of believing that the form itself is the assessment. Procedural tools can support the professional decision-making process, but not replace it (Barry, 2007, in Milner et al., 2015 [1998]). Forms are designed to meet the needs of the agency, prompting us about information that we need to gather. If we apply them mechanistically, they are very unlikely to help us to understand the individual experience of the person being assessed (Bolger and Walker, 2018). It is important that we are confident and flexible in our approach to assessments, so that rather than using a form as a script to be slavishly followed, we are able to use our professional curiosity to respond to the individual situation and ask questions about it.

Our practice assessments may be formal and informal:

> *Formal assessments* relate but are not exclusive to statutory assessment. They involve the practitioner in 'official' work-based assessments including initial, core and comprehensive assessments, which usually generate a paper or electronic product in the form of a report, assessment document or form.
>
> *Informal assessments* involve practitioners in continual or 'unofficial' assessment of a person or their situation, through the process of constructing more nuanced knowledge and understanding of their situation.

AUTHOR'S EXPERIENCE (PHIL)

Having qualified as a social worker, I immediately wanted to go out and help people. With little understanding about assessment and its importance to practice, I set about organising home visits and meetings. I did not realise my assessments were subjective because I did not know how to formally assess other than by using the guidelines provided by my employing local authority. Quite quickly, I found myself faced with many problems on my 'caseload' which overwhelmed me. I learned during practice about the need to assess before acting.

In contrast, some years later, the team manager told me not to 'do another assessment' because the family had already been assessed. This manager then shared with me her copy of Veronica Coulshed's *Social Work Practice: An Introduction* (Palgrave Macmillan, 1991). This text helped me appreciate that my manager was asking me not to undertake another *formal* assessment and to realise that I could and should continue to assess the family *informally*.

There is *a lot* going on during an assessment. A good and soundly constructed assessment will guide the practitioner's decision making, planning and interventions. Matthews and Crawford explain that there is a subjective element to professional assessments:

> Knowledge can only be gained and viewed through the prism of subjective interpretation. This subjectivity is not only unavoidable but should be embraced as a necessary component of the struggle to interpret and understand knowledge. This, however, should not be seen as an excuse to discard the search for evidence and knowledge that underpins social work practice. On the contrary we must be open to emerging knowledge and be willing to adopt a questioning stance that recognises that our existing evidence is never complete and that the search for knowledge is an ongoing quest. (Matthews and Crawford, 2011: 15)

AUTHOR'S EXPERIENCE (PHIL)

A Family Placement Officer once contacted me, requesting a placement for a young boy with 'asparagus (sic) syndrome – whatever that is'. She went on to describe his behaviour as challenging, an attribute that is wrongly associated with autism spectrum conditions. I worked on the assumption that she was referring to Asperger's Syndrome, but later I discovered that this boy had never been given any diagnosis of an autism spectrum condition. A lack of professional knowledge had mistakenly labelled the boy.

Whether assessments are being taken by local authority, private or third sector social workers, their core themes are the gathering, exchange and analysis of information. Smale and Tuson (1993) identify three different types of assessment: questioning, procedural and exchange models.

Three approaches to social work assessments

1. *Questioning model* – this approach is concerned with collecting data so that the practitioner can make decisions. The social worker is seen as the expert and the process reflects their agenda.
2. *Procedural model* – this approach fulfils the agency's function and relies on criteria and checklists filled in by the social worker.The process aims to ensure consistency and thoroughness in data collection and little judgment is required by the practitioner.
3. *Exchange model* – this approach regards the person as the expert about their own situation and is interested in their narrative. There is a reliance on the exchange of information between the person and the social worker, with the practitioner's problem-solving ability being viewed as their expertise. This approach readily fits in with strengths-based models, such as solution-focused and task-centred practice.

(Smale and Tuson, 1993)

AT NUMBER 1

Mary experienced a crisis following the death of her partner. They had been married for forty-two years, and although their marriage had its ups and downs, she found her bereavement difficult because this was the first time she had been alone. She asked her GP for support. He asked Mary many questions and then referred her on to adult social care. Mary was a little disgruntled because she had hoped the GP would talk to her about how she was feeling, rather than ask her questions about how she was coping.

Mary attended an initial assessment during which a social work student completed the agency's form. Mary liked the student but found this assessment difficult because she did not feel the form's questions really applied to her situation. Mary was referred on to a community project which arranged a home visit. The project worker showed a real interest in the stories Mary told about her life, her partner, her interests, and how she was feeling now. She enjoyed the session and felt that she had finally had a chance to express the things she had wanted to talk about when she first visited her GP. She was pleased to learn about how this project could help her make new friends and develop new interests after the isolation she experienced following her partner's death.

EXERCISE 1.3

Think about the questioning, procedural and exchange models:

- Which did the GP use and how do you know?
- Which did the social work student use and how do you know?
- Which did the community project worker use and how do you know?
- Which did Mary most appreciate and how do you know?

Social work assessments utilise analysis to make sense of information, and through this process we are able to plan how best to intervene with people who are experiencing adversity. In their analysis and critical thinking in assessment project, Brown et al. (2012) suggest there are clear steps in the assessor forming an analytical assessment, which include:

- stating clearly why the assessment is being completed;
- showing an understanding of family history and context;
- being specific about the person's needs;
- making a clear and evidence-informed prediction about the likely impact on the person if the identified needs are not met;
- supplying evidence to support decision making;
- giving clear views about what they think needs to happen – avoiding ambiguous language;
- being logical and free of social work jargon.

Social work assessments are influenced by societal expectations and public or institutional constructs of who does and does not deserve support or intervention. Our assessment task has varied from identifying needs so that they can be met, to identifying needs and then gauging whether they are severe enough to be *eligible* to be met. Social workers experience conflict because their role tasks them to both identify needs and act as gatekeepers of precious and finite public resources. People undergoing assessment have expectations of its outcome, and can often feel frustrated with the social worker who does not meet this expectation.

VALUES AND CONCEPTS KEY TO ASSESSMENT

Social work, in all of its broad scope, is identified as a value-based profession: Values & Ethics is one of the PCF's nine domains (BASW, 2018). A quick internet search of the term *value* will bring results which define it, firstly, as the regard that something is held to deserve, i.e. the importance, worth, or usefulness of something, and secondly, as the principles or standards of behaviour, i.e. one's judgement of what is important in life. Sarah Banks recognises that values may be:

> ... regarded as particular types of belief that people hold about what is regarded as worthy or valuable. In the context of professional practice, the use of the term 'belief' reflects the status that values have as stronger than mere opinions or preferences. (2006: 7)

Values are therefore quite subjective, and there may be some distinction between the values held by individual social workers and *social work values*. However, as professionals, we are expected to maintain the profession's standing away from practice too. Regulated expectations of professional conduct do not always relate specifically to social work practice and can extend into personal life choices, such as the values and views we present on social media.

EXERCISE 1.4

Exploring personal and professional values

Make two lists, one of your own personal values, and one of the values you associate with the social work profession:

- Which values only fit in one list? Why is this?
- Which values fit in both lists? Why is this?

Martin (2010) devotes a chapter of his book *Social Work Assessments* to the values underpinning assessment. He reflects on the assessor's duties and responsibilities to the employer, social work profession and society, emphasising the importance of valuing individuals and their unique needs, respecting diversity and observing confidentiality. For social work, values are closely related to professional codes and identity. This is somewhat problematic when the main code of ethics for social work is provided by BASW, an association that social workers may choose to become a member of, but which is not the profession's regulatory body.

Some values and concepts are integral to effective social work assessments. If we understand and employ these, our practice is elevated. The values and concepts we define here are not an exhaustive list; rather they are the ones that we will refer to frequently and repeatedly throughout this book.

Anti-oppressive practice (AOP)

Anti-oppressive practice acknowledges the socioeconomic and sociocultural oppression many people experience. Dominelli (2002) argues oppression is due to power and hierarchical relationships that see difference between sociocultural groups in superior and subordinate terms. Positions of power and subjugation are maintained due to socially constructed conceptualisations of gender, race, sexuality and other social relations (Dominelli, 2002).

Social workers can uses anti-oppressive practice to recognise and challenge oppressive, structural inequalities that maintain the subjectivity of social groups and promote equal and non-oppressive relationships. Anti-oppressive practice (AOP) has received a mixed press. For some it is the essential foundation of social work practice, and much more tangible and easy to define than social justice (see below). For others, it is about incorrectly politicising practitioners who should concentrate on delivering services (Narey, 2014).

Empowerment

Empowerment (sometimes also referred to as emancipation; see for example Dominelli, 1997) is a concept that has become increasingly central to social work practice. Adams describes it as:

> ... the means by which individuals, groups and/or communities become able to take control of their circumstances and achieve their own goals, thereby being able to work towards helping themselves and others to maximize the quality of their lives. (Adams, 2003: 3)

Social work exists to challenge inequality, promote rights and enable change. However, it is not sufficient for social workers to effect change, whilst the people we work with stay in a position of powerlessness. As social workers we do remarkable things, but we must be careful not to become susceptible to hero narratives that present us as rescuers and the people we work with as helpless. Empowering practice supports people to recognise, harness and develop their own power.

Collaboration

Social work is about working with people. Our profession has developed from the casework model with its professional/client-based relationship, to strengths-based models that seek to negotiate some form of partnership with people using social work services, enabling a collaborative approach. Collaboration focuses on working *with* people, to co-create an understanding of what is going on, to co-create an understanding of what (if anything) a person would like to change, and to co-create strategies to implement that change using existing strengths and assets, and/or additional resources.

The language we use to refer to the people we work with has long been the source of debate. The terms *client* and *customer* were prevalent throughout the 1990s and early 2000s. These are misleading and politically loaded terms, which have fallen from use due to unease around their association with business and marketisation. In the corporate world, clients and customers hold the power. They identify their needs and select how those will be met from a wide range of providers competing for their custom. This is vastly different from the situation of parents experiencing safeguarding assessments, who have little power or choice about social work involvement. We cannot regard people as customers of the child protection system when they have no option to take their custom elsewhere.

'Service users' is currently the most widely used term in UK social work, and yet it remains inadequate. The disability rights movement (which we will explore in Chapter 5) campaigned for people to stop being passive recipients of services and become in control of their support. Tom Shakespeare argues that the nature of the power relationship between a caregiver and care receiver changes positively when a customer-based approach is adopted (Shakespeare, 2000). Some people who use social work services may benefit from a customer identity; others will not. A problematic feature shared by the terms *client*, *customer* and *service user* is their effect of reinforcing power differentials by othering and dehumanising people who use services.

Working anti-oppressively and in collaboration requires us to actively work to reduce the dominant relations between the professional and the person using services. In this book, we consciously seek to use the terms 'person' and 'people who use social work services' in recognition that anyone, at any time of their life, can experience a situation that brings them into contact with social workers.

EXERCISE 1.5

What's in a name?

Think about all of the different ways people have referred to you in your life – e.g. your parents, your children, your teachers, your friends, your enemies, your employers, your neighbours, your doctor, your builder.

- Which ones do you like?
- Which ones do you tolerate?
- Which ones do you dislike?
- Could you influence the way in which people referred to you?
- Would you be happy to be referred to as a client, a customer or a service user?
- Which if any do you prefer?

Person-centred practice

Person-centred practice is closely allied to collaborative and partnership approaches. It is to tailor our practice to the individual we are working with, rather than adopting an inflexible 'one size fits all' approach. We live in a diverse society and we work with people, each one of whom is different. Recognising and embracing diversity is integral to our work, and assessments should be bespoke professional reflections on practice situations. Agency remits and processes can promote standard responses and depersonalised interventions that don't take into account the unique experience, needs, circumstances and preferences of the person. Person-centred practice seeks to consciously redress this. Collins (2014) identifies four principles of person-centred care:

1. Affording people dignity, compassion and respect.
2. Offering coordinated care, support or treatment.
3. Offering personalised care, support or treatment.
4. Supporting people to recognise and develop their own strengths and abilities to enable them to live an independent and fulfilling life.

Evidence-based practice

Evidence-based practice originated in medicine to enable clinicians to use current best evidence when making decisions (Lishman, 2018). It is practising in a way that is informed by knowledge from research. Taylor-Pillae states:

> Evidence-based practice (EBP) is the application of the best available empirical evidence, including recent research findings, to clinical practice in order to aid clinical decision-making. (Taylor-Piliae, 1998, in Hancock & Easen, 2004: 188)

Social work practice based purely on instinct and personal experience runs the risk of bias. Lishman (2015) believes that evidence-based practice strengthens social work by focusing practitioners on outcomes, requiring them to keep abreast of current research, and promoting the selection of approaches which fit the specific situation.

Social justice

Social justice represents a key concept in social work. Both the IFSW and BASW (along with other national social work bodies) embed social justice as a fundamental principle of social work practice (IFSW, 2017). The IFSW Statement of Ethical Principles states that 'Social workers have a responsibility to promote social justice, in relation to society generally, and in relation to the people with whom they work', and defines social justice as challenging discrimination, recognising diversity, distributing resources equitably, challenging unjust policies and practices, and working in solidarity (IFSW, 2012). However, there is not really a universally accepted concrete definition of social justice beyond the adherence towards sociopolitical notions of fairness. The application of social justice and the relationship with fairness can be highly subjective.

Social constructionism

Social constructionism is concerned with the ways in which reality is realised socially, rather than naturally formed. It challenges the idea that there is an objective, universal 'truth' to be discovered, and acknowledges that there are multiple, competing realities, dependent on perspective.

Wisdom and knowledge evolve, adapt and change over time. An easy way to understand this is by reflecting on the historical flat earth/round earth debate. For centuries, the earth was flat and the centre of the universe; it was a universally held truism. Now we know the earth as round and is located within, rather than central to, the universe.

Language and communication are important to social constructionism. Communication and social interactions between individuals, groups and institutions are the mechanisms through which we construct our understanding and reality. Just think about how language changes and how words take on new meanings over time. The notion of 'the teenager' emerged during the 1950s with the advent of commercially produced music and research on stages of human development. It is now a recognised identity stage related to hormonal growth and emotional development, but was unheard of before the twentieth century. Social constructionism influences social work practice by recognising diversity in the place of universal truth and therefore complexity in assessments.

Discourse

Discourse is a form of social interaction between people and within organisations (Van Dijk, 2011). Sociologically, it refers to the way in which a particular subject is conceptualised and discussed (Tulle and Lynch, 2011). Foucault (1978) shifted attention from language to discourse as a system of representation, arguing discourse is about the production of knowledge through language. By conceptualising language, Foucault reflected on its relationship to practice and how discursive practices, historically and culturally, set rules for organising and producing different forms of knowledge (Foucault, 1978; Foucault and Gordon, 1980). Language is not only a medium of communication but also a social action and way of 'doing' social practices (Wood and Kroger, 2000). Discourses are therefore systemised ways of talking and thinking (Holmes, 2007).

Narratives and stories

Narratives are the stories people recount about their lives, forming a sequential and consequential structure, as the storyteller interprets the world, makes sense of it and shares it with others. They are personal discourses, representing both conscious (intentional) and unconscious (unintentional) projections of identity. Narratives offer the opportunity to establish personal and collective identities, as through them we are able to hear the voices of not only individuals, but also many different and diverse groups (Riessman, 1993; Czarniawska, 2004; Elliott, 2005; Andrews et al., 2008). There is a wealth of literature on narratives, and the diversity of biographical research testifies to the variety of ways in which narratives can be interpreted.

An underlying feature of narrative is the principle that the ordering or sequencing of events shapes an account; that there is a beginning, middle and ending to stories (Riessman, 1993; Czarniawska, 2004; Elliott, 2005; Andrews et al., 2008). De Montigny (2016) proposes that:

> Assessment involves both listening – to what is said, how it is said, and not said – combined with a great deal of observation and reflection. Are the client's words and stories congruent with the client's tone, mannerism, emotion, and mood? Does the client's story make sense? Are events narrated in a logical chronology? Are details internally consistent? What is present and what is absent, or what is explicit and what is elided? (2016: 6)

The notion of recognising the distinct perspectives and giving voice to people using social care services is enshrined in our practice. We are expected to be expert listeners, good communicators and sound assessors. We are committed public servants and naturally want to provide the best possible service. There is an assumption that *giving voice* to people (such as infants during care proceedings in court) is a basic requirement and therefore an automatic and straightforward process. It is not. This is a highly skilled and contested area of practice (e.g. see Winter et al., 2017, and their exploration of social workers' communication with children and young people). It is more than regurgitating the expressed opinions of people who otherwise find it difficult to express themselves. The process of seeking to give voice and represent not only the expressed opinions but also the unique perspectives of people we work with is essential when seeking to work collaboratively.

Diversity and equality

Human experience is characterised by diversity and diverse identities. Race, disability, class, economic status, age, sexuality, gender, faith and belief form our identities, and recognising and valuing difference has long held importance in social work. Through difference, people may experience privilege and power, or oppression and marginalisation. Contemporary families and family life are very diverse; how people negotiate and perform roles within families is often difficult to understand and can appear fragmented, chaotic and complex. Fawcett suggests that when social workers recognise the diversity of people's needs, they deconstruct taken-for-granted prevailing knowledge, associated with a position of privilege and professional expertise, and move to an exploration of non-generalised needs (Fawcett, 1998; Boushel et al., 2000).

Understanding diversity is not only fundamental in helping us to assess people's needs, it is also a legal requirement. The Equality Act 2010 replaced and brought together 116 pieces of legislation concerning rights and discrimination into a single piece of legislation promoting individual characteristics and rights. The Equality Act 2010 positively promotes rights based on the nine protected characteristics, where are age, disability, gender reassignment, marriage or civil partnership (in employment only), pregnancy and maternity, race, religion or belief, sex and sexual orientation. The Act also protects people from *discrimination by association*, which is when someone is treated unfairly because another person in their life, such as family members or friends, have a protected characteristic.

Feminism, which is an influential body of work, has progressed from promoting women's equality to advocating for anti-oppressive practice in social work and general human rights (Dominelli, 1998). It is usual to think of feminism in three distinct waves. First-wave feminism was concerned primarily with woman's suffrage and occurred during the late nineteenth and early twentieth centuries. Second-wave feminism was more concerned with sexuality, family life and inequalities and originated in the 1960s. Currently, third-wave feminism, which began in the 1990s, is concerned with individuality and identity. The emergence of feminism has encouraged men's studies, which promote the discussion of masculinity and fatherhood (Connell, 1995; Hearn et al., 1998; Lamb and Tamis-Lemonda, 2004).

Feminist discourses have extended beyond woman's equality and encouraged thinking about diversity, inclusivity and non-hierarchical-based practice. At one level, this inclusivity and subversion of hierarchy are contradictory to professionalisation and registration in social work, and particularly with the focus on safeguarding and gatekeeping roles currently occupied by social work. Such is the complexity of practice; we have to manage agency expectations and legislative requirements with notions of social justice, inequality and people's empowerment in an ever-increasingly rich and diverse world.

EXERCISE 1.6

Diversity

Consider yourself and think about how you are different to other people, e.g. your age, gender, sexuality, height etc. Now consider the people we work with.

- How might they be different from you?
- How does the Equality Act 2010 relate to social work? (Think about the nine protected characteristics.)
- Can people experience multiple forms of discrimination?

Reflectivity, criticality and reflexivity in social work

Information floods in through our senses and we convert it into an understanding through rapid, instinctive mental processes. We don't experience our thoughts in a logical, consistent or reasoned order, and we are prone to taking action based upon flawed and incomplete evidence, for reasons that are not always known to ourselves. This very superficial approach is clearly unacceptable and inappropriate in social work practice, where we are required to address complicated, non-dualistic situations (Cottrell, 2011). We need to access and employ higher-level styles of analysis. Contemporary social work literature emphasises the central roles of reflection, criticality, and more recently reflexivity, as approaches crucial in assisting us to develop in-depth self-awareness in our practice and about our practice (e.g. see Fook, 2016).

We often find that students struggle to understand the difference between reflectivity, criticality and reflexivity and this is not surprising, because their definitions are contested and in social work literature the three terms are often used interchangeably. In addition, related terms are frequently used in conjunction with each other to create new terms, such as critical reflection, reflective analysis etc. The deeper we engage with the evidence base of any topic, the more we realise that definitions and understandings are subjective and interpretive, rather than objective and fixed. This can be very frustrating when you are trying to get to grips with new concepts!

Reflectivity

If we think about our most simplistic understanding of reflection, it is what looks back at us when we look in a mirror. Reflectivity is looking back on our practice, to develop a greater understanding of it, leading to the development of theory which can assist us in similar future situations. Schön (1983) distinguishes between reflection-*in-action* and reflection-*on-action*:

Reflection-in-action is concerned with practising critically (see criticality and critical reflection, below) by reflecting on an incident whilst it can still benefit that situation. Schön explains:

> When someone reflects-in-action, he becomes a researcher in the practice context. He is not dependent on the categories or established theory and technique, but constructs a new theory of the unique case. (Schön, 1983: 68)

Reflection-on-action occurs after the activity has taken place, through thinking about what you – and others – did, judging how successful you were and identifying why, and considering whether any changes to what you did could have resulted in different outcomes.

Criticality

The terms 'critical' and 'criticism' tend to have negative connotations; we often associate them with times we have been given unfavourable feedback. In social work practice, criticality is a thinking process through which multiple and alternative points of view are considered and contextual knowledge, e.g. political, social and values issues, is incorporated (Adams et al., 2005). Applying criticality in conjunction with our professional curiosity means that we question and evaluate evidence, rather than taking it at face value, making our assessments and decisions more robust. Payne argues that theory can be used reflectively, selectively, eclectically and through critical engagement, by applying theories critically against one another (Payne, 2002). Ford et al. (2004) suggest that intellectual resources for critical thinking include background knowledge, critical concepts, critical thinking standards, strategies and habits of mind (Ford et al., 2004, cited in Brown and Rutter, 2008).

Adams et al. (2005) set out five ways of thinking to add a critical element:

1. Being reflexive (identify 'taken for granted' knowledge).
2. Contextualising (policy and social contexts).
3. Problematising (debates about policy and law).
4. Being self-critical (do not assume our practice and agency are not problematic).
5. Engaging and transforming (recognising anti-oppressive practice).

Reflexivity

To be reflexive is to be 'taking account of itself or of the effect of the personality or presence of the researcher on what is being investigated' (*Oxford English Dictionary*, n.d.). In sociology, reflexivity refers to an act of self-reference where examination or action 'bends back on', refers to and affects the entity instigating the action or examination. In relation to social work, there are several different interpretations of reflexivity, which we will examine further below. In the simplest terms, we believe reflexivity is concerned with understanding *our own* impact on a situation.

The terms 'reflective' and 'reflexive practice' are often conflated – perhaps most obviously because of their phonetic similarities. Fook (2016) argues that this occurs because reflective processes should be underpinned by a reflexive stance. She suggests that the two have emerged from different discourses: reflectivity from practitioner and educational discourses; reflexivity from social science research. Therefore, reflectivity is the process of reflecting-on-practice, while reflexivity is concerned with how the practitioner influences practice through critical reflection and questioning of professional knowledge and practice assumptions (Fook, 2002; Fook and Gardner, 2007; Fook, 2016). Fook's understanding of reflexivity allows for a more complex understanding of the practitioner's influence upon assessments, by appreciating their individuality, values and personal traits.

Milner et al. (2015[1998]) offer more simplified definitions, whereby reflection is thinking about an action afterwards and possibly learning from a mistake, while reflexivity is reflecting during an action. In this way, reflection is a retrospective learning activity, which therefore leaves an action unchanged, whilst reflexivity is a real-time learning activity, and therefore influences action and effects change (Milner et al., 2015[1998]). Alternatively, Taylor and White (2000) see reflexivity as involving a deeper human subjectivity and critical self-awareness.

SUMMARY

In this chapter, we have unpicked exactly what assessment is, and offered an introduction to the standards and expectations of the social work profession. Performing social work requires us to move *beyond* our own personal perspectives, applying professional knowledge and skills, and being accountable for the decisions we take. We have explored approaches and models of assessment and defined some of the key values and concepts that inform social work assessment.

2 SOCIAL WORK'S EVOLVING CONTEXT: A BRIEF HISTORY

Learning in this chapter relates to

PCF	KSS Adult Services	KSS Child & Family
1. Professionalism 2. Values & Ethics 5. Knowledge 8. Contexts & Organisations 9. Professional Leadership	2. The role of social workers working with adults 4. Safeguarding 9. Organisational context 10. Professional ethics & leadership	1. The role of child & family social work 8. The law & the family justice system 9. Professional ethics 11. Organisational context

INTRODUCTION

In Chapter 1, we recognised that social work assessments cannot seek objective 'truth', because reality is not fixed; it is something that we construct socially, and therefore it changes over time. This chapter extends on this idea, offering insights into social work's contemporary identity by considering its historical context. We follow social work from its charitable and philanthropic beginnings, through to the establishment of the welfare state, regulation and professionalisation, and the contemporary context. It is not our intention to present a complete history of social work – there are many excellent books which do this (we recommend Terry Bamford's (2015) *A Contemporary History of Social Work*) – but to demonstrate how contemporary social work assessment practice has evolved and been shaped by changing times, changing attitudes and changing social policy.

THE BEGINNINGS OF SOCIAL WORK

The professional practice of social work evolved and adapted in a changing socioeconomic and political context, directed by social policy largely aimed at reducing poverty and engendering some form of civic responsibility. Social work is a complex activity; after all, we work with complex beings living in complex environments. Before we reflect on our history, it is worthwhile to recognise the tensions inherent in professional practice. Karen Postle states:

> Social work began, and continues to exist, in a state of ambiguity and tension, experiencing the difficulties inherent in both exercising compassion and control, and mediating between the State and the individual, the public and the private. (2002: 339)

This quote encapsulates the conflict inherent in the social work role from its very beginnings: how can we be agents of empowerment when we are also agents of the State, exercising powers that can be extremely oppressive? What marks the boundary where care becomes control?

AT NUMBER 6

Liam's mental health problems started during adolescence, when he was a child 'looked after' by the local authority. He had a lot of involvement with Child and Adolescent Mental Health Services (CAMHS), and when he reached 18 was transferred to adult services. Liam was allocated a mental health social worker, and having had previous negative experiences with social workers, he was quite reticent about this. However, he found that the social worker was genuinely interested in him, and he came to trust her. This social worker's non-threatening, compassionate approach enabled him to talk honestly about his current mental health, his past experiences and his aspirations for the future. She helped him identify strategies for managing his mental health, and worked in partnership with the leaving care team to support him to move into independent accommodation and start college. Liam did well, and after 10 months of working with the social worker, he was discharged, as he no longer needed support.

In his early twenties, his mental health deteriorated and he began to believe that he was being watched and filmed. He stopped going to work and barely left his room. He covered the windows with newspaper to stop anyone from being able to see in, and was uncharacteristically rude to his housemates, Sally and Adnan, whom he accused of 'being in on it'. Eventually, Sally and Adnan called the police because he had not eaten or slept for days and they feared for his safety. The police attended with two doctors, and the social worker who had previously been involved with Liam. She conducted an assessment and detained him under the Mental Health Act 1983 so that he could be assessed in hospital against his will. He felt totally betrayed by the social worker, and couldn't understand how someone who had previously been his ally was now responsible for depriving him of his liberty.

EXERCISE 2.1

Liam found his first involvement with the social worker extremely empowering, but his second encounter completely disempowering. In the first situation, she was able to act as an *Agent of Change*, but in the second, she was an *Agent of Control*.

- Which of these two roles do you identify with most strongly? Why?
- What ethical conflicts might you feel when asked to undertake the role you identify with less?

The history of social work is not straightforward. Generally, we can say that at different historical stages, different institutions provided social care or relief for poor persons. For instance, during the medieval period, support largely fell upon families, and during the seventeenth and eighteenth centuries, much support transferred to church institutions and charities. In the nineteenth and twentieth centuries, modern social work emerged alongside state-provided services.

Although philanthropy has always existed in some form, state-structured social intervention can be traced back to the Elizabethan (1558–1603) Poor Laws, created following Henry VIII's dissolution of the monasteries (Bamford, 2015). Through the Poor Law each parish became liable for its own poor, who could apply to them for poor rate/relief. Social work as a profession (albeit embryonic) is believed to have originated in the Charity Organisation Societies (COS), founded in England in 1869 (Wilson et al., 2011), following the 'Goschen Minute'.

The Goschen Minute

The Goschen Minute was a policy statement from the Gladstone government that provided instructions to local Boards of Guardians to work with charities to coordinate their efforts to provide support/assistance through Poor Law relief. George Goschen, as President of the Poor Law Board, was concerned that the Poor Law had become too generous and its administration too lenient, which promoted dependency and destitution. In 1869, he published a Minute on the 'necessity for co-operation between the London Boards of Guardians and London charities' (*The Spectator*, 1869). The basis of this Minute was to instruct both Guardians and charities to record and list assistance provided to people to prevent overlap between the Boards and charities, and to emphasise that the Guardians assist the 'totally destitute' with the charities helping before destitution.

The Charity Organisation Societies (COS)

The COS was concerned with social disadvantage and how social theory related to – and encouraged – this disadvantage. Wilson et al. (2011) argue it is important to consider how the COS conceptualised social theory, and the consequences this conceptualisation had on the development of social work. In the UK, the COS is associated with Helen Bosanquet and Octavia Hill, who believed that Poor Law relief, having been universally distributed rather than specifically targeted, fostered a reliance on charity, perpetuating morally defective attitudes without effectively tackling poverty. The COS advocated support through self-help and limiting government intervention to target the effects of poverty. It promoted the idea of *deserving* and *undeserving* poor, which often still resonates today in salacious characterisations which have been dubbed 'poverty porn' (Jones, 2016).

Bamford (2015) identifies the strengths of the COS as its administrative systems, systemic approach to the distribution of charity, use of volunteers and awareness of effective techniques of intervention. However, Bamford also acknowledges its weaknesses, such as the pursuit of self-reliance and rejection of collectivist approaches to solve poverty. The COS's use of employed staff, organisation and training of volunteers helped to initiate social work as a profession assessing need, and led to the creation of the casework model that is still fundamental to practice today.

Social casework

Mary Richmond (1861–1928) was a young American woman who worked for the COS in the United States. She trained to be a *friendly visitor to the poor,* attending people's homes to develop relationships and help them overcome difficulties. Over a number of charitable positions, Mary worked directly with families, searching for the causes of poverty and social exclusion and striving to develop structured and effective responses.

Mary set out the COS methodology in in her first book, *Social Diagnosis* (1917), conceptualising it as *social casework*. Her book presented instruction on what we now recognise as assessment, i.e. how to gather information, establish contact and conduct conversations. There was a strong emphasis on open and honest communication, without the barrier of formality. Social casework was premised on actively involving people in solving their problems and developing their resilience.

The COS believed that it was the individual's responsibility to draw on available support to better themself, and that the core principle of social casework must be to focus on the person *within their situation* (Richmond, 1917). Mary Richmond identified six sources of power available to those in social need:

1. The household.
2. The person.
3. The neighbourhood and wider social network.
4. Civil agencies.
5. Private agencies.
6. Public agencies.

In her second major publication, *What is Social Casework?* (1922), Mary presented and critically analysed six case studies, encouraging an approach she called 'learning from cases'. In the language of contemporary social work, she was introducing reflective practice.

Social reformers

Social researchers and reformers Charles Booth and Benjamin Seebohm Rowntree published studies of poverty in London and York respectively, revealing huge social inequality and unmet need. The Fabian Society, founded in 1844, was a socialist movement that argued for society's radical reconstruction. The Fabians were a collective of prolific thinkers and writers, including luminaries such as George Bernard Shaw, H.G. Wells, Ramsay MacDonald and Emmeline Pankhurst. The Fabians and the COS concurred that the Industrial Revolution had created significant social problems; however, whilst the COS believed that solutions lay with individual improvement, the Fabians believed that universal responses were required (Wilson et al., 2011). The Fabian Society published prolifically on political and economic approaches to social issues, and its key players, Beatrice and Sydney Webb, wrote numerous studies of industrial Britain. In 1900 Sydney incorporated many of the Fabian Society's ideas into the constitution of the Labour Representation Committee, from which the Labour Party grew.

THE EMERGENCE OF THE WELFARE STATE

In the early twentieth century, the UK social work that emerged from the development of social casework and the influence of social and political reformers progressed through the endeavours of charities such as the Children's Society, the Salvation Army, and National Children's Homes. Two world wars in rapid succession increased social need. The Beveridge Report of 1942 identified society's 'five evil giants' of Want, Idleness, Disease, Ignorance and Squalor, and suggested that rather than local discretion, a state-led response was required (Bamford, 2015). There was significant investment in social housing in the form of council estates and a social housing policy to reduce slum and substandard housing. Key industries were nationalised, for example, the Coal Industry Nationalisation Act 1946 established the National Coal Board, and the Transport Act 1947 established British Railways.

EXERCISE 2.2

Historically, different theoretical perspectives have contested the state, its function and purpose. For instance:

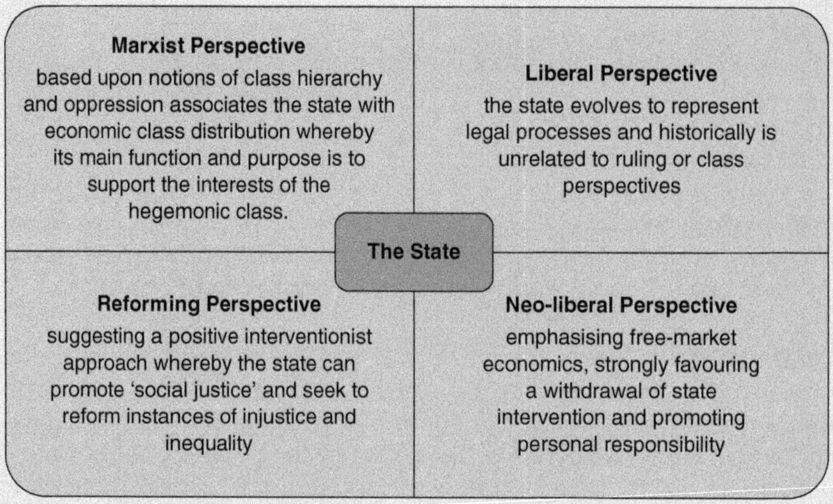

Marxist Perspective
based upon notions of class hierarchy and oppression associates the state with economic class distribution whereby its main function and purpose is to support the interests of the hegemonic class.

Liberal Perspective
the state evolves to represent legal processes and historically is unrelated to ruling or class perspectives

The State

Reforming Perspective
suggesting a positive interventionist approach whereby the state can promote 'social justice' and seek to reform instances of injustice and inequality

Neo-liberal Perspective
emphasising free-market economics, strongly favouring a withdrawal of state intervention and promoting personal responsibility

Figure 2.1 Theoretical perspectives on the role of the state

Which of the perspectives above do you most relate to? Why?

Should the state provide:

- universal services to improve the welfare of all?

or

- targeted services for those most at risk/in need?

At the end of World War II, cross-party support for Beveridge's recommendation of government policy aimed specifically at addressing social issues crystallised into the welfare state. The introduction of the National Assistance Act in 1948 formally abolished the Poor Law, and created a social safety net for older people, homeless people, disabled people and unmarried mothers, obliged local authorities to provide suitable accommodation for those in need, and enabled them to grant financial aid to voluntary organisations. Also receiving royal assent in 1948, the Children Act amalgamated legal processes to ensure local authorities had a responsibility to accommodate children and prevent their abuse.

The National Health Service Act 1948 established the NHS, its guiding principle – which remains to this day – to provide a universal service, free at the point of need. Hospitals were nationalised as part of the NHS, stripping local authorities of responsibility for inpatient health services. However, local authorities retained responsibility for a number of health functions in the community, such as public health and community nursing services. Whilst these services were a logical fit with other local authority responsibilities such as housing and social services, they were undoubtedly meeting health needs outside of the newly created NHS. Services provided by the local authority under the National Assistance Act 1948 could incur charges, whilst services provided by the NHS were free. The debate over the boundary between health and social care had begun.

With the welfare state providing support and protection for people living in the UK, including health, social benefits and social support, as well as affordable housing through council homes and employment for many in the nationalised industries, millions of Britons saw their standard of living rise. In 1957, full employment and an unprecedented rise in consumerism led the recently elected Prime Minister Harold Macmillan to make his infamous claim that 'most of our people have never had it so good!' However, as the 1950s gave way to the new decade, there was a growing sense of disillusionment that the post-war promise of a better, fairer society was not being fulfilled (Turbett, 2014). Economic stability was short-lived and by 1961 Macmillan's Conservative government had introduced a wage freeze in response to rising inflation. Societal inequalities were becoming more and more evident.

On the international stage, feminism's second wave was challenging traditional views about women, the civil rights and anti-apartheid movements were challenging the segregation of people of colour, and there was wide-scale opposition to the continuing war in Vietnam. The drug Thalidomide, prescribed as a treatment for morning sickness in 46 countries, had catastrophic and unanticipated side effects. In the three years during which it was licensed in the UK around 2,000 babies were born with severe birth defects; around half of these children died within a few months of birth. Sociologist Peter Townsend published his research evidencing that despite the welfare state, many older persons were still ending their lives in poverty and squalor. In 1966, Ken Loach's hugely influential TV play, *Cathy Come Home* (which included the mental health social worker David Brandon as a research advisor), revealed a national scandal of poverty and homelessness. A quarter of the UK population watched in anger and disbelief.

Seebohm and Kilbrandon

During the 1960s, two parallel committees looked at the organisation of social services and the role of social work: the Seebohm Commission in England and Wales, and a similar commission chaired by Lord Kilbrandon in Scotland. The reports of both commissions recommended broadly similar approaches of universal rather than targeted services. They advocated the establishment of new, unified, generic social services, premised on the assumption that social work had core, transferable skills which could be used with any group (Stevenson, 2005). From the late 1960s onwards, large social service departments developed to offer services to local people.

The implementation of the Local Authority Social Services Act 1970 placed a duty on local government to:

1. Provide training for social workers.
2. Coordinate responses to need based on casework.
3. Professionalise the social care task.

Training for social workers was formalised through the Central Council for Education and Training in Social Work (CCETSW). Social work seemed to prosper in the state sector through these reforms of social services, which gained access to considerable resources. However, its relationship with the state meant social work was embedded within public services – something that continues to this day. Social work emerged from supporting those experiencing poverty and the myriad of needs arising from or resulting in it, and has traditionally attracted social activists. This presents a dilemma when the occupation is *led by* state agencies, such as the NHS and local authorities. Radical social work emerged to criticise state-run social services and question how this could be reconciled with the core social work values around challenging structural oppression. Ferguson and Woodward suggest this criticism from radical commentators drew attention to the ongoing nature of oppression based on social divisions due to class, gender, sexuality and so on. The context of this criticism is significant because it highlights the debate and antenarrative within social work at a time when the profession was emerging with new vigour and credibility.

Social work's credentials were challenged by the tragic death of Maria Colwell in 1973. Maria had been returned to her mother and stepfather from foster care. Her stepfather cruelly and persistently abused Maria, ultimately injuring her so badly that she died. A public inquiry into the care and supervision provided to her was highly critical of the social workers involved, and led to early models of child protection. Social services faced criticism from both sides of the political spectrum. The conservative right felt (and continue to feel!) they lacked both efficacy and efficiency, whilst the socialist left was concerned (and continue to be concerned!) that by conceptualising social work as a direct relationship between provider and client, social issues were being individualised rather than addressed at their structural cause (Bailey and Brake, 1980). The New Right of the 1970s, led by Margaret Thatcher, redefined the agenda of public services from a universalist approach, towards a neo-liberal approach of personal responsibility. This Conservative movement argued for tighter fiscal control of public expenditure and more personal choice and autonomy; as a result, social services came under increasing attack. From the 1980s onwards, political agendas shifted the focus from public services towards using business solutions to tackle social problems, a trend supported by both Conservative and New Labour Governments.

The cornerstone of the New Labour government that came to power in 1997 was a *modernisation agenda*. Sociologist Ulrich Beck explains that modernisation involves:

> ... surges of technological rationalization and changes in work and organization, but beyond that includes much more: the change in societal characteristics and normal biographies, changes in lifestyle and forms of love, change in the structures of power and influence, in the forms of political repression and participation, in views of reality and in the norms of knowledge. In social science's understanding of modernity, the plough, the steam locomotive and the microchip are visible indicators of a much deeper process, which comprises and reshapes the entire social structure. (Beck, 1992: 50)

Labour's modernisation of public services extended Thatcher's neo-liberalism and was premised on managerial and market principles such as consumerism and performance management. Defining performance and establishing value for money is not as straightforward in social work as it is in commerce. Social work outcomes are dependent on many variables, and extremely difficult to predict. A 'good' outcome in one situation is a bad outcome for somebody else. As we highlighted in Chapter 1, people who use services do not have choice in the consumerist sense; often we cannot offer people the choices they would most like. The modernisation agenda's expectation was for public services to be accountable and meet measurable outcomes. The operationalisation of this through applying standardised performance management procedures to social work practice was felt by many to compromise relationship-based approaches and limit professional autonomy (Harris and White, 2009).

Technological advances occurred concurrently with this move towards managerial and process-orientated social work. Whilst computerised databases provided the means to more accurately record and collate information, the computer interface shifted practice away from default face-to-face contact, and against this context many social workers felt that they struggled to develop and maintain personalised social work.

> With social work being constructed increasingly as a failing profession, it is not surprising that governments wanted to be seen to respond formally, to lead this struggling profession into more 'efficient' and effective' ways of working. (Ferguson and Woodward, 2009: 60)

Ferguson and Woodward argue that this approach did not lead to improved services, but rather that it effectively moved the practice of social work away from delivering services towards gatekeeping access to services through assessment of needs based on statutory rights. This shift placed a strong emphasis on assessment and professional judgement.

The move away from universalism to responsibilisation has made the individual the responsible agent, resulting in a reduced role for the state. This neo-liberal and responsibilisation discourse has influenced thinking amongst social work practitioners. For example, Liebenberg et al. (2015) explore how social workers are now more likely to attribute a social issue, such as youth offending, to personal lifestyle choices, in contrast to the past, when they may have given more emphasis to contextual factors. Statutory social work has become increasingly confined to the execution of state functions to safeguard children and vulnerable adults, whilst also protecting the general public from their risky or undesirable behaviour. Notwithstanding personal, professional or even political opinion, social work and social work practice have evolved to become more focused on professional judgements based on rights defined by legislation. Social workers have always been involved in assessing needs to enable access to services, but it can be argued that the traditional debate around whether social workers are agents of empowerment or control (Freud and Krug, 2002) has been superseded by the increased emphasis on social workers gatekeeping access to public services.

AT NUMBER 1

As a young parent in the 1970s, Mary contacted her local community social work office following the birth of her second child. She had found the birth difficult and now with two children she wanted to find out what support was available to her. Within the context of universal welfare services, Mary was able to identify that she required support and to access this without need for consideration of whether or not she was eligible. Accessing support in this manner can support and maintain wellbeing and be seen as preventative – Mary got support before her situation was too bad, and because of the freely accessible support, her situation improved.

In the present day, her neighbour tells her daughter that she is concerned Mary isn't coping and seems confused and vulnerable. Her daughter contacts adult social care services, but Mary is reluctant to become involved with them.

EXERCISE 2.3

Consider the barriers to Mary's engagement with social care service:

- How could the changing model of social work be contributing to Mary's reluctance?
- How could Mary's stage of life be contributing to her reluctance?

THE PROFESSIONALISM OF SOCIAL WORK

What is professionalism?

Social work gained structure and mandate through the creation of the welfare state and the direction of the Seebohm and Kilbrandon Reports, but it was not formally recognised as a profession until 2001. Professionalism is broadly defined as possessing specialist knowledge and qualifications, meeting high standards and being self-regulatory with a degree of autonomy (Larson, 1977; Macdonald, 1995; Neal and Morgan, 2000). There are several critical elements to professionalisation, including having an agreed body of knowledge and adherence to a code of ethics (Hugman, 1991; Hugman 2003). The process of professionalisation was initially described in the 1920s by Carr-Saunders as emerging from a wave of associations by various occupations during the nineteenth century (Carr-Saunders, 1928). In the 1950s Caplow, following on from Carr-Saunders' work, classified several steps by which occupations become professional, most often beginning with the creation of an occupational association leading to a code of ethics and finally legal restriction to the profession (Caplow, 1954). Larson (1977) argued that professions made themselves into special and valued kinds of occupations during the great transformation of European societies brought about by the reorganisation of society through industrialisation and market-led economies. Therefore, for Larson, professionalisation is a process of translating special knowledge and skills into social and economic reward.

This relatively early work on professionalism tends to relate how the economic value placed upon certain occupations enabled their practitioners to command a higher financial reward and achieve professional status. The history and high status afforded to occupations predominantly associated with men, such as medicine and law, can be contrasted with a comparably much lower status afforded to occupations predominantly associated with women, such as nursing and social work (Halford et al., 1997). The allocation of high status to male-dominated professions strongly suggests how hegemonic social constructions of gender are formed. The professionalisation of social work seems to have been impeded by its identification as a woman's occupation (Dominelli, 1996). Dominelli argues that attaining professional recognition was difficult for social work because it was not seen as necessarily skills-based in the traditional manner of male-orientated professions. Indeed, the very attempt to achieve a transparent and accessible service seems to have downgraded the apparent skills and knowledge of social work practitioners.

Professional identity

Professionalism regulates and offers some standardisation to occupations. Society values professionalism, and at its most basic level, professionalism involves the payment (or remuneration) for a service. Social work is now a recognised profession, with regulatory bodies throughout the UK. Professional identity further develops our appreciation of professionalism and is broadly defined as an individual's professional self-concept related to motives, values, beliefs and attributes (Ibarra, 1999; Slay and Smith, 2011). Therefore, practitioners adopt the professional identity associated with their profession. As we have seen, social work has gone through significant changes in line with public perceptions of social services. Our practice remains central to the assessment of need and the allocation of public services.

Social work is a legally defined title with a requirement to register with an appropriate regulatory body in order to practise, which make practitioners more accountable. Ferguson and Woodward (2009) welcome this potential for social care services to be more accountable, with practice becoming more in tune with the wishes of people using services and carers. However, they are concerned that these regulatory bodies have little appetite to challenge dominant business discourses, and fear this lack of criticality will move the profession in the direction government wishes. The response to Ferguson and Woodward's concerns would seem to hinge on how independent and robust our professional independence is.

Wiles (2013) identified three aspects of professional identity in the social work context:

1. The desired traits of a profession.
2. A collective sense of professional identity.
3. A subjective perspective of what each individual believes is the identity of the profession.

AUTHOR'S EXPERIENCE (PHIL)

As a support worker before I became a qualified social worker, I – like many others – described myself as 'doing social work'. The implication was that social work is somehow intuitive and does not require specialist skills and knowledge. When I went on to study for a social work qualification, I naively believed that by qualifying I would become – almost mystically! – a very professionally skilled person, and that this professionalism itself would enable me to work with people successfully and 'know what to do'.

Ten years after qualifying as a social worker, I still felt some professional insecurity about my skills and knowledge. I reflected on how long I had been involved in the activities of social work – in my unqualified practice, my social work education and my qualified practice. As an experienced practitioner, I realised that I was knowledgeable and skilled and had some awareness of my own professional practice, as well as the very complex nature of my work. I had replaced my naive hopes of exalted uber-professionalism and always knowing what to do, with a much more realistic appreciation of my practice depth, specialist knowledge and professional skills. Furthermore, I had not changed but matured, and while I had developed and acquired new skills and knowledge, I still utilised my own highly personalised skills.

Payne reflects on the relationship between personal identity, social identity and professional identity, stating 'Our professional identity as practitioners is a social identity, interacting with personal identities' (Payne, 2011:163). The ways in which identities have evolved and been created have changed over time. Postmodernism and technology, such as social media, have facilitated the growth of multiple identities. However, the construction of professional identity is potentially more complex than that of personal identity. There are competing discourses and a wide range of factors involved in the construction of professional identity. The general assumption is that professional identity adapts through the socialisation of professional meanings and personal adaptation during career transitions (Slay and Smith, 2011). A study focusing on African American journalists, by Slay and Smith (2011), explored the relationship between professional identity and social stigma, and suggested that professional identity emerges through redefinition rather than adaptation. The implication here is that professional identity is more than simple adaptation through identifying with role models, socialised professionalism or professional transitions, because both the individual and the profession are constantly being redefined.

What does this mean for our professional identity? Have we been part of an adaptation or redefinition of social work? These are important questions to ask, but remain difficult to answer at this stage. We have certainly seen the transformation of social work coinciding with an emerging professional identity. Hatton (2015) reflects on the coming together of two professional identities through social and community work, but recognises subtle differences between the two in their relationships with the welfare state. Essentially, Hatton argues they apply different sociological approaches, with community work espousing challenge to power at the political level, while social work is much more concerned with promoting change through individual psychological processes. In contrast, and more practically driven, Rogers et al. (2017) suggest professional identity promotes more effective collaboration and inter-professional work. Therefore recognising our professional identity is not only helpful personally, but is also a framework on which we can organise our practice.

Social work qualification

The Health Visiting and Social Work (Training) Act 1962 established the Council for Training in Social Work. This body was renamed the Central Council for Education and Training in Social Work (CCETSW) in 1971 by the Local Authority Social Services Act 1970. CCETSW was responsible for overseeing the education and training of social workers by recognising courses and awarding qualifications – the taught Certificate Qualification in Social Work (CQSW) and the work-based Certificate in Social Services (CSS). In 1991, the CQSW and the CSS were replaced by the Diploma in Social Work (DipSW). From 2003, degree-level social work qualifications in the form of Bachelor's or Master's degrees became more common, and the DipSW was finally phased out in 2009.

Social work regulation

The UK-wide CCETSW was abolished in 2001 and replaced by national bodies: in England, the General Social Care Council (GSCC); the Scottish Social Services Council (SSSC); the Care Council for Wales (CCW); and in Northern Ireland, the Northern Ireland Social Care Council (NISCC). These national bodies were set up to raise the standards of social work. The GSCC, established in 2001 following the Care Standards Act 2000, launched the regulatory procedures for social workers in England and set up the first register of social workers in England. The GSCC was abolished in 2012, with its regulatory duties transferred over to the Health Professions Council which was renamed the Health and Care Professions Council (HCPC).

Currently in the UK, regulation and registration are provided by: the Scottish Social Services Council; Social Care Wales; the Northern Ireland Social Care Council; and the newly established regulator, Social Work England. Like its predecessor the HCPC, Social Work England will approve all social work education and training courses in England; however, it has a new power to suspend courses, and it is planned to introduce a register for student social workers (Department for Education and Department of Health and Social Care, 2018).

AUTHOR'S EXPERIENCE (CAT)

My qualifying DipSW was, like Phil's CQSW, issued by CCETSW. Although Phil and I undertook different social work qualifications, in different decades, we both became registered social work professionals at the same time, when the GSCC was created in 2001.

Professional leadership

Following the tragic death of Peter Connelly (also known as Baby P) in 2007, an inspection of the services involved with Peter and his family uncovered a catalogue of safeguarding failings and inconsistent practice. Evidence from other inspections and serious case reviews suggested that such issues were endemic throughout the country, and the former Department for Children, Schools and Families recommended a Social Work Task Force be established to advise on reforms and to improve the recruitment, training and quality status of social work. Its final report in 2009 made 15 core recommendations, which the Social Work Reform Board (SWRB) was set up to carry out. The SWRB developed the professional standards for social work in England, i.e. the Professional Capabilities Framework (PCF).

In 2010, Professor Eileen Munro was commissioned to conduct an independent review of child protection in England. The press release for the Review of Child Protection Final Report, published in 2011, stated:

> It is the government's view that we need fundamental reform to frontline social work practice and to make sure that we liberate the skills and talent of professionals. The Government wants a strong profession so that social workers are in a better position to make well-informed judgements, based on relevant evidence, in the best interests of children, free from unnecessary bureaucracy and regulation. (gov.UK, 2010)

AUTHOR'S EXPERIENCE (CAT)

I was a social worker in adult services when the extent of systemic failings in child protection practice became apparent following Peter Connelly's death. The impact on social work was enormous, and reflecting back on that time I can see how in many ways, rather than uniting as a profession, adults' and children's social workers became unhelpfully polarised. Adult social work did not come under the same public, government or media scrutiny that children's social work did; however, I believe that if it had, sadly, similar issues would have been uncovered. In the anger and upset that followed Peter's death, I spent a lot of time explaining that adult social work was very different from child protection social work. I realise now that rather than acknowledging and explaining the difficulties of the profession as a whole, I was distancing my area of practice from blame, and allowing it to be located with my colleagues in children's services.

EXERCISE 2.4

There can be a 'them and us' divide between children and families' social workers and adults' social workers, which is entirely incongruent with the profession's values of inclusivity.

- Have you come across any examples of this?
- Why do you think this happens?

The profession frequently separates itself into a focus on children or adults.

- What are the positive aspects of this?
- What are the negative aspects of this?
- Is social work a single profession?

The College of Social Work was created in 2012 to be an independent organisation leading and representing the profession. This resulted in a very public dispute with BASW, which had existed since 1970 and regarded *itself* as leading and representing the social work profession. The College of Social Work was launched with three years of government funding, and given ownership of the PCF. Social workers, who were already paying registration fees to the HCPC, struggled to see a reason to pay an additional and non-mandatory fee for membership of The College of Social Work. Having failed to develop a self-sustaining funding model, when its government funding ran out in 2015, the College closed.

In 2013, two new senior civil service roles were created to provide leadership to the profession and expert advice to ministers: the Chief Social Worker for Adults, based within the Department of Health (now the Department of Health and Social Care) and the Chief Social Worker for Children and Families based within the Department for Education. From 2014 onwards, the Chief Social Workers have issued Knowledge and Skills Statements (KSS), which articulate what a social worker should know, and be able to do, within specific practice settings and roles.

Following the closure of The College of Social Work, BASW became the custodian of the PCF, hosting it on behalf of the profession. This was contentious: like The College of Social Work before it, BASW is not the regulator of social work in the UK, and there is no requirement for practising social workers to take up membership. There was much speculation about the future place of the PCF, and whether it would be retired in favour of the KSS that the chief Social Workers continued to issue (BASW, 2018). However, BASW launched a refreshed PCF in 2018, and in a joint statement with the Chief Social Workers, outlined how the PCF and KSS should be used in conjunction with each other (see Chapter 1).

Contemporary professional practice

With social work rooted in the welfare state and local authority social services, social workers helped to deliver public services at the point of need. However, notwithstanding the positives of the welfare state, there were also many instances where state intervention was unacceptable when viewed from a modern perspective, e.g. orphaned or poor children were relocated to Australia as late as the 1970s (Child Migrant Trust, n.d.), and people with learning disabilities and mental health problems were routinely admitted into long-stay hospitals where their links with family were reduced and family life was regulated. Until the Suicide Act of 1961, suicide was a criminal offence, and people who survived an attempt to end their own life were routinely prosecuted. Sex between adult men was not legalised until 1967. Our contemporary understanding of social work practice is very different from that of social workers who practised during the 1960s.

Wilson et al. (2011) suggest that early twenty-first century understandings of assessment in social work have been shaped by two factors: firstly, the impact of public inquiries on perceived social work shortcomings; and secondly, the Labour Government's (1997–2010) modernising agenda. The relationship between social work and safeguarding has become more pronounced following numerous serious case reviews of significant harm or fatality to children, and safeguarding adult reviews into the abuse and neglect of adults. The first two decades of the twenty-first century have seen an extensive overhaul of welfare provision. The nature of our work has changed and altered in line with the state, directed by an increased emphasis upon personal responsibility. Society has gradually moved away from viewing social work as a radical or emancipatory activity, towards it becoming a *profession* (Gilbert and Powell, 2010). What was once a voluntary activity is now a state-prescribed, heavily regulated profession with a registration process.

Assessment has always been an intrinsic part of social work practice. The attention it is afforded, however, is variable. Milner et al. state:

> Having agreed on the centrality of assessment in the social work process, some texts, over the last 20 years, then dismissed the subject in a few pages. (2015[1998]: 3)

This seems to present a professional contradiction: whilst assessment may be accepted as integral to social work, it is not always clearly linked to practice and often overlooked within literature which focuses on other aspects of the social work role. This may be connected to the trend within social work education since the Social Work Reform Board, to focus on *thinking processes* such as reflection and professionalism, rather than on the *practice skills and tools* that support assessment.

Social work assessments are diverse, and assessment has become increasingly more important as social policy has shifted away from a model of universal support to alleviate social needs such as poverty, towards an expectation of individual responsibility. Successive governments have introduced austerity measures that have drastically reduced spending on public services, adding a further facet of complexity to social work practice. Budgetary cuts to local authorities have created a need to 'ration' services through the application of narrower and narrower eligibility criteria. Social work assessments have taken on a significant gatekeeping aspect. The identification of needs does not necessarily result in social work involvement; the needs must be great enough, and the threshold keeps rising.

The role of the social worker has changed significantly since the radicalism of the 1970s (Lee, 2014), when a context of universal welfare support and services enabled case management approaches based on prevention, emancipation, empowerment and community development. Social policy, with an increasing emphasis on individual responsibility and the rationing of services to those perceived to be at most need or risk, has resulted in both child and adult services seeing an exponential focus on safeguarding. Despite the prominence the 2014 Care Act gives to promoting wellbeing, cash-strapped local authorities have increasingly focused on those services that they have a statutory duty to provide, at the expense of preventative services, many of which have been withdrawn. Higher threshold criteria for involvement, in combination with a reactive rather than preventative model of service delivery, means involvement is triggered by crisis, and assessment is focused on risk and safeguarding. Most people now access social work services at a point when they are already in crisis, vulnerable, and at risk of significant harm.

Damned if you do and damned if you don't

Social work decisions, like those taken by doctors or fire fighters, may have enormous impact on people's lives, but there is a significant difference. Should you find yourself in a fire, you will most likely be extremely grateful to the firefighters who attend and rescue you. Although you may not enjoy going to the dentist, you will almost certainly be relieved when they identify what is causing your pain (by undertaking an assessment) and provide appropriate treatment, which eases it. Although doctors receive much criticism if they make an incorrect diagnosis, generally speaking, when we are ill, we are very appreciative of their support and diagnosis (another type of assessment!).

The act of social work occurs during crisis, and unlike the other professions we have mentioned, is often in conflict with the people we work with or their families. The outcomes of social work assessments are frequently unwelcome, unpopular and upsetting, even though they are correct. Social work assessments may result in a child being separated from their birth family and placed in foster care, or a person being detained against their will (commonly referred to as being 'sectioned') under the Mental Health Act 1983. In *getting it right,* social workers seldom receive praise or gratitude. However, on those occasions when social workers *get it wrong*, the consequences can be catastrophic, and may at times contribute to serious harm. Although such mistakes are not common, when they occur they often attract a significant media profile, which in some cases has vilified the social work profession as a whole. The lack of profile around positive social work means that there is little to offset this negativity, and social workers often describe themselves as feeling 'damned if you do and damned if you don't'. The Channel 4 sitcom about child protection social work is entitled *Damned* for precisely this reason.

Given the obvious concerns of many social workers, it is reasonable to ask, 'Why does anyone choose this profession?' Quite simply, social workers are uniquely placed to contribute to positive change in people's lives. Making 'good' assessments, and seeing their impact, is enormously rewarding.

SUMMARY

In this chapter, we have set out the historical context in which the practice and subsequently the profession of social work has evolved. Hennessey (2011) talks about the importance of self-awareness in social workers, and how we must reflect on our past to recognise how it influences who we are and how we practise. It is equally important for us to understand our profession's past, and to recognise how this influences what it is and how it is practised today. We have considered how social work has shifted its focus from a generic occupation targeted at helping people to a specialised, needs-led, assessment-based profession. This transformation has happened across a landscape of continuing policy changes, a movement away from universal public services to responsibilisation, and the focusing of service provision on statutory rights and safeguarding concerns. Our brief journey through key aspects of social work's history shows that there has always been conflict and differences of opinion about why social issues exist, and how they should be addressed. However, whilst the professional context changes and social work practice evolves, the central role of assessment in social work practice remains.

3 RISK AND PROFESSIONAL JUDGEMENT

Learning in this chapter relates to		
PCF	**KSS Adult Services**	**KSS Child & Family**
1. Professionalism 2. Values & Ethics 5. Knowledge 6. Critical Reflection & Analysis 9. Professional Leadership	2. The role of social workers working with adults 4. Safeguarding 6. Effective assessments & outcome-based support planning 8. Supervision, critical reflection & analysis 9. Organisational context 10. Professional ethics & leadership	1. The role of child & family social work 4. Abuse & neglect of children 5. Effective direct work with children & families 6. Child & family assessment 7. Analysis, decision making, planning & review 9. Professional ethics 11. Organisational context

INTRODUCTION

This chapter examines two interrelated features of social work assessment: risk and professional judgement. Responding to actual or potential risk permeates all that we do, and in 2013 The College of Social Work encapsulated this when it stated, 'Social workers are society's safety net as they are professionally qualified to intervene in people's lives for the protection of children or adults at risk of abuse or neglect who could otherwise be harmed' (The College of Social Work, 2013:1). Whilst there is truth in this statement, it tasks us with a huge and somewhat overwhelming responsibility. Social work is a difficult profession involving professional judgements about some of society's most at risk children and adults. We are expected to always *get it right*, but sadly this is not always possible. In this chapter we consider how concepts of risk are constructed and recognise how unrealistic expectations, combined with cultures of blame, can result in defensive practice, which acts as a barrier to effective professional decisions. We explore features of professional judgements, notions of professional autonomy and accountability, and discuss approaches and models for decision making. We suggest critical reflection and professional values based on anti-oppressive practice, working with hope, compassion and unconditional positive regard are vital, but acknowledge the realities of practising under seemingly ever-increasing demands at a time of reduced resources.

RISK

As we have already mentioned, social work has become indelibly linked with risk and risk assessments. In this section, we reflect on risk and begin by looking at how it is constructed.

Constructing risk

Social constructionist perspectives identify the term 'risk' as a contentious concept, which can have either positive or negative connotations depending on how it is located within particular historical and political contexts (Berger and Luckman, 1979; Hothersall and Mass-Lowitt, 2010). You will find an endless number of definitions of risk; we particularly like the elegant simplicity of Alberg's (1996) definition concerning the possibility of beneficial and harmful outcomes and the likelihood of their occurrence in a particular timescale (cited in Smethurst, 2011). Alberg recognises the potential for risks to have positive as well as negative outcomes, and engages with the fluid concept of possibility (likelihood) as distinct from probability: just because something is possible, it does not mean it is probable. Time is a key variable because the types of risk we encounter in social work practice usually fluctuate markedly over time.

Adams described risk as 'the world's largest industry' (1995: 31). Think about representations of risk in the media and news. On a daily basis, we are bombarded with information about risks to our health, our safety, the environment and so on. Risk and the avoidance of risk are a constant preoccupation. The concept of the *risk society* was first introduced in the 1980s, by the German sociologist Ulrich Beck, in work published in the aftermath of the Chernobyl nuclear power plant disaster. British sociologist Anthony Giddens was also a proponent of this concept, which he described as 'a society increasingly preoccupied with the future (and also with safety), which generates the notion of risk' (Giddens and Pierson, 1998: 209). Giddens and Beck argued that whilst society has always been exposed to risk from non-human forces (such as natural disasters like famine, flood and disease), modern societies experience risks created by the modernisation process itself (e.g. pollution, industrial accident, crime). Both Giddens and Beck suggested that because it is possible to assess and take preventative measures where risks are the product of human actions, society becomes orientated towards the systematic reduction of risk in *all* areas of life.

Webb (2006) observed that social work's increasing dependence on process and rules – in the form of statutes, guidance and policy – has moved the profession's focus from need to risk, prioritising safety over all other aims. Bamford cautions that 'the shades of grey in which social workers often operate do not lend themselves easily to schedules and protocols that often fail to capture the multi-faceted nature of the difficulties faced by clients' (2015: 167).

Cultures of practice

Negative constructions of risk have led to a 'blame culture' in social work, which can result in risk averse, defensive and even oppressive practice where bureaucratised responses emphasise following procedure, rather than applying knowledge and skill. Eileen Munro (2011) talked about such approaches being negative 'compliance' cultures, rather than cultures of learning. As a regulated profession, social workers must adhere to standards in order to maintain their registration; where this is in question, they can be subjected to disciplinary proceedings and possible deregistration.

Through the lens of hindsight, it is possible to make unduly critical assessments of professional judgements, but life is lived forwards, not backwards. Risk taking is a core facet of life in the mainstream – *we all* take risks. However, the responsibility we accept for our own risk-taking behaviour is different from that which we feel towards those persons for whom we have a professional responsibility. Identifying and responding to the risks faced and posed by some of society's most at risk citizens can weigh heavily on social workers, creating a further risk of slipping into risk-averse practice. Working with our profession's key values of empowerment and anti-oppressive practice means recognising people's right to take risks:

> Choice and control are what everyone wants for themselves and those they care for, but sometimes the decisions they make may seem to others as too risky. Risk is a concept that tends nowadays to have mainly negative connotations ... But avoiding risk altogether would constrain the choices people can make. (Department of Health, 2007)

A 'Health & Safety' model, which seeks to avoid or eliminate all risk may be appropriate and desirable in industry, but does not work in the context of relationships and lives lived. If we take a risk-averse stance and prioritise safety over all else, we disregard the very nature of humanity. A person cannot fully experience the scope of life and relationships without risk, as Sir James Lawrence Munby, former President of the Family Division of the High Court of England and Wales noted:

> ... all life involves risk, and the elderly and the vulnerable are exposed to additional risks and to risks they are less equipped than others to cope with. But just as wise parents resist the temptation to keep their children metaphorically wrapped up in cotton wool, so too we must avoid the temptation always to put the physical health and safety of the elderly and the vulnerable before everything else ... Physical health and safety can sometimes be bought at too high a price in happiness and emotional welfare. What good is it making someone safer if it merely makes them miserable? None at all! And if this is where safeguarding takes us, then is it not, in truth, another form of abuse – and, moreover, abuse at the hands of the State? (Munby, 2012)

Unrealistic perceptions of social workers' 'duty of care' – whether held by ourselves or others – can result in great anxiety and promote risk-averse practice.

THE SLUG IN THE BOTTLE

In 1928, May Donoghue and a friend met at Frankie Minghella's 'Tally café' in Paisley, near Glasgow. May's friend bought her a ginger beer float, which came in a brown frosted bottle. On pouring out out the last of the drink, May was horrified to discover a partially decomposed slug. She suffered from shock and was treated for gastroenteritis, so decided to sue the café owner.

Mr Minghella successfully defended that as May Donaghue had not purchased the drink herself, she was not his customer, and he had no legal responsibility towards her. May decided to sue the manufacturer of the ginger beer, Paisley soft drink maker David Stevenson. Her lawyer argued that Stevenson had a 'duty of care' to those consuming his product, even without a direct contract. The case went all the way to the House of Lords, where May Donoghue finally won her battle in 1932.

Two common phrases are derived from this ruling:

1. Can I have a slug of your drink?
2. Duty of care.

The principle of Mrs Donaghue's win has since been applied in every court action where a person suffers injury or loss. In Scotland, it is known as delict – the law of negligence and liability. In North America, it is known as tort. Millions of damages actions around the world now regularly begin with Lord Atkin's ruling in the Paisley slug case, which states:

> You must take reasonable care to avoid acts or omissions which you can reasonably foresee would be likely to injure your neighbour.

EXERCISE 3.1

- How does this apply to social work?
- How much risk should social workers try to eliminate?
- Can all risk ever be eliminated?

Unlike many other professions, we often only become involved with people during periods of crisis in their lives. Some people we work with may want our service, though many don't. They may or may not be aware of the crisis, and the crisis itself may be temporary or permanent. It is difficult to legislate for other people's crises and every person is different. As we have recounted, as social workers we often receive no acknowledgement when we get it right, but can be vilified when we get it wrong. Even when we do everything right, we don't always know how to stop children and adults from getting hurt because risk is not always predictable or preventable. There are many potential courses of action available in response to a particular problem, but it can be difficult to predict exactly how circumstances may alter or interact to affect the outcome. Consequently, it is impossible to remove an element of uncertainty in decision making.

Faulkner identified that 'frontline staff are often afraid of being held responsible should something happen "on their watch". Hence members of staff will often act defensively, and may themselves feel disempowered in a situation that does not support them to take risks with and for their clients' (2012:17). Ayers (2017) argues that the blame culture in social work is dictated by central government's persistent lack of faith and confidence in the profession, which is transmitted to the media, the public and organisational cultures, and even internalised by social workers themselves. She suggests that rather than blame, social work needs a *just* culture, where 'errors and unsafe acts will not be punished if the error was unintentional. However, those who act recklessly or take deliberate and unjustifiable risks will still be subject to disciplinary action' (Ayers, 2017). Social work education, whether delivered through traditional university programmes or work-based routes, must establish a safe and just learning culture, where students can learn to practise defensibly, not defensively.

Risk assessment

Risk assessment is the process of identifying, estimating and evaluating the risk. Kemshall stresses that risk assessment 'is not an end in itself; however, it must be purposeful' (2013: 9). Linking to comments we have already made in this chapter, Hothersall and Maas-Lowitz (2010) caution us that risk assessments cannot prevent risk, they can only identify the probability of harm, assess the impact of it on key individuals, and pose intervention strategies that *may* diminish or reduce the risk of harm. When assessing risk, we need to establish the following:

- What the specific risk is.
- What the significance is, i.e. the probability and seriousness.
- Its currency.
- The context: internal and external factors.
- An awareness of probable sources of error.
- Current or past strategies for managing these.
- The different perspectives on risk.

Kemshall (2013) identifies three approaches to risk assessment – actuarial, unstructured clinical and structured professional judgement.

Actuarial

Based on scientific models of risk, actuarial approaches draw upon statistical and quantitative analysis of data to calculate probability. They do not provide an individualised assessment, do not identify strengths, and are not good predictors of serious and uncommon behaviours/risks.

Unstructured clinical

Based on the subjective knowledge, skills and experience of the assessor, unstructured clinical approaches are individualised and contextualised. However, they are very subject to bias.

Structured professional judgement

This approach seeks to combine positive elements of actuarial and unstructured clinical approaches.

We find the risk assessment matrix (see Figure 3.1) to be a very useful tool (in both teaching and practice) for establishing specific concerns, context and perspectives.

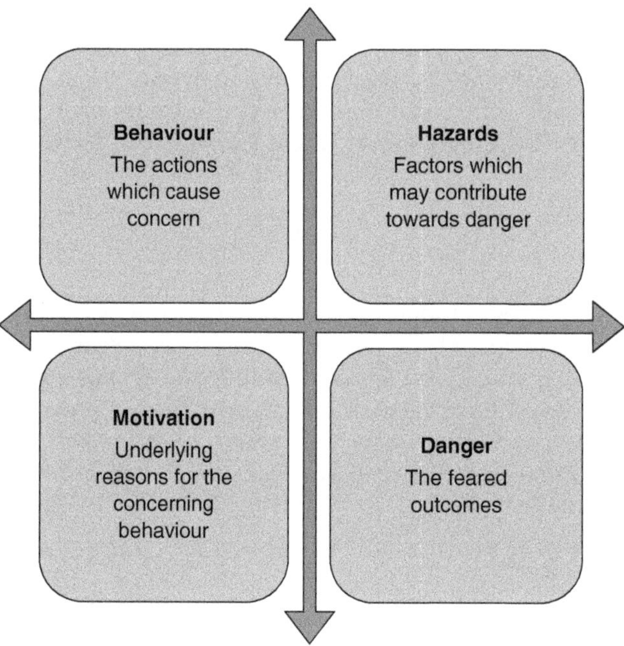

Figure 3.1 Risk assessment matrix

AT NUMBER 5

Prior to his stroke, Max and Samantha enjoyed a very active social life. They both pursued sports and hobbies, and together they enjoyed dining out and going to concerts, the cinema and theatre. Now they very rarely go out at all. Max reluctantly accepts support from carers during the day when Samantha is at work, but once she comes home she provides all of his care, as well as looking after Tyra. Max's speech therapy is going well, but talking is still very tiring for him. He needs a lot of rest, so he likes Samantha to help him to bed after the family's evening meal. After Max and Tyra go to bed, Samantha often feels bored and lonely and longs for adult company. She started drinking a couple of glasses of wine on an evening a few months back, but now she regularly drinks one to two bottles a night. Sometimes when Tyra gets up on a morning, she finds Samantha asleep on the sofa with the TV still on, and has to go to school without breakfast because mummy has a headache and is late for work.

EXERCISE 3.2

Apply the risk matrix above to Samantha's situation to identify the behaviour, hazards, motivation and danger.

AUTHOR'S EXPERIENCE (CAT)

I took a telephone call from a district nurse who wanted to make a safeguarding referral in respect of a woman in her late thirties with physical and learning disabilities. District nurses regularly attended the house where the woman resided with her maternal uncle, who was her main carer. The nurse was clearly very concerned, but quite ambiguous about the nature of her concerns. I asked her to explicitly explain what she believed the risks to be, and she said that the situation of an uncle providing personal care for his adult niece was highly unusual and not normal. I agreed that it was not a common situation and asked again what she felt the risks were. She said it was obvious, everyone who knew about the situation thought it was risky. I asked whether she had seen any evidence of injury, neglect or improper care. She told me that despite her complex needs, the woman was well cared for; however, the situation was not right. I explained that I would need more information to start a safeguarding inquiry, and at this point things got quite bizarre. The nurse told me that I was being obstreperous, and then said, 'He wears a wig! You know exactly what I am getting at!'

I wasn't being intentionally obstreperous, but I was a little frustrated that the nurse clearly expected me to investigate a risk that she wasn't prepared to name, and I felt that a lot of value judgements had been made. I suspected that the nurse was worried about the potential for sexual abuse, but her marked reluctance to express this was extremely unhelpful. Eventually I asked her outright if this was her concern and she acknowledged that it was. I asked if her concern was based on any evidence (other than her apparent beliefs about people who wear wigs!) and she told me that it was not. I agreed to undertake some initial inquiries, but not on a safeguarding basis.

Historical records established that the uncle had always lived there with his mother and sister. When his niece was born, it was apparent that she would need a great deal of care for the rest of her life, and the grandmother, mother and uncle believed it was their duty of love to provide this. Over time, the man's mother and sister died, leaving him as sole carer – a role he intended to continue as long as he was physically able. A colleague and I visited the pair at home, and although

(Continued)

the woman had no verbal communication, we observed her face light up whenever her uncle spoke to or came near. Her needs were being met and there was no evidence of abuse or neglect. The GP was frequently involved and had no concerns at all. We persuaded the uncle to have a carer's assessment and an OT referral to consider a hoist.

”

Risks in social work are primarily responded to through safeguarding, a process which was initially described as child protection or the protection of vulnerable adults. Terminology has shifted in recognition of the oppressive power dynamics, value judgements and potential for victim blaming inherent in the ideas of professionals protecting 'vulnerable' people from abuse. Rights-based approaches recognise that people have the right not to be subjected to inhuman or degrading treatment (Human Rights Act, 1988, Article 3) but also the right to respect for a private and family life (Human Rights Act, 1998, Article 8). They require social workers to actively ensure children and adults are fully involved in the safeguarding process. We believe that to effectively safeguard children and adults, social workers must be trained and supported to apply the full range of their knowledge skills to undertake thorough, personalised and analytical safeguarding assessments.

It is very easy to view risk one-dimensionally, and this is encouraged by some of the commonly used dyadic language associated with risk, e.g. victim/perpetrator, abused/abuser, vulnerable/controlling. People and relationships are complex. A person can be both victim and perpetrator, but if the lens of our assessment is too narrow, we may miss this. The murder of Steven Hoskins in 2006 remains one of the most horrific and high profile UK disability hate crimes (see the serious case review by Flynn, 2007). Steven had a learning disability and mental health problems. He was targeted by a gang led by Darren Stewart, who was also identified as vulnerable adult, because of his chaotic childhood, mental health and substance misuse issues and history of self-harm and suicidal behaviours. Steven's body was found at the base of a railway viaduct. He had been forced to dangle and then drop by Darren and his accomplices. Steven's post-mortem examination found extensive evidence of torture in the form of cigarette burns, neck bruises from the dog collar and lead he had been dragged around in, a lethal dose of paracetamol and alcohol in his system and footprints on his hands, which finally caused him to fall 30 metres to his death.

Smethurst (in Mantell and Scragg, 2011) asserts that good risk management processes are systematic, participatory, proportionate, least restrictive, clear, and are regularly monitored and reviewed (see Table 3.1).

Table 3.1 Risk management processes (based on Hothersall and Maas-Lowit, 2010)

Systematic	Involving accurate analysis of all available information
Participatory	Involving service user and carers as much as practicable
Proportionate	To the degree of perceived risk and available resources
Least restrictive	Maximising individual rights and freedoms
Clear	Involve shared plans outlining who is to do *what* and *when*
Regularly monitored and reviewed	

EXERCISE 3.3

In the first part of the exercise consider risk on a sports playing field or arena: you can be either a spectator or participator in any team sport of your choosing. You notice an opposing team member is playing very hard and recklessly and you are concerned about the risk this person represents. Now ask yourself:

- Who is at risk – is it the player, the opponent or the spectators?
- Try to identify three types of risk posed by this player.

In the second part of the exercise consider yourself as a social worker in a children's residential home. You are concerned about 15-year-old Liam in particular ('At Number 6') who you feel is vulnerable yet persists in risk-taking behaviour. Liam is spending time with people who are much older than him, staying out late and coming back to home intoxicated. You don't think he is aware of the personal risks and are concerned he may influence others to take part in risky behaviour. Now ask yourself:

- Who is at risk – is it Liam, other young people or practitioners?
- Try to identify three types of risk posed by Liam.

PROFESSIONAL JUDGEMENTS

Social workers make sense and form professional judgements about risks. Our role requires that we make practice decisions when people are experiencing or presenting risky behaviours. 'Judgement' and 'decision making' are terms that are often used interchangeably within the social work literature. Taylor (2013) differentiates between the two, describing decision making as 'a conscious process [individually or collectively] ... leading to the selection of a course of action among two or more alternatives' (p.164), and judgement as the 'considered evaluation of evidence by an individual using their cognitive faculties so as to reach an opinion on a preferred course of action based on available information, knowledge and value' (p. 165).

Making decisions

We make decisions – choosing between alternatives with a greater or lesser degree of deliberation – all of the time. A 2017 Microsoft advertisement campaign was premised around the claim that adults make around 35,000 decisions a day. Unfortunately, they didn't provide a reference so we don't know whether this figure is true! However, if we consider that every word we speak and every move we make required us to make a choice, we can begin to see how we may well be making tens of thousands of decisions. Many of these decisions are so implicit and instinctive that we are not even aware we are making them.

EXERCISE 3.4

How did you decide what to have for breakfast today? Think about all of the factors you took into consideration. How significant were the following factors:

- The time of day, your location, your normal routine and habits, your likes and dislikes, the weather, your mood, your skills?
- The available time, resources, options and finances?
- The influence of other people on your decision making?

Were you able to gather all of the information you needed as part of your assessment, or was your assessment compromised in any way?

Now we can start to see how many variables we have to consider – often unconsciously – in an assessment to inform a simple, everyday decision. Was your decision robust? What were the consequences of it? Did it result in a breakfast you were delighted with, satisfied with or unsatisfied with? How will your decision about today's breakfast inform tomorrow's breakfast?

Heuristics (or rule of thumb)

In reflecting on your decision in the exercise above, you become aware of the multiple factors and influences that guided it. In the moment when you were actually deciding what to have for your breakfast, you were almost certainly not aware of these multiple factors. If we stopped and analysed the possible options and consequences of every trivial decision we made, our lives would simply grind to a halt. We use heuristic techniques to allow us to take mental shortcuts and make quick, practical decisions that will meet our immediate needs. We are describing heuristics when we talk about using rule of thumb or common sense, making an educated guess or guesstimating. Heuristics are very helpful, but can also be dangerous. Relying on heuristics usually means that we accept information uncritically, at face value. Stereotyping, bias and assumption are all types of heuristic or a rule of thumb principle.

Social work decisions

When we are faced with a more complicated decision, or when the consequences of our decision are greater, we may become aware of ourselves stopping and thinking. We may defer the decision until we have more information, or have sought the views of others. Social work decisions are professional judgements, made using our professional knowledge, skills, values and experience to consider and analyse evidence about a person or situation, and reach a conclusion or recommendation:

> ... social work decisions are often problematic balancing acts, based on incomplete information, within time constraints, under pressure from different sources, with uncertainty as to the outcome of different options, as well as a constant fear that something will go wrong and the social worker will be blamed. (O'Sullivan, 2011: 2)

There is great value in this honest acknowledgement of the limitations of social work decision making. Social workers are people who work with people, and as we all know, people are flawed, fallible and imperfect. Recognising our limitations enables us to consider how we might address them. It does not guarantee that we will always get things right, but it is a helpful way of identifying our blind spots and checking our assumptions in order to promote defensible practice. Professional judgement is an essential element of our professional practice, and it is intellectually and emotionally challenging.

Barlow and Scott describe professional judgement as:

> ... the use of clinical expertise both to undertake contextual assessments and to make decisions about the necessary standardised tools to be used as part of an actuarial assessment of risk. Clinical judgement/skills are then used to translate the information from both of these processes into decision-making about evidence informed interventions and services. (Barlow and Scott, 2010: 16)

Rutter and Brown explain that 'professional judgement is a crucial aspect in the development of professional expertise' (2015: 17). Dunne rather helpfully proposes that 'professional judgement involves the ability to actuate knowledge with relevance, appropriateness, or sensitivity to the context' (2011: 18).

Reflective decision making

Social workers aim to practise non-judgementally, but are required to make professional judgements, and this often leaves our students feeling conflicted and confused. We all have our own individual beliefs, values, preferences, likes and dislikes, and some of the exercises we introduced you to in Chapter 1 encouraged you to identify these. Taking steps to recognise when our personal beliefs and values may be influencing our professional judgements can help us identify when we are being judgemental and counter this. Employing reflectivity, criticality and reflexivity can help us to be more objective in our decision making, increase our self-awareness, and facilitate more person-centred assessments. Dunne (2011) makes the point that when practice is reduced to a technical process, it ceases to be reflective or person oriented. Rutter and Brown (2015: 17) suggest that 'high quality professional practice encompasses individual leadership based on sound judgement derived from a set of professional moral standards'. There are several models of reflection, and the one we use most often with our students is Gibbs's (1988) reflective cycle:

Description – what happened?

Feelings – what were you thinking and feeling?

Evaluation – what was good and bad about the experience?

Analysis – what sense can you make of the situation?

Conclusion – what else could you have done?

Action plan – what will you do next time?

AT NUMBER 4

Following a disturbance at her home, police arrested Olivia's partner for domestic violence and referred Olivia and her children, Matty and Georgia, to children's services. The referral was prioritised with a social work visit because of Georgia's learning disability. During the home visit, Olivia was very concerned about her children's welfare and impressed the social worker with her child-centred house. There were lots of toys and learning materials, and Olivia and her children interacted well. The social worker's interview focused on the current situation and allowed Olivia to reflect on her experiences with social workers. The reports from nursery were positive about her. The social worker's professional opinion was that she was maintaining her children's welfare and seemed able to protect them.

EXERCISE 3.5

Use Gibbs's cycle to reflect on this situation.

- How might Olivia have felt about the police referring her to children's services?
- What pressures may she have felt during the assessment?
- What emotions might she have felt during the assessment?

Consider the social worker's response to this situation.

- What pressures may the social worker have felt?
- What emotions might the social worker have felt?
- What contributed to the social worker's professional judgement?

Taylor and White (2000) argue that in order to enhance a critical approach to judgement and decision making in social work, practitioners need to develop reflexive practice (see Chapter 1). Reflexive practice is concerned with our capacity to critically question our intuitive and analytical reasoning and consider the influence the 'taken-for-granted dimension' has had on our formulation of judgement. Taken-for-granted dimensions of practice include dominant discourses, knowledge, language and 'normative' cultural rules and practices informing our reasoning and judgement. For example, being critically aware of how our anxieties about risk can encourage defensive and risk-averse approaches to judgement and decision making. Reflection and reflexive approaches can help us to become aware of potential barriers to effective decision making, such as:

Deflection/routine categorisation	Accepting information uncritically and unquestioningly
Pattern making	Viewing a situation as typical and making judgements accordingly, e.g. 'This referral is similar to one I had last week, therefore I will make the same decision I did then.'
Bias	The influence of your beliefs and values that confirm an initial interpretation, e.g. one based on prior knowledge

	of the family, experience of the family (hostile, compliant, engaged etc.).
Framing bias	Judgement influenced by emotional statement or frame of reference.

Autonomy

In previous chapters, we have talked about how many social work assessments have been increasingly standardised through agency pro forma documents. However, and in contrast to this standardisation process, Trevithick (2014) suggests that the wide range of social work assessments and the diverse purposes of these assessments have effectively shifted them away from standardised formats. Therefore, we seem to have opposite trends in social work assessments: at one end there is the agency's desire for standardisation, which conflicts with the opposite end and the proliferation of assessments requiring a wider range of non-standardised assessment formats. In developing this argument, Trevithick refers to investigative assessments (e.g. safeguarding children risk assessments); eligibility/needs-led assessments (e.g. community care or child in need); multidisciplinary assessments (e.g. for hospital discharge); suitability assessments (e.g. foster carer assessments); and third party assessments (e.g. pre-sentence reports). It is therefore impractical to suggest a one-size-fits-all approach to social work practice, and the proliferation of diverse assessments at the very least implies a significant role for professional autonomy.

Autonomous practice exists in the space before populating the form, in the acts of information gathering (observations, questions, curiosity) and assessment forming (intuition, analysis, values) to make sense and form a professional judgement. Neil Thompson (2015) highlights that professional practice involves discretion and judgement, and argues that practice is more than following procedure. He suggests that despite the bureaucracy and layers of policy and legal context, there remains a considerable degree of professional autonomy for social workers. In a similar vein, Rutter and Brown (2015) acknowledge that prescribed procedures can be helpful for practitioners, but also suggest that prescriptive responses can fall short when practitioners are confronted with new and unusual practice situations. After all, one size cannot fit all social work issues. Despite the movement towards a heavily regulated and prescribed profession, evidence of autonomous practice remains during professional judgements.

AUTHOR'S EXPERIENCE (PHIL)

Autonomy is how we formulate our judgements and decisions to make recommendations and does not reflect notions of autonomously activating services or professional power. This is an important distinction, which I only learned through years of experience, denial and insecure practice. As a student I presumed I would act autonomously when I became a social worker, and in my first social work role I was shocked by mechanisms which I felt held me back, such as supervision and having to report to managers and other

(Continued)

professionals. I now recognise how good a supervisor my first social work manager was; she explained to me that you can only ever control yourself, and then only what you think.

Recently, I was teaching a newly qualified social worker undertaking his Assessed and Supported Year in Employment (ASYE) who recounted a similar story of realisation. He told me he was surprised to discover that in practice he only really had any autonomy over what he thought and what recommendations he could make to his manager to influence what the manager thought.

Accountability

We are rightly accountable for our professional practice. This accountability can seem like a heavy burden when we seek to make sense of highly complex needs and social contexts within a more prudent social care environment. The movement towards marketisation and customer-based services has seen the emergence of a complaint and litigation culture. This may be more sharply felt when social workers are seen to gate keep and restrict access to seemingly ever-reducing public services. Working within a hierarchical structure, social workers are part of a managed workforce. Supervision (which we will consider in more detail in Chapter 6) is important as both a management exercise and reflective tool, but it does not remove professional accountability. We are accountable to the people with whom we work, accountable within our employment structure, and accountable to our regulatory body. We may, retrospectively, be called upon to articulate our professional decision, and here 'I informed the manager' is no longer acceptable.

Van der Gaag et al. (2017) identified that when expectations are not met because of decisions taken at a strategic service level – e.g. funding decisions, service redesign, multiple changes of allocated worker – individual social workers may be blamed and reported to their regulator. They also found that many fitness to practise referrals to the HCPC related to disagreement with professional decisions and a desire to see them changed (Van der Gaag et al., 2017). In light of this, the reluctance to be accountable for professional decision making which we have previously highlighted becomes an understandable response.

AT NUMBER 2

Alfie and Suzie were initially assessed six years ago as foster carers by their local authority through what is known as a Form F assessment (Chapman, 2016). The 'CoramBAAf Form F. assessment' is the most commonly used format to assess prospective foster carers. There are generally two stages in the Form F assessment:

- Stage 1 is the completion of several different checks, including criminal records and medical, in order to either screen people out of the assessment or identify that they are appropriate to proceed to Stage 2 of the process.
- Stage 2 is a more personal assessment process involving a number of regular meetings with an assessing social worker to reflect on childhood, adult life, relationships, caring and personal experiences.

Aside from the two stages to this process, the assessment of prospective foster carers has two connecting aspects: firstly, an evaluation of what a candidate can offer, their suitability along with their strengths and weaknesses; and secondly, to assess and develop that candidate's ability to change or grow with fostering (Chapman, 2016). The implication is that the assessing social worker must not only assess the fostering candidate's experiences, attitudes and reflections, but also make some judgement to predict their capacity to care for fostered children and young people. The difficulty here is that many foster carers' past experiences do not equip them with any understanding of the possible adversities looked after children may have encountered. Essentially, the assessing social worker is making a calculated guess based on their practice knowledge and assessment skills. The possible consequences of 'getting it wrong' are almost impossible to calculate but very easy to imagine.

EXERCISE 3.6

- Is the social worker autonomous in this situation? What is your evidence for your answer?
- To whom is the social worker accountable? How?
- What might the consequences of a poor assessment of Alfie and Suzie be?

The interaction between professional autonomy, professional judgement and opinion forming is part of contemporary social work practice, where we are often required to reach professional judgements during conflict. This conflict may be directed at the social worker, other professionals, family members, the community, or even internalised to the self. A process does not and cannot fit all scenarios. It is therefore in the gaps where process does not fit that we make autonomously based decisions that are most challenging to social workers' sense of self-risk and fear of consequences. We believe this is why practitioners may at times be reluctant to accept the autonomous nature of our role. After all, clinical expertise takes time to develop and until we feel comfortable, we will inevitably feel some insecurity about making decisions.

Defensible decisions

It is vital to differentiate between defensible practice and defensive practice. Defensive practice describes insecure practice that does not accept any challenge to professional opinion. It is our contention that social work should seek to promote defensible assessments and practice, rather than inflexible, risk-averse assessments constructed around the fallacy that it is possible to never make a mistake. Defensible decisions are those which, when viewed in hindsight, we are able to demonstrate were based on sound evidence and assessment. In forming defensible assessments, Kemshall (2013) proposes that we ask the following questions:

- Were all reasonable steps taken?
- Were reliable assessment methods employed, using information gathered and methodically analysed?
- Were decisions recorded and acted upon?
- Is there evidence that agency policy and procedures were adhered to?
- Have practitioners and managers been analytical and proactive, using sound sources of knowledge?

Most social work teams will include practitioners who explain 'we don't use theory here' or 'you only read articles at university'. To develop robust and defensible practice our profession has to embrace all available and up-to-date evidence. Our practice often has to be defended in retrospect, and therefore we must explain 'I chose this course of action because the evidence from research indicated ...' Unfortunately, as we have explained in earlier chapters, events move on: time does not stand still, and our work with vulnerable people in crisis may seem right at the time but who knows what the future will bring. Taylor explains that:

> We need to use sound professional knowledge in our judgement so as to be transparent and fair in our decision processes, and so as to achieve the best possible outcomes for our clients. This has come to be known in recent decades as *evidence based practice*. (Taylor, 2013: 66)

APPROACHES AND MODELS OF DECISION MAKING

Earlier in the chapter, we set out Kemshall's three approaches to risk assessment: actuarial, unstructured clinical and structured professional judgement. These relate directly to the three broader models of decision making which we will now explore below.

Technical-rational approaches

Related to actuarial risk assessment, technical-rational approaches are also referred to as analytical, prescriptive approaches. They are concerned with calculated, deliberated, prescriptive and analytical judgements, and are considered a reasoned, structured, logical and probabilistic approach to decision making. They often incorporate cognitive linear models, e.g. flowcharts, decision-making trees to aid professional practice, and use step-by-step rules/processes to inform decision making.

Working Together to Safeguard Children (HM Government, 2018) and the *Framework for the Assessment of Children and Families* are two examples of guidance that promote a technical-rational approach. Decisions are based on 'evidence based practice, grounded in knowledge with finely balanced professional judgement' (Department of Health et al., 2000: 16). The performance management culture of statutory social work practice often privileges technical-rational approaches as a means of managing the volume of work in high pressure environments, e.g. by applying thresholds, eligibility criteria, timescales etc. This can contribute to a conveyor-belt culture (Ferguson, 2003), which discourages practice-depth (Chapman and Field, 2007) and stifles the development of skilled intuitive reasoning. It raises concerns about whether the contemporary social worker's primary function is as a practitioner resource, or simply as an audit tool. Research studies (e.g. Hackett and Taylor, 2014; Platt and Turney, 2014) suggest that the technical-rational approach is most useful when time is on your side, the level of error is high and you need to demonstrate clear and accountable decision making.

Intuitive approaches

Related to unstructured clinical risk assessments, intuitive approaches are also referred to as descriptive approaches, practice wisdom, real world decisions, bounded rationality and naturalistic approaches. They describe knowing how to proceed without necessarily deploying a cognitive analytical approach to the task in hand, and recognise the value of practice intuition, practice experience and practice wisdom in challenging contexts. The more experienced the worker, the more likely a reliance on intuition based on prior experience when quick decisions need to be made, reflecting our accumulation of an intuitive knowledge bank as we move through the PCF continuum from novice to expert.

However, it is difficult to establish the reliability and validity of such a subjective approach, or to achieve consistency across a social work team made up of different workers with different levels of experience. The potential for bias and error in intuitive decision making has influenced the move towards more analytical approaches.

Integrated approaches

Related to structured professional judgements in risk assessment, integrated approaches to decision making advocate systems analysis that aims for a balance between technical-rational and naturalistic approaches. The importance of intuition is recognised, alongside the need for reflective space and supervision to try to counter the potential for bias (Taylor and White, 2001). Hackett and Taylor's (2014) research followed social work decision making in practice and identified that a combination of technical-rational and intuitive approaches were used when:

- the decision(s) involved assessment of harm and risk;
- there was previous knowledge of the service user;
- the stakes were high and there was a need for a strong evidence base, e.g. mental health tribunal, care proceedings;
- practitioners were part of action/feedback loops, e.g. formal review processes;
- the environment was uncertain and changing.

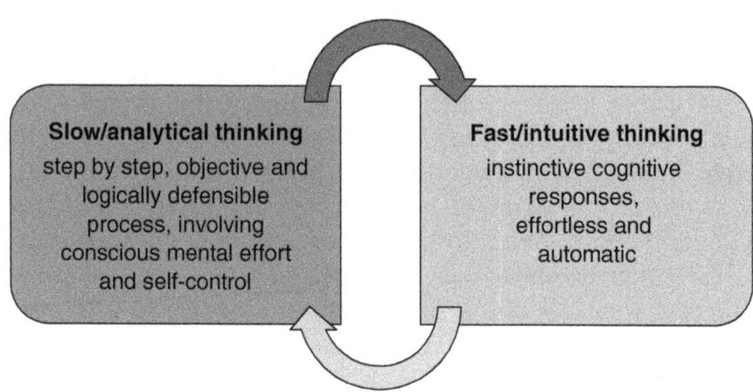

Figure 3.2 Kahneman's interrelated dimensions of thinking

Kahneman (2011) suggests that we use two interrelated dimensions of slow and fast thinking (see Figure 3.2). In contrast to accepted wisdom, he argues that fast, intuitive thinking is valuable when making decisions. He suggests that slow thinking can overturn effective judgements by allowing us to overthink something to the point of hesitation, or persuade ourselves to ignore our intuitive, fast thinking-based judgement.

In a similar vein to Kahneman, Klein (1998, 2004) developed a naturalist model of decision making, which he calls *recognition-primed decision-making*. In the recognition-primed decision-making model, the decision maker sizes up the situation through pattern matching and recognising relevant cues. Through the pattern, the decision maker gets a sense of the situation, knowing which cues are important and need to be monitored. We know what goals we might be able to accomplish and have an idea of what to expect next. When we analyse, our brain is balancing a complex interplay between different neurological processes.

We should not discount the fact that we analyse on a daily basis in order to understand, explain, propose and decide. Crossing a road is a very hazardous activity, but through a complex combination of factors, we are able to use our existing knowledge and memories, apply this to interpret a dynamic situation, weigh up possible outcomes, and make a judgement about when to cross the road. Our analytical skills have evolved through our personal history; however, as practitioners we need to formulate *professional* judgements. To know when to cross the road we use fast and slow thinking as well as recognition-primed decision making. We essentially use similar processes when making professional judgements.

AT NUMBER 1

Mary was very lonely and depressed after her husband's death. She lost a great deal of weight and her Type 1 diabetes became unstable. With time and support, she began to feel better and her physical and mental health improved. She started to attend a luncheon club at the local community centre and this led to her developing a number of good friendships. She also got a part-time job running the community centre coffee bar, and was extremely proud that her friendly attitude and attention to detail increased the takings significantly.

Mary's daughter always calls round to Number 1 on Friday afternoons for a catch-up with her mother. For the last three Fridays, she has noticed that Mary looks tired and seems forgetful. Today Mary kept getting her grandchildren's names wrong, and complained that she couldn't find her mobile phone anywhere; her daughter eventually found it in the fridge.

EXERCISE 3.7

- What is the first explanation for Mary's situation that springs to mind?
- What evidence is there for this?
- What assumptions are present in this?
- What might be the consequences of you basing your professional judgement on this instinctive explanation?
- What module of decision making have you applied?

Develop three alternative explanations for what might be happening with Mary. How could you test these out?

Overview of professional judgement

We have set out a number of models and theories, which are helpful ways of understanding and approaching decision making, but we are not suggesting that any model will fit a situation entirely, or that applying a model simplifies professional judgement. Social workers are masters of eclecticism; we rarely work from a purist model of anything, because this simply does not fit with the way that lives and relationships are lived. We take pieces of theory, research and knowledge and weave them together to help us understand and explain enormously complicated situations. We suggest the following process of reaching professional judgement:

1. Throughout the assessment process, develop explanations to understand the situation and test these using your observations and interactions with the person/family, together with the information you collate from historical records and other professionals. Develop and test multiple explanations/hypotheses: the more open-minded you are, the more robust your decision making will be.
2. Critically analyse the collated evidence by applying knowledge. Link theory to the evidence and ask yourself what matches? What does the research tell you? What does your practice wisdom tell you?
3. Critically reflect on your process. What decision-making framework is guiding you? What are the strengths and weaknesses of your evidence gathering and analysis? What do you

not know? Has anything biased your decision making? Has your decision making considered the long-term as well as the immediate impact of possible outcomes?
4. Draw a clear conclusion – this is your professional judgement. Make recommendations that are achievable and will address the risks identified.

SUMMARY

In this chapter we have explored the nature of risk, recognising that safeguarding children and adults from harm is social work's key role. Sadly, the unpredictable nature of people and relationships makes this extremely difficult and sometimes unattainable. The expectations that we place upon ourselves, and that are placed upon us by others, must be realistic and bounded by what is achievable. Similarly, the requirements we place on the people we work with must be realistic and recognise that human life involves risk. Cultures of practice have a significant influence on whether practitioners promote rights and positive risk taking, or become risk averse. If our professional judgements are to be robust and evidence based, it is important that we critically reflect on our own decision-making processes to identify any shortcomings or assumptions. We have offered tools and approaches which can support social work approaches to risk and decision making, and we concur with contemporary research which suggests that defensible decision making requires social workers to use a combination of technical-rational and intuitive approaches.

4 ASSESSING CHILDREN, YOUNG PEOPLE AND FAMILIES

Learning in this chapter relates to

PCF	KSS Adult Services	KSS Child & Family
1. Professionalism 2. Values & Ethics 3. Diversity & Equalities 4. Rights & Justice 5. Knowledge 8. Contexts & Organisations	7. Direct work with individuals & families	1. The role of child & family social work 2. Child development 3. Adult mental ill health, substance misuse, domestic abuse, physical ill health & disability 4. Abuse & neglect of children 5. Effective direct work with children & families 6. Child & family assessment 7. Analysis, decision making, planning & review 9. Professional ethics 11. Organisational context

INTRODUCTION

This chapter reflects on the assessment context when working with children and their families. We begin with a brief history of childcare social work practice, highlighting key legislation that has shaped social work practice in this arena and exploring public debates behind policy changes. Any contemporary work on childcare assessment considers safeguarding children, young people and their families from risk and harm. We reflect on assessment perspectives, and seek to give the assessment of children's needs fresh impetus by drawing on notions of childhood, family and gender. As we write this book, the implementation of the Children and

Social Work Act (2017) has begun to take shape through the setting up of Social Work England, the Child and Family Social Work National Assessment and Accreditation System (NAAS) and the National Child Safeguarding Practice Review Panel.

BRIEF HISTORY OF CHILDCARE SOCIAL WORK PRACTICE: WORKING WITH FAMILIES AND CHILDREN

To our contemporary minds, the fact that children require care and protection seems natural. However, society has not always recognised children as being more than just smaller adults. In our previous chapters, we have shown how social needs alter over time and welfare services have moved away from seeking to meet universal needs and towards responsibilisation. Many social workers and social commentators regret this shift from a welfare state with the subsequent reduction of services. We have suggested this transformation, occurring incrementally over time, has refocused social work practice onto assessment. In childcare social work, the focus is heavily placed upon safeguarding and child protection. Whilst this emphasis is perhaps most acutely felt in childcare social work, *all* contemporary UK social work is generally premised on safeguarding and responsibilisation. With a reduced welfare state and in the electronic age, with virtual teams, video interviewing and e-mails, it is tempting to see practice as less intimately involved with people. Harry Ferguson argues that the tendency to see child protection as more of an organisational, desk-bound, case management exercise has devalued the importance of professionals assessing the space where the child lives, and he advocates for a more intimate rather than distant and desk-bound child protection practice (Ferguson, 2011).

Historically, the state in the UK was not concerned about safeguarding children. Child protection appears to have originated during the 1870s in the USA and thereafter spread to Europe and Australasia. Specific concern about the welfare of children in the UK does not fully develop until the latter part of the nineteenth century, with the move to reduce child cruelty and the establishment of the National Society for the Prevention of Cruelty to Children (NSPCC, 2009a). Similar organisations, like Action for Children and Barnardo's, also chart their foundations to this period. The first Prevention of Cruelty to Children Act (1889) provided guidelines on the employment of children and outlawed begging. It was not until the Children Act 1908 that the state was first mandated to investigate sexual abuse of children within families. Until this Act, any such investigations within families had been traditionally the preserve of the clergy (Batty, 2004). While much of this early legislation appears outdated, the NSPCC, early on in its history, adopted the practice of home visiting, which Ferguson (2011) considers integral to safeguarding children. Policy and practice evolve. Reductions in public services and alternative methods of gathering information make it possible for home visiting to be perceived as outdated during the digital age. We feel nothing could be further from the truth, and agree with Ferguson's continued support of home visiting because it ensures we see children in their home environment.

In previous chapters, we have reflected on how legislation and social policy resulted in increased state responsibilities in family life. However, the UK has not acted in isolation and during the 1980s the United Nations Convention on the Rights of the Child promoted universal concepts of childhood and the rights of children (United Nations, 1989). Following this international precedent, England and Wales legislated to safeguard children initially through the Children Act 1989, and later on, in response to the public inquiry into eight-year-old Victoria Climbié's tragic death, with the Children Act 2004 (Home Office, 1991; Social Services Inspectorate, 1995; Department for Education and Skills, 2006). The Children and Social Work Act 2017 established a new English social work regulatory body (Social Work England) and National Child Safeguarding Practice Review Panel, as well as local panels (replacing Serious Case Reviews) to identify safeguarding issues and learning. This Act seeks to provide some clarity on the corporate parenting role of local authorities for care leavers and educational achievement for children looked after by local authorities.

In just over a century, we have witnessed not only the evolution of social work as a profession, and the emergence and retraction of the welfare state with a shift from universal need to responsibilisation, but also the growth of legislation and an emphasis on safeguarding children. Social work has taken, and been given, lead responsibility to ensure all children are safe. Professional practice has become focused on this aspect of social need and our profession receives much criticism when children are not kept safe. The state's withdrawal from welfare services aimed to meet universal need has become more sharply focused, primarily through local authorities, trusts (Northern Ireland) and boards (Scotland), on the responsibility to safeguard children. A prime role of social work is to assess childcare need in response to safeguarding concerns and then, where assessed appropriate, to intervene to protect children.

ASSESSING CHILDREN'S NEEDS: CONTEMPORARY PROCEDURES/ PERSPECTIVES

We have discussed assessments and reflected on professional decision making. In this section, we introduce procedures for assessing children's needs because in childcare social work safeguarding and the child's welfare are paramount. We suggest practice depth and professional analysis are important, and we agree with Marion Bogo and her colleagues that:

> ... professional judgment is based on the links between a practitioner's thoughts and feelings and the reflective and critical thinking she or he brings to the judgments and decisions made. (Bogo et al., 2014:10)

Yet we also recognise the central aspect of procedures in childcare social work. Later on in this chapter we discuss more complex aspects of childcare social work, but it is important to locate the procedural context to childcare social work at the beginning of this section on assessing children's needs.

Contemporary application and procedures

Through the Children Act 1989, local authorities have a duty to 'safeguard and promote the welfare of children who are in need'. Social workers, as local authority employees, are legally obliged under this Act to assess child welfare and reports of child abuse. The *Working Together to Safeguard Children* (HM Government, 2018) guidance provides a series of flowcharts detailing the appropriate actions. For instance, Figure 4.1 (below) refers to the action following a child's referral to a local authority.

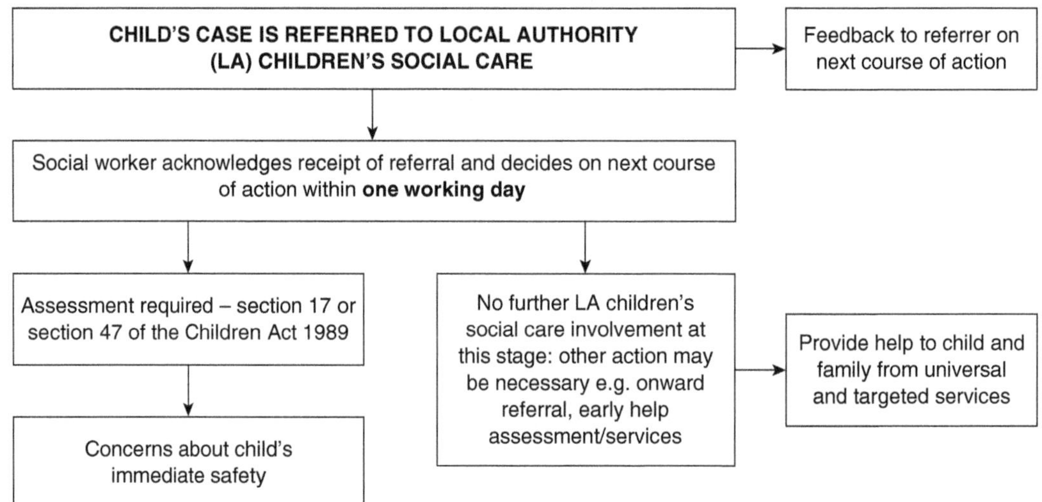

Figure 4.1 Action taken when a child is referred to local authority children's social care services (HM Government, 2018: 33; reproduced under Open Government Licence v3.0)

The flowchart suggests that practice in childcare social work is technical-rational (see Chapter 3) and very much prescribed. This impression is further supported by Figure 4.2, which relates to the statutory assessment of children and their families and provides guidance on actions and timescales for the assessment.

However, whilst the statutory social work response is prescribed, the expectation is that within this process, social workers operate autonomously, undertaking robust professional decision making. The guidance stipulates the analytical component of the assessment and states:

> The social worker should analyse all the information gathered from the assessment, including from a young carer's, parent carer's or non-parent carer's assessment, to decide the nature and level of the child's needs and the level of risk, if any, they may be facing. The social worker should receive insight and challenge to their emerging hypothesis from their practice supervisors and other relevant practitioners who should challenge the social worker's assumptions as part of this process. An informed decision should be taken on the nature of any action required and which services should be provided. (HM Government, 2018: 29)

The guidance, therefore, while offering a clear process, also recognises the importance of professional judgement. It calls for an integrative approach utilising both technical-rational and intuitive approaches to professional judgement to create defensible decisions and recommendations. It also includes the framework for assessing children in need (see Figure 4.3).

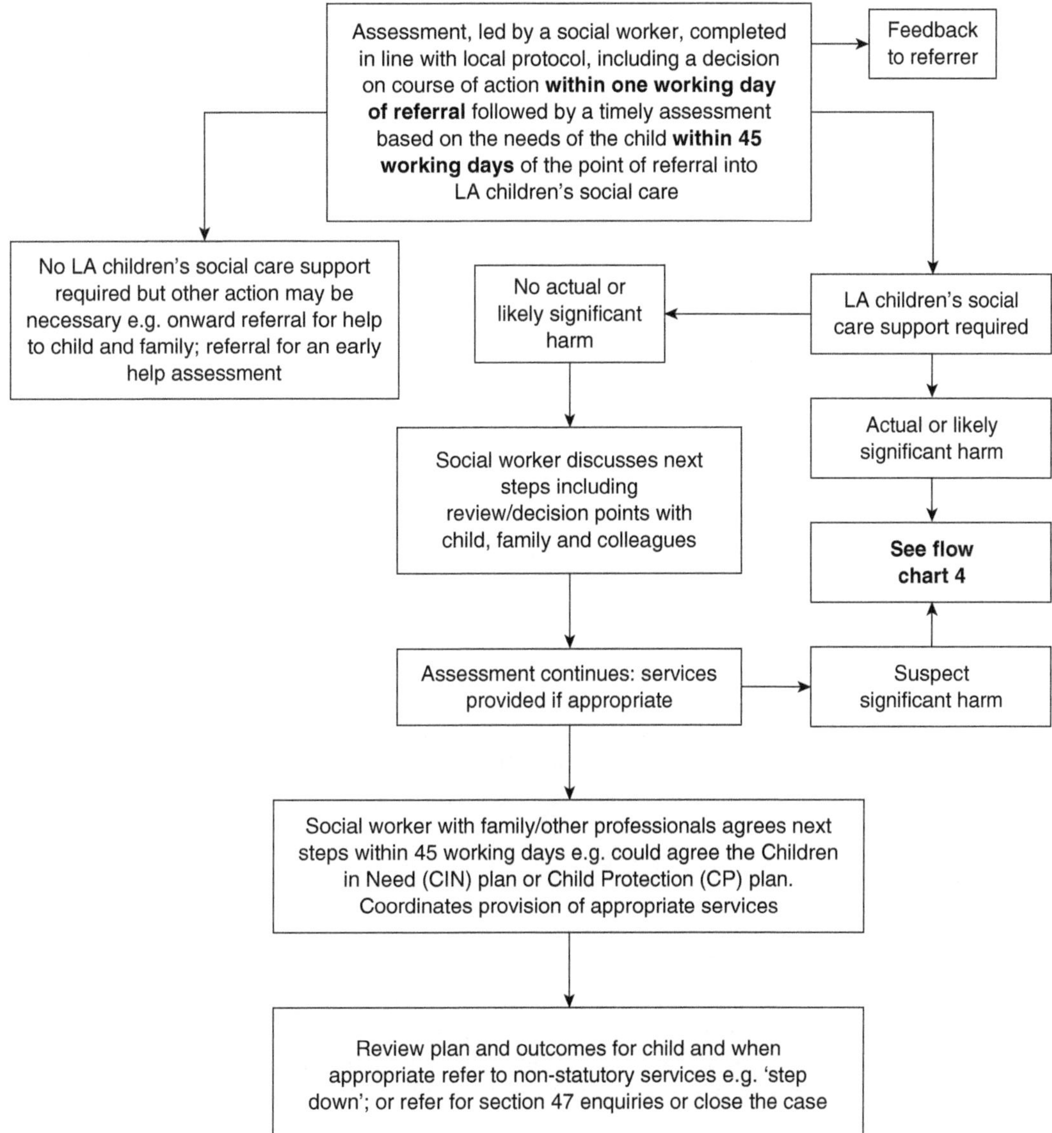

Figure 4.2 Action taken for an assessment of a child under the Children Act 1989 (HM Government, 2018: 38; reproduced under Open Government Licence v3.0)

First introduced by the Department of Health in 2000, the *Framework for Assessment of Children in Need and their Families* sought to address perceived shortfalls in childcare assessments and encourage more holistic and less prescriptive assessments (Calder, 2003; Wilson et al., 2011). The basic aim of any assessment is to reach a judgement, and in relation to childcare social work is about identifying the nature and level of needs and/or risks that the child may be facing within their family. The Department for Education guidance for childcare planning reflects on the Assessment Framework's three domains of parenting capacity, child's developmental needs and family and environmental factors (see Figure 4.3), and explains:

> The seven dimensions of developmental need will feature prominently in care planning, placement and review. (Department for Education, 2015b: 4).

(We explore planning and reviewing in Chapter 6.)

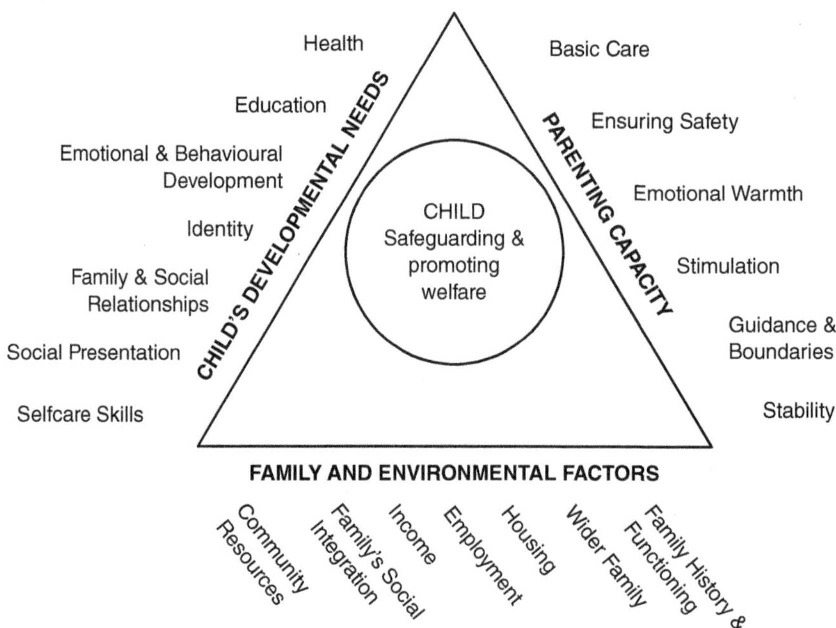

Figure 4.3 The Assessment Framework (HM Government, 2018: 28; reproduced under Open Government Licence v3.0)

The *Working Together to Safeguard Children* guidance has been updated several times (most recently in 2015 and 2018) and the current guidance states:

> Whatever legislation the child is assessed under, the purpose of the assessment is always:
>
> - to gather important information about a child and family;
> - to analyse their needs and/or the nature and level of any risk and harm being suffered by the child;
> - to decide whether the child is a child in need (section 17) or is suffering or likely to suffer significant harm (section 47);
> - to provide support to address those needs to improve the child's outcomes and welfare and where necessary make them safe. (HM Government, 2018: 24)

Working Together to Safeguard Children includes guidance on Early Help assessments (which replaced the Common Assessment Framework [CAF]) and states:

Providing early help is more effective in promoting the welfare of children than reacting later. Early help means providing support as soon as a problem emerges, at any point in a child's life, from the foundation years through to the teenage years. Early help can also prevent further problems arising. (HM Government, 2018: 13)

AT NUMBER 6

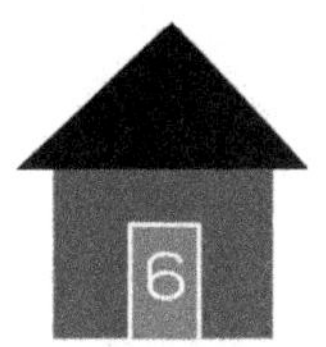

Sally became pregnant when she was living in foster care aged 15. At that time, she refused to say who the father was and because she was living in foster care there was an unborn baby conference. At the conference, and due to Sally's childhood experiences, foster care circumstance and her age it was agreed to place her in a parenting assessment placement. Her foster carers were not approved for babies and had no experience of assessing birth parents, so Sally moved to live with a single female foster carer approved as a parent and child foster carer. This upset Sally because she was happy living with her foster carers, liked the area and enjoyed school, and now had to move from the city to live in a small rural village.

Sally was unsure if her foster carer was there to help care for her and her baby, or whether she was there to assess Sally's parenting skills. Sally fell asleep without feeding her baby because she was tired, and the foster carer's recording detailed how she had to intervene to feed the baby because Sally would not wake up. Another day, the foster carer's recording reported Sally had asked her to babysit because she wanted a night out with her friends. There was a tense scene when Sally's social worker asked about these events. Sally swore at the social worker and told her she didn't want to be a mother anyway. The assessment concluded Sally was ill prepared, too immature, not attentive enough and too aggressive to care for a young baby.

EXERCISE 4.1

Using the Assessment Framework how would you assess Sally in relation to:

- the child's developmental needs?
- her parenting capacity?
- family and environmental factors?

How would you reflect that you had adhered to the *Working Together to Safeguard Children* (HM Government, 2018) guidance on how:

- to gather important information about a child and family?
- to analyse their needs and/or the nature and level of any risk and harm being suffered by the child?
- to decide whether the child is a child in need (section 17) or is suffering or likely to suffer significant harm (section 47)?

Childcare assessments are not easy or straightforward. Assessments are more comprehensive than identifying a child's needs and the mother and father's parenting capacity; they extend to assessing other family and community members. Within the assessment process, the gathered information must be analysed and different variables identified and considered before a decision is reached. Childcare assessments seek to secure the child's immediate safety, but also inform planning for the rest of the child's life. Contemporary life expectancy is such that assessments and professional judgments made in respect of a five-year-old child now will potentially have impact for the next eighty-five years of their life.

What is a child?

At first glance, this question seems redundant: surely everyone knows what a child is? Actually, it is surprisingly complicated to quantify what – and *when* – a child is. We frequently talk about young people being very grown up, or old beyond their years, and about older people being childlike and immature. This suggests that childhood and adulthood are not exactly fixed states, that they have strong behavioural elements. We tend to view childhood through the lens of our personal experience, so conceptualising it can be a highly emotive exercise.

Objectively, childhood refers to a chronological period of human growth and development, and biologically it is considered to end once a person reaches sexual maturity. However, we don't usually start to treat someone as an adult simply because they have entered puberty. In addition to physical maturity, we construct adulthood around a range of social and legal concepts such as independence, self-sufficiency and responsibility. Childhood, therefore, is constructed around somewhat negative notions of dependence, vulnerability, innocence, and often powerlessness.

Article 1 of the United Nations Convention on the Rights of the Child (1989) declares that 'A child means every human being below the age of 18 years unless, under the law applicable to the child, majority is attained earlier.' UK legislation takes various stances about when childhood ends and adulthood begins. No single law defines the age of a child and things differ between the UK nations. In all four the legal remit for child protection/safeguarding is a child who has not yet reached their 18th birthday. The Children Act 1989 mainly applies to those under the age of 18, but young people who are considered particularly vulnerable, such as those with some learning disabilities, may continue to be supported by children's care services after they reach this age. Under the Children (Leaving Care) Act 2000, local authorities in England and Wales have responsibilities towards care leavers until they are at least 21 (and these extend beyond 21 if the young care leaver is in education or training), and the Children and Social Work Act 2017 requires local authorities to produce a *Local Offer* for care leavers. In England and Wales, the Mental Capacity Act 2005 uses the term 'children' for those below the age of 16, who do not have legal autonomy over decisions. It states that provided that they have the mental capacity (see Chapter 5), those aged 16 and over have legal autonomy over the decisions that they make. This is consistent with the age of sexual consent in England and Wales, which the Sexual Offences Act 2003 sets at 16. It may seem surprising then, that the age of criminal responsibility is set much lower, at 10 in England, Wales and Northern Ireland, and 12 in Scotland.

EXERCISE 4.2

Thinking back to your own childhood:

- What status did you have? How did this feel?
- In what situations did you value/enjoy your status as a child?
- In what situations did you dislike/resent your status as a child?
- When did you stop thinking of yourself as a child and why?

INTRODUCING CHILD DEVELOPMENT: RELEVANCE FOR ASSESSMENTS

Child development is the biological, emotional and psychological changes experienced by humans from birth until adulthood and the end of adolescence. The expectation is for children to progress from dependency to increasing autonomy as they mature. Childhood is generally perceived as a continuous process with predictable sequences; however, the maturation process from childhood to adulthood is unique for every child. Children experience many differences so that 'childhood' is a generic term, which belies the unique circumstances of each child. Children within families have different experiences and are genetically different from their siblings. Therefore, an understanding of child development requires the practitioner undertaking an assessment to appreciate the unique circumstances and personality of each child.

AUTHOR'S EXPERIENCE (PHIL)

The trainer said 'all children's behaviour is understandable'. Someone asked, 'What about a child on the autism spectrum who presents bizarre and difficult to understand behaviour?' The trainer, quick as a flash, retorted – 'The explanation there is autism.' Since that session, I have become more knowledgeable about autism and have written quite a few magazine articles about it. I now think that the trainer's answer was at most only partially correct. An adult on the autism spectrum explained to me behaviour is neither the autism, nor the person, but simply something we objectively witness and describe.

Behaviour is understandable, though it may be unfathomable and incomprehensible to the assessor. As a practitioner, I have worked with many young people who repeat problematic actions – actions almost predestined to have a negative impact on them. Once while piloting a comprehensive recording system we were able to

(Continued)

identify a fostered child's 'aggressive' behaviour directed at the foster carers' child as frustration and boredom, rather than something malicious. Unfortunately, we only managed to gain this understanding following the breakdown of his foster placement and his moving to another home. The fostered child suffered the consequences of his behaviour being misunderstood.

Childhood stages

Child development is the progression from infant dependency to increasing autonomy and adulthood, during which time the child will experience different stages of biological, psychological and emotional development. It is mostly recognised as a continuous process with a predictable sequence; however, each child is unique and therefore there is considerable variation, with different rates of progression and each stage affected by the preceding developmental experiences. Naturally, not all children achieve adult autonomy. It does not progress at the same rate, and alternative and complementing models of childhood growth include: identity formation (Erikson, 1968); staged schematic progress (Piaget & Gruber, 1977; Piaget & Inhelder, 2000; Piaget, 2001); mentored progress (Vygotsky, 2016); social learning (Skinner et al 1988); role modelling and self-efficacy (Bandura, 1978, 1994); and ecological systems connections (Bronfenbrenner, 1979). Erikson, developing Freud's delineated five stages that children negotiate through, proposed eight stages of human development (Erikson, 1965):

- Infancy (0–18 months).
- Early childhood (2–4 years).
- Preschool (4–5 years).
- School age (5–12 years).
- Adolescence (13–19 years).
- Early adulthood (20–39 years).
- Adulthood (40–64 years).
- Maturity (65 plus).

Piaget, through observations of well-known experiments such as the Conservation of Volume test and Mountains test, concluded that there are four distinct cognitive stages through which a child progresses (Piaget, 1955 [1976]):

- Sensorimotor Stage: 0–2 years.
- Preoperational Stage: 2–7 years.
- Concrete Operational Stage: 7–11 years.
- Formal Operational Stage: 11 years and older.

While Piaget emphasised a staged version of child development, the Russian developmental psychologist Vygotsky, writing in the 1930s, identified the role of mentors in children's learning and the importance of play for childhood learning as well as the potential to retain knowledge once learned (Vygotsky, 1978). Bruner built on Vygotsky's work by conceptualising support as being scaffolded around a child/learner (Stewart, 2012), and viewed people as being active in their own learning by selectivity and discovery rather than mimicry and recollection. Therefore Vygotsky's, and Bruner's, understanding of childhood development were more fluid than Piaget's four stages.

The Russian-born American psychologist Urie Bronfenbrenner formulated Ecological Systems Theory, identifying four types of nested environmental systems relating to childhood development:

- Microsystem – initially reflected the dyadic mother–child relationship but has expanded to those relationships that most immediately and directly affect the child's development including family and school.
- Mesosystem – the relationships and interconnections between the microsystems, e.g. between family and teachers.
- Exosystem – refers to those social settings in which the child is not actively involved, e.g. parent's place of work.
- Macrosystem – the wider social, cultural, legislative and community networks that affect family and child, such as laws.

Bronfenbrenner later added a fifth level, the chronosystem, which considers the aging process.

Childhood developmental stages are important for us as social workers when assessing children's needs, but they are not definitive indications of exactly what should be expected. We need to recognise each child's unique and individual experience, and use our knowledge of child development with discretion, as guidelines that can help us make assessments. The application of Fraser Guidelines when working with young people highlights how chronological developmental stages are open to professional judgement.

Fraser Guidelines/Gillick competence

At what point may we assume children and young people can make adult-type decisions and exercise adult choices, particularly regarding sexual activity if aged under 16, the legal age of sexual consent? This is a moot and important question for social workers. We are guided by case law emanating from the *Gillick v West Norfolk* (1985) judgement. Victoria Gillick challenged the medical right to theoretically prescribe contraception to her under-age daughter without seeking parental permission. The judge concluded:

> ... whether or not a child is capable of giving the necessary consent will depend on the child's maturity and understanding and the nature of the consent required. The child must be capable of making a reasonable assessment of the advantages and disadvantages of the treatment proposed, so the consent, if given, can be properly and fairly described as true consent.

Practice decisions on a child's capacity to consent and make decisions are known as Gillick competence (after the parent). Fraser guidelines (after the Law Lord making the judgment) relate to whether or not a child can consent to contraceptive or sexual health advice and treatment. Gillick competence and Fraser Guidelines are widely used to assess a child's maturity and capacity to make their own decisions.

BIRTH FAMILIES, FOSTER CARE, ADOPTIVE FAMILIES AND KINSHIP CARE

Birth families remain the most common family type for children. The assessment of child needs and parenting capacity should follow the *Working Together to Safeguard Children* guidelines (HM Government, 2018) and the Assessment Framework (see Figure 4.3 above). The assessment should consider family members, their roles and parenting capacity. There are several birth-family parenting types: two birth parents, a single birth parent, and birth parent and step-parent families. Within each of these three family types are variations, e.g. same sex and different sex, and seemingly unquantifiably diverse ways of organising individual family contexts, roles and relationships. Most birth families successfully care for children without social work intervention. However, in England there are currently over 72,000 children looked after by local authorities (Department for Education, 2017).

Foster care in the UK is a state-regulated activity where children deemed unable to reside with their birth family are looked after by approved fostering families (Department for Education, 2011). Foster carers look after children on behalf of the local authority and parents, and do not assume parental responsibility. Adoption is distinct from foster care and can be defined legally as the permanent transfer of parental responsibility from birth to adoptive parent. Adoptive parents are granted an adoption order and parental responsibility for a child through court proceedings. Residential care is a professional service, mainly delivered by employed care workers (Smith, 2010). From the 1970s the focus of childcare has shifted away from residential childcare to caring for children in families, which Fulcher (2009) suggests mirrors a trend for family-based placements. Over time, fostering has become the most common type of placement for looked after children, as the percentage of looked after children in English foster placements has risen from 36% in 1979 (Berridge & Cleaver, 1987) to 74% in 2017 (Department for Education, 2017). The prioritising of fostering in the UK reflects a movement away from residential homes in preference to placements within families, which Butler and Charles (1999) argue, mirrors an ideological assumption based on the primacy of the Western nuclear family.

AT NUMBER 2

When facing redundancy and unemployment, Alfie saw an advert for foster care, which read, 'Do you have room in your heart and home for a child? Would you like a career in childcare which pays an allowance to look after children?' Alfie liked children and talked to Suzie who agreed that they should apply to foster. It is assumed that mainly women choose to foster, but most fostering households include men and women, and research by Heslop (2016) indicates that foster fathers are often the prime motivators to foster in their families. Alfie and Suzie were enthused by the prospect of looking after children. They thought they would have a child live with them quickly and were surprised by the length and rigour of the assessment process. They attended the foster-care training and found it really interesting; however, they were distressed when the social workers talked about some of the safeguarding situations that led to children living in foster care. Realising how hard life can be for some children made Alfie and Suzie determined to 'pass' the assessment, and when they did they celebrated together by going out for a meal.

EXERCISE 4.3

- How well prepared do you think Alfie and Suzie are to foster?
- Identify three difficulties you think they may encounter as foster carers.
- How would you go about supporting/supervising them as foster carers?

It is rare, in the UK, for children to be looked after by a local authority or trust for any other reason than parental capacity or concerns about parenting. Officially, only 3% of children are looked after by an English local authority due to the child's disability, while abuse or neglect, at 62%, is the main category of need experienced by children who are looked after by an English local authority. It is important to point out that children may experience several needs concurrently, e.g. a disabled child may experience both family dysfunction and abuse and neglect.

Kinship care refers to the care of children by relatives or close family friends. Through kinship placements, children continue to live with extended family or friends. Kinship fostering provides identity and attachment benefits for children (McFadden, 1998). This type of placement has experienced popularity in the USA, where in the 1990s McFadden (1998) estimated that 38% of fostered children were placed with kinship carers. Kinship care is not as prevalent in the UK but one estimate is that 16% of children placed in local authority placements live with kinship carers (Murphy-Jack & Smethers, 2009), and we are witnessing increasing numbers of children living with kinship carers or 'connected persons' (Wijedasa, 2015). The Children Act 1989 stipulates kinship care is the initial placement option to be considered by children's services in England and Wales for children who cannot live with their birth parents. Former family judge Justice Munby ruled that kinship carers should have equitable payments with stranger foster carers (Broad, 2007) and social workers should consider family placements alongside adoption (Stevenson, 2014). It has been reported that there has been an international upturn in vulnerable children being supported through extended family and community networks (Connolly et al., 2017). Wyke suggests kinship care involves relatives stepping in to care for children to preserve family and community connections while helping protect children (Wyke, 2013). This preservation of family connections is emphasised when slightly more than half of the children in kinship care live with grandparents and 23% are looked after by siblings (Wijedasa, 2015).

AUTHOR'S EXPERIENCE (PHIL)

When I carried out parenting assessments early in my career, I followed best practice and agency guidance, but this did not involve extending assessments to include fathers or extended family beyond the immediate maternal grandparents. Now on reflection, I recognise how possible sources of support for mothers and

(Continued)

their children went unrecognised because of gendered attitudes, which prioritised women as mothers and carers. Unfortunately, this meant they were assessed against a societal understanding of mothering which blamed women and did not view men as possible carers in their own right. Whilst I thought I practised anti-oppressively, I was in fact accepting the dominant discourse uncritically. More recently, I have provided training and support to kinship carers through a locally based Grandparents Plus project, and am a trustee with a local young dads' project. Due to my conversations with parents and kinship carers, I have become increasingly aware of the need to assess both parents along with community and extended family members, maternal and paternal, before considering substitute stranger families for children.

SAFEGUARDING AND RISK ASSESSMENT

Having detailed the procedures for assessing risk and safeguarding children, we now incorporate additional elements to consider when assessing children's needs.

Domestic abuse within families

Domestic abuse is any type of controlling, bullying, threatening or violent behaviour between people in a relationship. Historically we referred to domestic violence, however the terminology has moved on in recognition that alongside violence, people also experience emotional, physical, sexual, financial and psychological abuse. Domestic violence was traditionally viewed as something that men perpetrated on women, but abusive behaviour can occur in any relationship and often continues after the relationship has ended. Statistics demonstrate that domestic abuse is startlingly common. An average of two women per week are killed by a partner or ex-partner in England and Wales, and domestic violence cases account for 10% of total crime (Office for National Statistics, 2017; Women's Aid, 2017). The prevalence of domestic abuse means that regardless of their practice setting, all social workers encounter people who are in, or have been in, abusive relationships.

The sociologist Michael Johnson classifies four types of domestic violence with *common couple violence* appearing to be the most common category. Johnson suggests this form of domestic abuse is likely to go unnoticed by child welfare agencies because it rarely comes to the attention of health, police or child welfare agencies (Johnson & Ferraro, 2000). The other three categories he collectively terms as 'intimate partner violence' (IPV) and argues conclusively that IPV is damaging to children though there are differentials within the categories and that interventions should relate to these variables (Johnson, 2008).

The impact of childhood abuse and maltreatment is well documented (Stevenson, 2007), though also much debated. Social work's concern with child welfare and the paramountcy principle, as well as our genuine desire to reduce discrimination and oppression, makes this a difficult practice area. Our values can be tested, particularly when an adult takes a decision to remain with an abusive partner. In earlier chapters, we have discussed instances where children have died as a result of familial and domestic abuse, resulting in criticism of social workers for erring on the side of optimism when assessing parents.

Language is telling. Practitioners can easily fall into the trap of referring to people as 'victims' or 'perpetrators'. In the previous chapter we introduced the multidimensional nature of risk. In all practice situations, it is critical to remember that people are seldom one thing or another. Our advice is to gather all the information you can, formulate a hypothesis, and then test it with the evidence by looking at different perspectives. In this way, you may recognise the *victim* of domestic abuse as someone more than a victim and similarly with *perpetrators*. Consider your language; reflect on issues such as culture, gender and disability to formulate effective and defensible assessments. Children after all deserve no less.

Once someone is identified as a perpetrator of domestic abuse and therefore a risk to children, common safeguarding practice is to request that the risky person move out of the family home. Research highlights that this practice assumes the person deemed risky will remain faithfully out of the home and not return – essentially, a false assessment of the situation (Featherstone, 2003; Scourfield, 2006; Brown et al., 2009; Featherstone, 2014). Relationships are complicated, and occur predominantly outside of our gaze. A person may agree to leave only to avoid the alternative of their children being placed elsewhere, or a broken relationship may be repaired. In either situation, the risky person may return or be a frequent visitor to the home without our knowledge. Our assessments must be robust and consider the dynamic nature of relationships.

Relationship with social class, 'troubled families' agenda, poverty etc.

Social work practice, throughout its history, has been linked with poverty and notions of deserving/undeserving poor relief. Lambert and Crossley (2017) suggest that a wide spectrum of policies have located 'troubles' or 'problems' in the family itself, without regard to social or economic considerations. They highlight the negative language contained in policies, e.g. *unemployable, social problem group, problem family, cycle of deprivation, underclass*, and more recently, *troubled*. The New Labour Government's (1997–2010) *Family Intervention Projects* (FIPs) were derived from the Social Exclusion Task Force, which identified 120,000 families 'at risk' because they were experiencing multiple disadvantage evidenced by at least five out of seven of the following problems: parental unemployment, maternal mental health, parental disability, poor housing, poverty, overcrowded living conditions and parents unqualified (Lambert & Crossley, 2017).

The Coalition Government's (2010–2015) *Troubled Families Programme* (TFP) was initially based on Louise Casey's reappraisal (Casey, 2012) of the Social Exclusion Task Force's work, and the Families and Children Study carried out in 2004 (Bostock et al., 2005). Lambert and Crossley argue that the implementation of this programme should be seen, along with other global-wide policies, as 'a central pillar in efforts to shape a "new" form of state in the UK and beyond, with "the family" often placed at the centre of these efforts' (Lambert & Crossley, 2017: 93).

Possible impact of disabilities

The relationship between parenting and disability can be another area that presents conflict in our practice. On the one hand, social work promotes the social model of disability, whereby it is the way society is organised which *disables* people with different abilities, rather than the medical model, which locates the disability within the person. On the other hand, parenting and certain disabilities, such as learning difficulties and mental health, almost always lead to involvement and scrutiny from children's services. This indicates pathologising assumptions and automatic negative beliefs about the parenting capacity of parents who have disabilities (Olsen and Wate, 2003).

While parents with disabilities experience disproportionate child welfare concerns, there is a growing body of research (Lightfoot et al., 2010) that does not necessarily support the assumption that disabled parents are more likely to abuse or neglect their children. Indeed, many disabled parents succeed in raising their children when provided with appropriate support services. Research indicates that disability alone does not necessarily have a negative effect on parenting (Collentine, 2005), and that predictors of parenting problems are often found to be the same for disabled and non-disabled parents (Olkin et al., 2006).

Serious Case Reviews (SCR)

Serious Case Reviews (SCRs) take place in England following a child death or significant injury due to possible abuse or neglect. The purpose of these reviews is to learn lessons to help prevent similar incidents being repeated. SCRs take place in England (in Wales, *child practice reviews* are a similar process; in Scotland they are *significant case reviews*; and in Northern Ireland are referred to as *case management reviews*) when: a child has died; a child has been seriously harmed and there are concerns about how organisations or professionals worked together to safeguard the child; a child dies in custody; or a child has died by suspected suicide. Following any of these concerns, the Local Safeguarding Children Board (LSCB) should conduct an SCR within one month of notification of the incident and should aim to complete the SCR within six months. The Panel of Independent Experts and Ofsted should be notified of any decisions made by the SCR. The LSCB must publish the SCR findings on their website within 12 months. The NSPPC, in association with the Association of Independent LSCB Chairs, provides an online repository SCRs which can be found at www.nspcc.org.uk

Following criticism of the effectiveness of SCRs to effect changes to safeguarding procedures (McNicoll, 2016), the Children and Social Work Act 2017 set in place procedures to replace SCRs in England with the National Child Safeguarding Practice Review Panel. The Act also abolished Local Safeguarding Children Boards (LSCB), replacing them with locally arranged Child Safeguarding Practice Review Panels.

Rescuing children: heroic social work

We have identified the challenging and emotional nature of social work which focuses on the welfare and safeguarding of children. Within this context we need to carefully balance our emotions and motivations with professionalism, otherwise it is all too easy to fall into *heroic* practice and cast ourselves as *rescuers* of children.

AUTHOR'S EXPERIENCE (PHIL)

A senior practitioner explained to me, 'I've taken more children into care than you've had hot dinners.'

A reviewing officer said, 'I'll notify anyone regardless of their rights if it protects a child.'

EXERCISE 4.4

- Can we ever disregard the rights of people, even if we are protecting children?
- Why might these professionals have held these views?
- How can we promote best practice when safeguarding children and promoting people's rights?

Social work exists to challenge inequality, promote rights and enable people to achieve change (IFSW, 2017). We do some remarkable things, in some extremely challenging and emotional circumstances; however, to believe that we are somehow heroes actually intensifies the oppression of those we work with. Hero narratives are premised on exploitative narratives where:

- people who use services are dehumanised and not viewed in context, but unhelpfully simplified down to caricatures;
    - The 'bad' parent is demonised and represented as the villain.
    - The 'poor' child is disempowered and represented as helpless/clueless.
- conversely, the social worker is elevated from a professional undertaking a role for which they are trained, prepared and remunerated;
    - The 'brave' social worker is powerful and heroic, without the social worker, 'they' would be doomed.

In this narrative, the only person with any strengths, agency or power is the social worker. Heroic and rescue-based social work is not robust or effective practice; best practice requires that we work with people and recognise their multidimensional nature. As Ferguson (2011) explains, it remains important that social workers knock on doors and visit children in their home environment to understand their situation, and not to take on a saviour or heroic role that is based on the practitioner's perception.

AUTHOR'S EXPERIENCE (PHIL)

Newly qualified and in my first post in a children and families social work team, I felt proud but also daunted by the prospect of saving children and working with families. I remember my first phone call about a possible child protection situation. The family were new to the area and lived in cramped conditions. Both parents were unemployed and the father experienced mental health problems. He was also abusive towards his wife, who spent time in a women's refuge. I liked both parents; they were struggling to make sense of their lives and made mistakes. I now appreciate that what I perceived as chaos when I walked into their lives made sense to them. I was applying my own values to people whose lives and experiences were very different from mine. I oscillated between being their saviour and their friend, neither of which was the right role. Looking back, I realise that I was too empathetic and insufficiently critically reflective, but in the early 1990s these were not concepts that I had yet discovered.

SUMMARY

We have reflected on working with children and young people, contextualising social work practice historically and contemporarily. As we write this book there are many new developments in childcare social work, but however childcare social work evolves, it remains embedded in concepts of childhood and notions of family. We have introduced childhood development theories and discussed family diversity and perceptions of problematic family practices, such as domestic abuse and troubled families. Childcare social work is challenging and rewarding, and through this chapter we emphasise that we should seek the best for children and young people and aim for robust practice and defensible assessments.

5 ASSESSING ADULTS' NEEDS

Learning in this chapter relates to

PCF	**KSS Adult Services**	**KSS Child & Family**
1. Professionalism 2. Values & Ethics 3. Diversity & Equalities 4. Rights & Justice 5. Knowledge 6. Critical Reflection & Analysis 7. Skills & Interventions 8. Contexts & Organisations 9. Professional Leadership	2. The role of social workers working with adults 3. Person-centred practice 4. Safeguarding 5. Mental capacity 6. Effective assessments & outcome-based support planning 7. Direct work with individuals & families 8. Supervision, critical reflection & analysis 9. Organisational context 10. Professional ethics & leadership	3. Adult mental ill health, substance misuse, domestic abuse, physical ill health & disability 5. Effective direct work with children & families 6. Child & family assessment 7. Analysis, decision making, planning & review 8. The law & the family justice system 9. Professional ethics

INTRODUCTION

This chapter reflects on the context of assessment with adults. We begin with a brief outline history of adult social work policy and practice, considering human rights and noting the complicated and evolving relationship between health and social care. We will explore the myriad legislation that has been significantly simplified by the Care Act 2014, which sets out how adults' and carers' social care needs are assessed. We will introduce concepts key to the assessment process, including wellbeing, autonomy, personalisation and mental capacity, and consider the critical issues when assessing people with disabilities, older people, people experiencing mental distress and safeguarding adults.

BRIEF HISTORY OF ADULT SOCIAL WORK PRACTICE

During the post-war establishment of the welfare state, responsibilities for meeting the welfare needs of adults were – and largely still are – structured around health and disability. The local authority Welfare Departments were responsible for older people and people with disabilities (referred to in post-war UK as physically handicapped). Medical Officers of Health were responsible for needs relating to mental health and learning disabilities (referred to as mental handicap). Needs arising from deafness and visual impairment tended to be addressed by voluntary organisations, albeit funded through local authority monies. Practice with individuals and families largely followed Mary Richmond's social casework methodology, but was also beginning to be influenced by ideas from the growing psychotherapy movement.

The legal definitions and mechanisms for the protection of human rights emerged rapidly in the post-war period, becoming intrinsically linked to social work. A strong desire to learn from and protect against a future reoccurrence of the atrocities of World War II, coupled with concerns about the growth of communism in central and eastern Europe, led the Council of Europe to draft the European Convention on Human Rights (ECHR). This international treaty protects human rights and fundamental freedoms in Europe (Liberty, n.d.), was ratified by the UK in 1951 and came into force in 1953. The ECHR established the European Court of Human Rights (ECtHR), and was later enacted in UK primary legislation through the Human Rights Act 1998.

THE HUMAN RIGHTS ACT 1998

Human rights are the basic rights and freedoms everyone is entitled to from birth until death; they are fundamental to everything that we do as social workers. There are 16 basic rights within the Human Rights Act 1998:

- Article 2: Right to life.
- Article 3: Freedom from torture and inhuman or degrading treatment.
- Article 4: Freedom from slavery and forced labour.
- Article 5: Right to liberty and security.
- Article 6: Right to a fair trial.
- Article 7: No punishment without law.
- Article 8: Respect for your private and family life, home and correspondence.
- Article 9: Freedom of thought, belief and religion.
- Article 10: Freedom of expression.

- Article 11: Freedom of assembly and association.
- Article 12: Right to marry and start a family.
- Article 14: Protection from discrimination in respect of these rights and freedoms.
- Protocol 1, Article 1: Right to peaceful enjoyment of your property.
- Protocol 1, Article 2: Right to education.
- Protocol 1, Article 3: Right to participate in free elections.
- Protocol 13, Article 1: Abolition of the death penalty.

Some rights are absolute, and can never be legitimately interfered with (e.g. Articles 2 and 3); some rights are limited, meaning they can be restricted for reasons established within the ECHR (e.g. Article 5 following criminal conviction and sentencing). Other rights are qualified, meaning that they can be restricted to protect the rights of others (e.g. Article 10 if it is being used to incite racial hatred).

The Human Rights Act 1998 places an obligation on public bodies – which tend to be the main employers of social workers – to act (as far as possible) in compliance with human rights, and places an obligation on the state (the functions of which are often carried out by local authorities and health bodies) to protect against breaches of human rights. Our practice is complex, so upholding one right may mean that we impinge on another – e.g. in order to safeguard someone from abuse (upholding their Article 3 rights), we may need to impinge on their liberty (Article 5 rights) and their private and family life (Article 8 rights).

However, the establishment of defined, protected human rights had minimum impact on people with significant and ongoing social care needs. The dominant model of care provision remained exactly as it had been before the war, i.e. institutionalisation. It was commonplace for people born with physical and learning disabilities to spend their entire lives in institutions. People could be involuntarily detained in mental health hospitals on the basis of issues such as prostitution, promiscuity and bearing children outside of marriage, up until the Mental Health Act 1959 finally abolished the category of 'moral imbecile'. National and local government gave very little consideration to alternatives to institutionalisation until a series of high profile cases of abuse, culminating in the Ely Hospital scandal, forced the issue. In 1967, the *News of the World* reported allegations from a nursing assistant at Ely Hospital about widespread ill treatment and theft from patients with learning disabilities. Public outrage led to an inquiry which considered the 20-year-old NHS's whole approach towards people with learning disabilities. It uncovered institutional cultures characterised by a complete lack of expertise, controlling and abusive practices, and no real attempt to provide quality of life, let alone habilitation or rehabilitation (Department of Health and Social Security, 1969). The report became significant for generating the momentum to close long-stay hospitals that heralded the dawn of community care, shifting the primary responsibility for meeting the needs of people with disabilities away from the NHS and onto local authorities.

The legislative landscape of practice with adults is enormously complex, being bound up in law and policy which is concerned with both health and social care – but seldom addresses the two together. The Audit Commission's 1986 report, *Making a Reality of Community Care*, found that responsibilities had transferred from the NHS to local authorities without corresponding finances. In 1988 the *Community Care: Agenda for Action* Green Paper (also known as the Griffiths Report; Griffiths, 1988) identified that neither the NHS nor local authorities wanted to accept the responsibility for community care. It recommended that social work departments be responsible for long-term and continuing care, whilst health bodies took responsibility for primary and acute care – arrangements which persist in the present day. Griffiths (1988) also recommended the use of independent and voluntary service providers.

The NHS and Community Care Act 1990 was the first post-war legislation to attempt to bridge the gap between health boards and local council social services, giving local authorities responsibility for developing home, day and respite care to enable people to live in their own homes wherever possible. This Act progressed recommendations from the Griffiths Report (1988) by instigating the 'purchaser/provider split'. Up until this point, social care services had been predominantly provided on an in-house basis, using local authority staff and facilities. The Thatcher government (1979–1990) argued that social care needed a marketplace that could offer choice and, through competition, better value for money. The purchaser/provider split left the budget and responsibility for assessing needs and purchasing social care with local authorities, but directed them to purchase suitable provision externally. The impact of this is very evident today as more and more local authority functions – including assessments – are tendered out to private and third sector agencies.

AUTHOR'S EXPERIENCE (CAT)

In the 1990s, before I started my social work training, I worked as a residential support worker with people with learning disabilities. I came to learn that some people are habitually and blatantly oppressed without political outcry or media attention. As I saw how commonplace it was for people with learning disabilities to be denied or stripped of power and status, I began to understand how much of my privilege I had taken for granted, and to realise human rights are unfortunately not universal if you are denied the power to assert them.

Most of the people living in the small, group homes where I worked had recently been resettled to the community from large, long-stay institutions, and would freely share their experiences of institutional life with me. They talked of a routine lack of privacy and no influence or choice over even basic decisions. Many people had experienced habitual abuse and neglect. Individualism or attempts at autonomy were classed as 'challenging behaviour', and often addressed through chemical or physical restraint. Any expression of sexuality was thwarted or ridiculed.

Perhaps most shocking to me was the realisation that the homes in which I was working, whilst a huge leap forward from institutions, were not perfect either: there was still a power imbalance between staff and residents, and I was part of this. I began to realise that care itself can be a mechanism for stigmatisation and control. I was starting to understand the need for something more than a well-intentioned approach, but I had not yet discovered rights-based or anti-oppressive practice.

Something that has always stayed with me is the absolute delight I witnessed people experience from simple, everyday freedoms they had been denied when living in institutions: carrying their own cigarettes and choosing when to smoke without asking permission, going to the corner shop and back alone, getting up late – or not at all. Eleanor Roosevelt encapsulated the importance of small, ordinary freedoms in her 1958 speech on human rights:

Where, after all, do universal human rights begin? In small places, close to home – so close and so small that they cannot be seen on any maps of the world. Yet they are the world of the individual person; the neighbourhood he lives in; the school or college he attends; the factory, farm or office where he works. Such are the places where every man, woman and child seeks equal justice, equal opportunity, equal dignity without discrimination. Unless these rights have meaning there, they have little meaning anywhere. Without concerned citizen action to uphold them close to home, we shall look in vain for progress in the larger world.

"

The contemporary context of social work with adults has been most significantly shaped by two arenas which we will explore further on in this chapter: the disability rights movement, and the abuse and neglect of adults. Both highlighted significant shortcomings in both legal frameworks and models of service delivery. In 2011, the Law Commission concluded that adult social care legislation was too fragmented and recommended that a single, unified act should be developed (Law Commission, 2011). The Health Select Committee's 2012 report on social care identified that many older people and those with disabilities and long-term conditions were being badly served by fragmented services. In 2012, the Department of Health set out the Draft Care and Support Bill, which ultimately received royal assent as the Care Act 2014, and was enacted the following year.

SOCIAL CARE NEEDS

People are not homogeneous, and neither are their needs. We support person-centred approaches that are informed by intersectionality, but we recognise that adult services are still most commonly configured around the most prominent presenting need. In the next section of this chapter, therefore, we explore considerations for assessment practice relating to disability, older people and mental health.

Disability

Unfortunately, society's default stance on disability continues to be a medical model, which sets a normative expectation of cognitive, physical or mental function, and views anyone who deviates from this as disabled. The World Health Organization recognises that:

> 'Disabilities' is an umbrella term, covering impairments, activity limitations, and participation restrictions. An impairment is a problem in body function or structure; an activity limitation is a difficulty encountered by an individual in executing a task or action; while a participation restriction is a problem experienced by an individual in involvement in life situations. Disability is thus not just a health problem. It is a complex phenomenon, reflecting the interaction between features of a person's body and features of the society in which he or she lives. (World Health Organization, 2016)

In the UK during the 1960s, people with disabilities took inspiration from the American civil rights movement, and began to look for ways to emancipate themselves and gain control of their own lives. Statutory social work responses to people with physical, mental and learning disabilities often perpetuated exclusion and stigma, whilst in charitable organisations people with disabilities were often portrayed as objects of pity in need of patronage. The legitimacy of large charities made up of non-disabled people representing the experience of disabled people was questioned, with many feeling that this actually compounded and contributed to their stigmatisation (Cameron, 2014). What was needed was *self-representation*. These arguments still resonate today, with recent criticism of the charity Comic Relief for using celebrities to talk about the experience of poverty in Africa, rather than African people (Lammy, 2017).

Paul Hunt was a man with disabilities whose 1966 book, *Stigma: Experience of Disability*, documented the experiences of 12 people with disabilities without sentimentality, demonstrating society's part in perpetuating their exclusion. The book was used as a text in the first UK disability studies course, and Paul became recognised as an authority on the experience of people with disabilities. Paul and Vic Finkelstein established the Union of the Physically Impaired Against Segregation (UPIAS) (Cameron, 2014), and in 1975, together with the Disability Alliance, published the *British Fundamental Principles of Disability*, declaring:

> In our view it is society which disables physically impaired people. Disability is something imposed on top of our impairments by the way we are unnecessarily isolated and excluded from full participation in society. Disabled people are therefore an oppressed group in society. (p. 4)

Finkelstein (1980, 1981), Barnes (1999) and most notably Mike Oliver (1990, 1996) developed these ideas into the *social model of disability*. Medical models of disability problematise

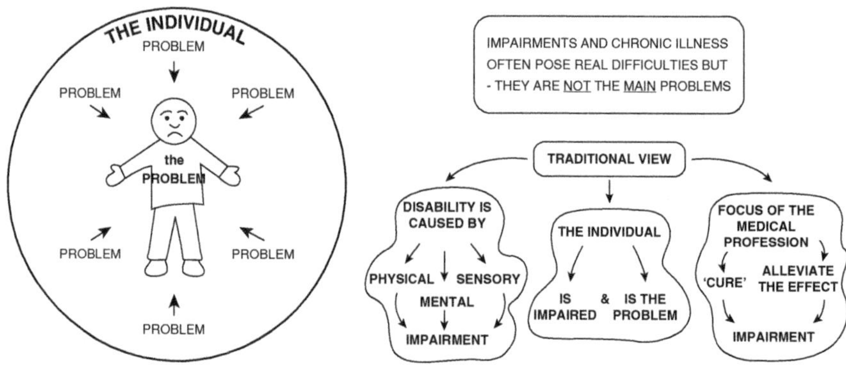

Figure 5.1 Medical model of disability

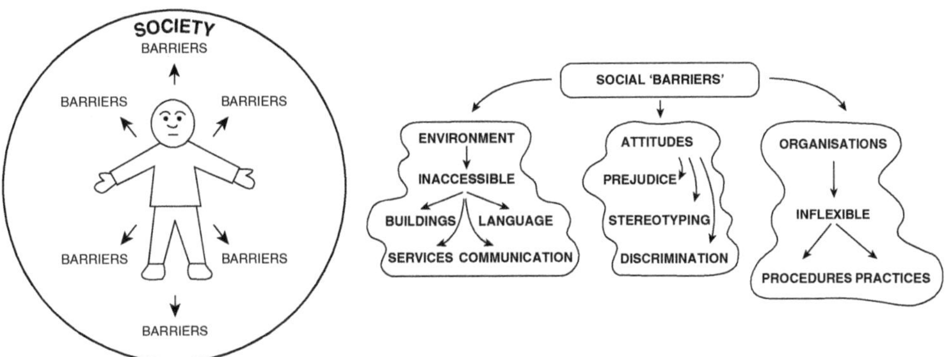

Figure 5.2 Social model of disability

the person, locating the disability within them (Figure 5.1). The social model of disability (Figure 5.2) makes a distinction between the impairment a person has and the oppression they experience, defining disability as the product of the oppression, rather than the impairment (Shakespeare and Watson, 2002).

AT NUMBER 5

It is two years since Max had his stroke. Speech and physical therapy have helped him a great deal and he no longer needs support with his personal care. Max uses a wheelchair, which he can transfer in and out of, and is able to drive his adapted car. He would like to return to work.

EXERCISE 5.1

What barriers to employment do you think that Max might experience?

In 2006, the United Nations General Assembly created an international human rights treaty, the Convention on the Rights of People with Disabilities (CRPD), which reaffirms that all persons with all types of disabilities must enjoy all human rights and fundamental freedoms. The UK ratified the CRPD in 2009, committing to promote and protect the full human rights of disabled people and ensure their full equality. In 2017, the UK's progress against the convention was reviewed, and the UN Committee was concerned that 'some people think that disabled people's lives are less valuable than the lives of non-disabled people. In addition, there are gaps in the UK's anti-discrimination laws' (EHRC, 2017b: 9). Other significant concerns were that living independently and being included in the community are not recognised as human rights in UK law; public services do not provide enough accessible information; availability of high-quality sign language interpreters is poor; disabled people are less likely to be in employment, and are paid less on average than non-disabled people; austerity measures have had a severe impact on disabled people and their families (especially families with disabled children), leading to increased reliance on food banks (EHRC, 2017b).

Social workers recognise that human life is characterised by difference, and that embracing diversity is a critical step towards an inclusive society. Understanding the social model of disability and challenging oppressive and discriminatory attitudes are critical elements of our practice.

Older people

Older people are currently a very significant area of social, economic and political focus. The life expectancy for babies born in 1901 was 45 for boys and 49 for girls; in 2014, the corresponding life expectancies were 79 and 83 (ONS, 2015). Our extended life expectancy is the result of universal access to healthcare, better housing, economic security and social support. It is arguably the greatest achievement of the welfare state, and yet 'the aging population' is rarely portrayed positively in the news media; in fact, it is most often presented very negatively as an economic time bomb. As we write, the government is preparing its Green Paper on care and support for older people, which will set out its plans for meeting – and critically funding – the care and support needs of an aging population.

Whilst all of us want to live longer, few people relish the thought of being old. In 2009, the Centre for Policy on Ageing compared the experiences of older people to those of younger users of social care, and found that older people were culturally stereotyped as vulnerable and burdensome, and widespread ageism existed at both institutional and structural levels (Centre for Policy on Ageing, 2009). Older people are diverse, with unique, individual biographies (Ray and Phillips, 2012), but sadly after the age of retirement, their value and contribution often cease to be recognised. Such attitudes have negative consequences for the individual person's wellbeing, and also prevent society from benefiting from their experiences and skills. Meeting the needs of an aging population is not simply about how to meet the social care costs associated with extended life expectancy, it is also about how we reconceptualise aging to harness the resources that older people present and enable them to live a full and active part in society.

The Centre for Aging Better commissioned research that identified three, interrelated dimensions of a good later life which were consistent regardless of gender, ethnicity or other socio-demographic characteristics: health, financial security and social connections (Ipsos MORI, 2015). Social work practice with older people must not simply seek to address basic needs – although these are important – it must recognise that life experience is a valuable asset, and the need for purpose, fulfilment and quality of life exists at every age.

Mental health

In the UK in any one year, one in four adults will experience a diagnosable mental health problem, suicide is the biggest killer of people under the age of 35, and the estimated cost of mental health problems to the UK economy is £70–£100 billion, around 4.5% of GDP (Mental Health Foundation, 2015). Mental health has traditionally been conceptualised as an illness requiring a medical response, and this has at times left mental health social work ambiguously placed. The growing evidence base for social explanations of mental distress now presents an undeniable challenge to the dominance of medical models, and highlights the need for social responses.

Psychiatry is premised on the biomedical model of mental illness, which has been the dominant model throughout the western world for the past century. Psychiatry views mental illness as a disorder in the functioning or chemical balance of the brain, which is either genetically predetermined (faulty genes) or spontaneously occurring (disease). The primary treatment is pharmacological, aiming to rebalance neuro-chemistry or to subdue (tranquilise) symptoms. Mental health research funding is almost exclusively channelled into biomedical studies, and mental health services are overwhelmingly constructed around this model, and yet recovery rates for severe mental illness have not changed since the end of World War II (Bentall, 2010).

Critics of psychiatry arose from within the profession (e.g. Szasz, R.D. Laing, Rosenhan, Fernando) and the mental health user movement grew out of the wider disability rights campaign, arguing for recognition of the individual experience. Both groups highlighted how psychiatry and the biomedical model disempower people experiencing mental distress, and fail to account for the impact of traumatic life experiences or structural issues. Writing in support of an increased social work role in mental health, Goemans argued:

> ... while we pretend that madness can be cured with pills, we can conveniently ignore all the massive social problems within our communities which directly impact upon mental wellbeing. (2012: 68)

The United Nations' official statement for World Health Day in 2017 declared that approaches to mental health,' need to move from focusing on "chemical imbalances" to focusing on "power imbalances"'.

Social models of mental health draw upon knowledge from sociology about the impact of poverty and discrimination; labelling theory and social constructionism; social work, and its focus on anti-oppressive practice and empowerment; transcultural psychiatry, which recognises that there are different ways of expressing and dealing with mental distress in different cultural contexts (see Tew, Fernando etc.); and the social model of disability which we explored earlier in this chapter. An ever-growing body of research demonstrates evidence of a link with future psychiatric disorder for poverty in childhood (Wicks et al., 2010), early exposure to urban environments (Vassos et al., 2012), migration (Cantor-Graae & Selten, 2005), belonging to an ethnic minority (Veling et al., 2008), early separation from parents (Varese et al., 2012) and childhood sexual, physical and emotional abuse (Varese et al., 2012), suggesting that the behaviours and experiences we have constructed as mental illness are actually responses to long-term unmet needs. The biopsychosocial model (see Figure 5.3) recognises the interconnected nature of biological, psychological and social factors that affect our mental wellbeing.

Needs relating to mental wellbeing are so prevalent that we encounter them whatever the focus of our social work practice. Understanding social models of mental health can equip us to adopt a compassionate approach, which seeks to understand what has happened to someone, rather than what is wrong with them.

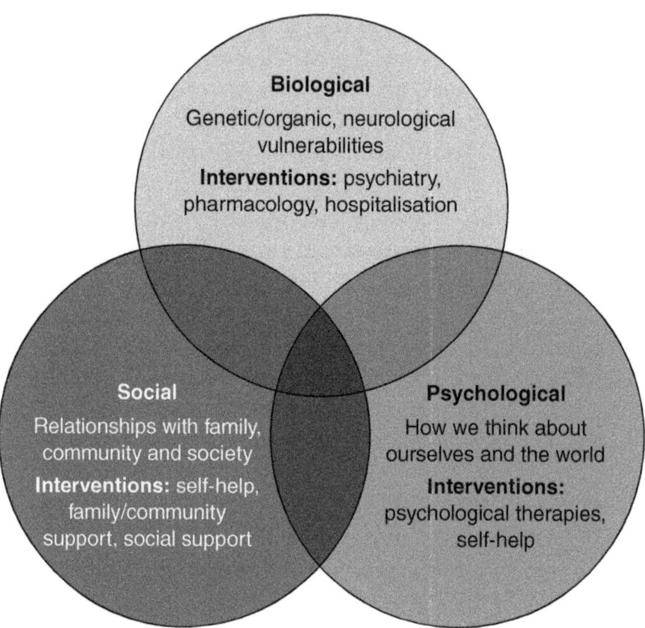

Figure 5.3 The biopsychosocial model

ASSESSING ADULTS' NEEDS

Autonomy and self-determination

In the last chapter, we spent time considering the biological, legal and social constructions of childhood and saw that defining when childhood ends and adulthood begins is far from straightforward. Children are viewed as inherently vulnerable, and the welfare of the child provides an automatic mandate for social workers to intervene (whether welcome or not). As children progress towards adulthood, they are assumed to become more autonomous and less vulnerable. Social work involvement with adults is premised primarily on consent.

Notions of autonomy and self-determination are implicitly bound up with human rights. Much of our contemporary practice has been established through legal and ethical debates around consent to medical treatment. In 1908, Mary Schloendorff refused surgery to remove a suspected fibroid tumour, but did consent to be examined under anaesthetic. During the procedure the tumour was removed, and subsequently Mary developed gangrene, which resulted in the loss of some of her fingers. Mary successfully sued the hospital for having carried out the surgery without her consent and against her expressed wishes. The resulting judgement declared that:

> Every human being of adult years and sound mind has a right to determine what shall be done with his own body, and a surgeon who performs an operation without the patient's consent commits an assault. (*Schloendorff v. New York Hospital*, supra note 1 at 129–30, 1914)

The implications of this case are much broader than consent to medical treatment; it established the legal and ethical protection for libertarian principles of autonomy and self-determination. This means that a capacitated adult is free to refuse social work involvement, and this refusal must be respected, even if the consequences may be catastrophic. Section 11 of the Care Act 2014 recognises that an adult or carer may refuse an assessment and this must be respected unless the person lacks the capacity to refuse an assessment that would be in their best interests, or the adult is experiencing, or is at risk of, abuse or neglect.

Assessment under the Care Act 2014

The Care Act 2014 revised and collected together duties and powers previously scattered over a raft of acts. It cannot, however, be viewed as a single framework for assessing and responding to adult needs in the same way that the Children Act 1989 is for children. Social work with adults requires us to comprehend and navigate overlapping – and sometimes competing – legislation. Whilst other legislation is relevant in particular situations, assessment under the Care Act will always require consideration of the Human Rights Act 1998 and the Mental Capacity Act 2005. In teaching, we encourage our students to use the model below (see Figure 5.4) to recognise that legislation does not work in isolation, it requires integration!

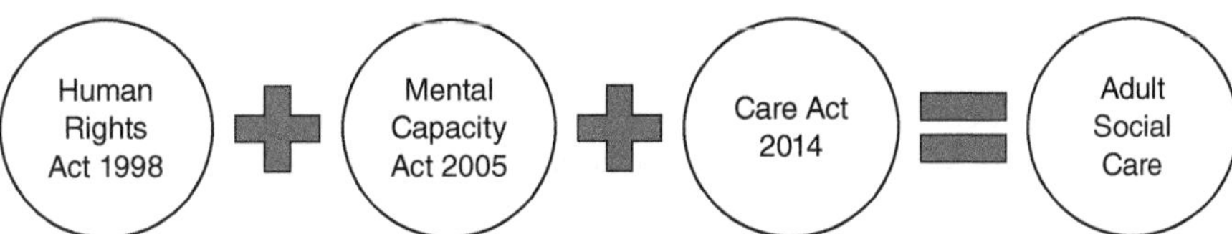

Figure 5.4 Legislation – integration not isolation

The statutory guidance accompanying the Care Act 2014 states that:

> The core purpose of adult care and support is to help people to achieve the outcomes that matter to them in their life ... Local authorities must promote wellbeing when carrying out any of their care and support functions in respect of a person. (Department of Health and Social Care, 2018: 1)

This clearly directs that our assessments and interventions with adults must be outcomes based (see Chapter 6), and establishes the Act's central 'wellbeing principle', which applies equally to adults with care and support needs and their carers. The guidance further defines wellbeing as 'a broad concept', and it is described as relating to the following areas in particular:

- Personal dignity (including treatment of the individual with respect).
- Physical and mental health and emotional wellbeing.
- Protection from abuse and neglect.

- Control by the individual over day-to-day life (including over the care and support provided and the way it is provided).
- Participation in work, education, training or recreation.
- Social and economic wellbeing.
- Domestic, family and personal.
- Suitability of living accommodation.
- The individual's contribution to society.

(Department of Health and Social Care, 2018: 1)

This list does not represent a hierarchy; all of these factors should be considered holistically within the person's situation. The concept of wellbeing therefore includes traditional areas of social focus, such as mental and physical health, safety, economic and domestic situation, but self-determination, personalisation and citizenship (we will explore these concepts in more detail later on in this chapter) have parity. Local authorities must assume that the individual is best placed to judge their own wellbeing, minimise restrictions on their rights, and encourage them to participate as fully as possible in the assessment process (Care Act 2014, s 1 (3)).

In previous chapters, we have considered the increasing 'rationing' of social care resources, and the impact of austerity. Section 9 of the Care Act 2014 places local authorities under a duty to assess the needs of any adult who may have needs for care and support, regardless of whether the local authority believes that they are likely to be eligible for social care services, and section 10 creates exactly the same duty for carers. The entitlement to assessment *before* determination of eligibility is important. There are many ways of meeting needs outside of social care services, and a statement of assessed needs may help a person to understand their needs, strengths and desired outcomes, in order to arrange their own care and support.

Section 6 of the Care Act 2014 directs that assessment of adult and carer needs must consider the outcomes the person wishes to achieve, whether any identified needs impact on the person's wellbeing, and whether the provision of care and support to meet the needs could contribute to achieving the outcomes. A strengths-based (see Chapter 11) and, where appropriate, whole family approach, is encouraged (Department of Health and Social Care, 2018, 6.63–6.73). The Social Care Institute for Excellence (SCIE) (2015a) set out an overall process map for assessing adult/carer needs and eligibility (see Figure 5.5).

Eligibility and funding

Everyone has needs, but not all needs are eligible for local authority involvement. Criteria are applied to determine if a person is eligible to have their identified needs met by the local authority. The Fairer Access to Care (FACS) eligibility criteria which existed prior to the Care Act 2014 were applied differently across local authorities and were much criticised for enabling a 'postcode lottery', where needs which might make a person eligible for services in one geographical area would not in another. The Care Act introduced a national minimum eligibility threshold for accessing social care services, and the process for determining eligibility (see Figure 5.6).

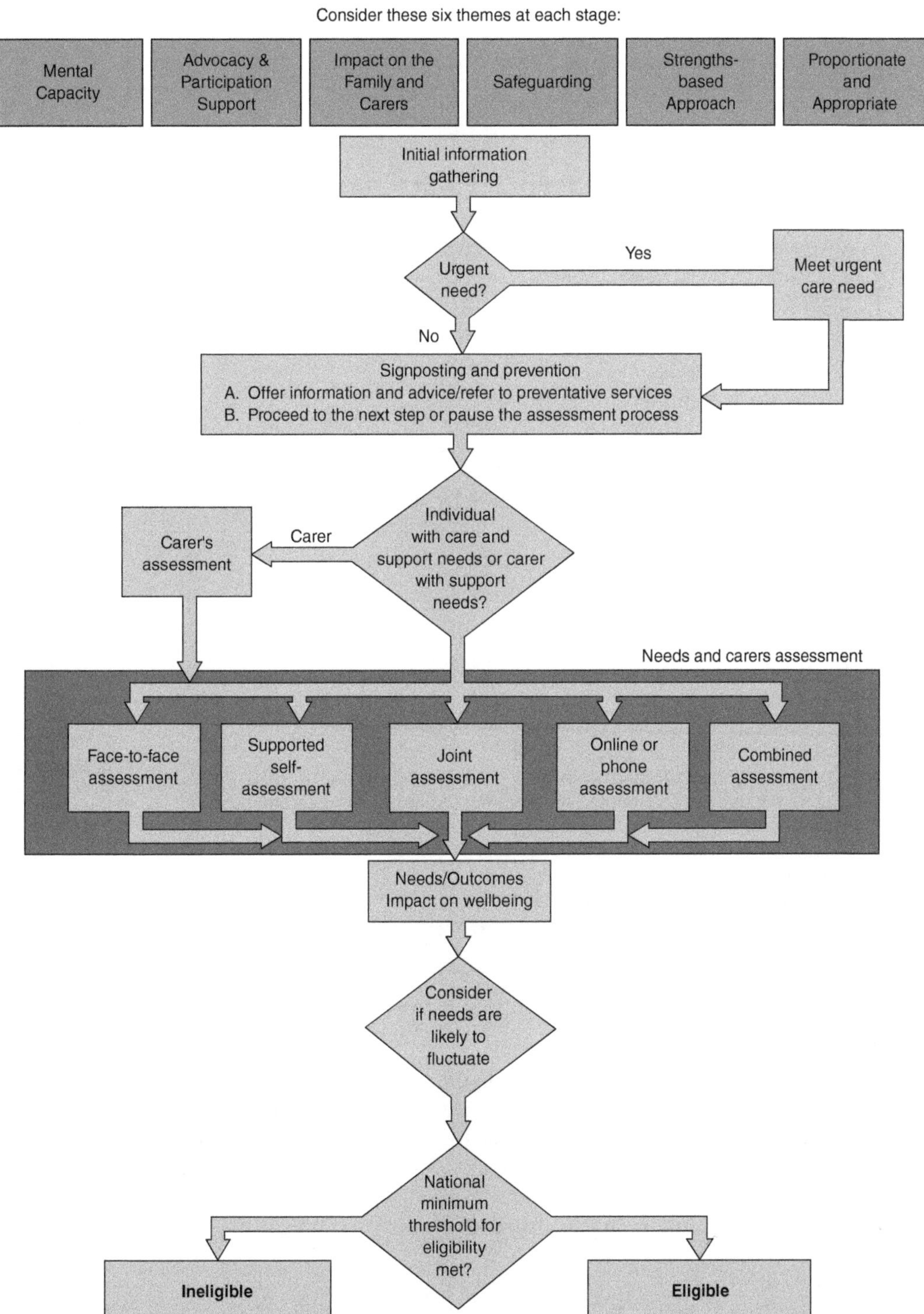

Figure 5.5 Assessment and eligibility process map (SCIE, 2015a; reproduced under Open Government Licence v3.0)

Needs
The adult's needs arise from or are related to a physical or mental impairment or illness

Outcomes
As a result of the needs, the adult is unable to achieve 2 or more of the following:
a) managing and maintaining nutrition
b) maintaining personal hygiene
c) managing toilet needs
d) being appropriately clothed
e) maintaining a habitable home environment
f) being able to make use of the home safely
g) developing and maintaining family or other personal relationships
h) accessing and engaging in work, training, education or volunteering
i) making use of necessary facilities or services in the local community including public transport and recreational facilities or services

Wellbeing
As a consequence, there is or is likely to be a significant impact on the adult's wellbeing, including the following:
a) personal dignity (including treatment of the individual with respect)
b) physical and mental health and emotional wellbeing
c) protection from abuse and neglect
d) control by the individual over day-to-day life (including over care and support provided and the way it is provided)
e) participation in work, education, training or recreation
f) social and economic wellbeing
g) domestic, family and personal relationships
h) suitability of living accommodation
i) the individual's contribution to society

Figure 5.6 Eligibility decision process

It is important to differentiate between eligibility and funding: being eligible for services does not necessarily mean that the local authority will meet the cost of those services. If a person is eligible for services, they will be financially assessed to determine whether they are able to contribute to some or all of their care costs. Some people with long-term complex health needs qualify for free social care arranged and funded solely by the NHS. This is known as Continuing Health Care, and it engages separate eligibility criteria.

Advocacy

The person whose needs are being assessed should be involved in the process as far as possible, and this may mean that we need to consider whether reasonable adjustments under the

Equality Act 2010 can support the assessment process. If it appears that the person will have substantial difficulty in being involved with their assessment or care and support planning, and has no friends or family available to support and represent their wishes, then they are entitled to an independent advocate (s 67 Care Act 2014). SCIE (2015b) states that within this context, advocacy means 'supporting a person to understand information, express their needs and wishes, secure their rights, represent their interests and obtain the care and support they need' (p. 6). The requirement to provide independent advocacy applies equally to carers with support needs. The purpose of involving an advocate – regardless of whether this role is being undertaken by a friend, family member or advocacy professional – is to facilitate the person's involvement and support them throughout the process.

Personalisation

The term 'personalisation' is often used very reductively. Although it led to the creation of what we now know as personal budgets (see Chapter 6), in its true sense, it describes a shift in power, rather than a process of service delivery. The concept of personalisation emerged from the disability rights movement as a means to move power away from the centre (the state, health and social care professionals) towards the individual. Personalisation requires 'thinking about public services ... in an entirely different way – starting with the person rather than the service' (Carr, 2010: 67), but there is much debate about whether successive governments have embraced personalisation in order to promote citizenship or consumerism (see Ferguson, 2007; Scourfield, 2007; Roulstone and Morgan, 2009; Lymbery, 2010).

Assessment and provision of services was traditionally premised on what Duffy (2006) termed the *professional gift model*. In this model, all of the power and decision making rests with the social worker, who uses their professional expertise to assess and determine needs, and then decides how these should be met. Having designed the package of care – usually by fitting the person into existing services – the package is then costed. The professional gift model disempowers people by expecting them to passively and gratefully receive whatever the assessor decides that they do or do not deserve.

Duffy (2006) argues that this model maintained disabled people in a position of powerlessness and exclusion, and that the aim of care and support should be to facilitate full participation in society – citizenship. The Community Care (Direct Payments) Act 1996 established the right for people to receive direct cash payments from local authorities to arrange and procure their own care. This presented the possibility for people to challenge the professional gift model and employ their own expertise to design care more individually tailored to their needs. The 2003 'In Control' pilots pioneered the concept of self-directed care by involving people with learning disabilities in their own care planning (Poll et al., 2006). People's own expertise was harnessed through self-assessment of needs and the identification of an approximate sum of money to which these needs entitled them at the beginning of the process, rather than the end, so that individuals could plan how to allocate that money to secure the outcomes they desired.

In Control demonstrated sustainable benefits with no increase in costs, and evaluations showed that the majority of participants were happier with their care (Glasby and Littlechild, 2009). Personalisation appealed to the New Labour government's neo-liberal ideas about choice, consumerism and a free market economy, and was a prominent element of their 'Putting People First' policy (Department of Health, 2007). Personalisation, however, was not without its critics. Ferguson (2007) argued that consumer choice did not address structural issues of poverty, inequality and multiple discrimination, and questioned whether services would become individualised rather than collective, and provided by profit-making organisations rather than social enterprises. Scourfield (2007) was concerned that personalisation was transferring public responsibilities to individuals, requiring them to fulfil a number of new roles for which they may not be well equipped. Glasby and Littlechild (2009) found that social workers were themselves resistant to personalisation and direct payments. This was supported by Bola et al. (2014), who found that professionals were concerned about the potential for mismanagement of public funds, and in some cases had limiting, discriminatory attitudes about the capabilities of people who use services to determine their own needs and arrange their own support. Needham (2014) argued that the focus of successive governments on personalisation during a climate of austerity has resulted in people becoming responsible for arranging their own care at a time when local authority services are being withdrawn.

The Care Act statutory guidance directs that local authorities facilitate personalisation, and this means that at the assessment stage if appropriate, self-assessment can be employed to allow the person to identify their own needs. This raises the potential for someone to over- or under-report their level of need; however, this risk applies equally to professional assessment. The guidance suggests that social workers can confirm the accuracy of the person's needs by consulting with other relevant professionals and people who know the person (Department of Health and Social Care, 2018: 6.3)

AT NUMBER 6

Liam was placed under s 2 of the Mental Health Act 1893, which provided a legal authority to detain him in hospital for assessment for up to 28 days. He responded well to treatment and his section was lifted; he is now a voluntary patient. Liam has been diagnosed as having a psychotic episode triggered by post-traumatic stress disorder. His doctor believes he can soon be discharged from hospital. He will access psychological therapy in the community and has been referred for a social work assessment to determine his needs and desired outcomes.

EXERCISE 5.2

Use the current information and what you know about Liam's situation before he came into hospital (see Exercise 2.1).

- Consider the Care Act Assessment and eligibility process map (Figure 5.5). How are the six themes currently relevant to Liam's assessment?
- Consider the Eligibility decision process (Figure 5.6). Is Liam eligible? Give specific evidence.

The Mental Capacity Act

We have identified the significance of autonomy and self-determination, but many of the people that we work with in social care have conditions that affect their ability to make decisions. The ability to make a specific decision at the time it needs to be made is referred to in UK law as mental capacity; it is helpful to think about being able to make an informed choice. Historically, people with learning disabilities and mental health problems were frequently regarded as globally lacking capacity, and therefore denied decision-making autonomy outright. The Mental Capacity Act 2005 (MCA) was a response to shifting attitudes around the balance of power between professionals and people who use services, personalisation and citizenship. The MCA provides a statutory framework to support personal autonomy. It sets out when and how capacity should be assessed, and where it has been established that a person lacks the capacity to make a particular decision, sets out the process that must be followed to make decisions in their best interests (Department for Constitutional Affairs, 2007). It became operational in 2007, and applies from age 16. It states that:

> ... a person lacks capacity in relation to a matter if at the material time he is unable to make a decision for himself in relation to the matter because of an impairment of, or disturbance in the mind or brain. (Department for Constitutional Affairs, 2007: 42)

The Act stipulates that unjustified assumptions about capacity must not be based on age, diagnosis or behaviour. The person's inability to make a decision must be as a result of an impairment of, or a disturbance in, the functioning of the mind or brain, and this is known as the causal nexus. It does not matter whether the impairment or disturbance is permanent or temporary, and mental capacity may be affected by a range of conditions, e.g. any mental health condition, any learning disability, a brain injury, the effect of a stroke, delirium arising from infection or dehydration. The decision-specific nature of capacity is critical; a person may not be able to make one decision but be perfectly capable of making another – e.g. someone may not be able to make a complex decision about their accommodation, but they may well be able to decide who they want to provide their care.

The MCA has five statutory principles, the first three of which relate to capacity, and the final two of which relate to substituted decision making for a person who has been assessed as lacking capacity:

1. A person must be assumed to have capacity unless it is established that they lack capacity.
2. A person is not to be treated as unable to make a decision unless all practicable steps to help him to do so have been taken without success.
3. A person is not to be treated as unable to make a decision merely because he makes an unwise decision.
4. An act done, or decision made, under this Act for or on behalf of a person who lacks capacity must be done, or made, in his best interests.
5. Before the act is done, or the decision made, regard must be had to whether the purpose for which it is needed can be effectively achieved in a way that is less restrictive of the person's rights and freedom of action. (Section 1, MCA, 2005)

Assessing mental capacity

The MCA sets out a four-stage test, sometimes referred to as the functional test of capacity, which requires the assessor to give the person information relevant to the decision that needs to be made, and then determine whether they are able to do the following:

1. Understand information about the decision to be made.
2. Retain that information in their mind.
3. Use or weigh that information as part of the decision-making process.
4. Communicate their decision (by talking, using sign language or any other means).

If any one of these four stages is not evidenced, the person is found to lack capacity in relation to that specific decision at that specific time. Separate capacity assessments must be conducted for separate decisions, and consideration should be given to whether the person is likely to regain capacity. The person assessing someone's capacity is usually the person directly concerned with the individual at the time the decision needs to be made, and different people will be involved in assessing someone's capacity to make different decisions. Assessing capacity is a communicative process, which requires the assessor to provide the person with the relevant information, which will differ from situation to situation. Before you attempt to assess capacity, make sure that you fully understand:

- the nature of the decision;
- the reason why it is needed;
- the likely effects of deciding one way, or another, or making no decision at all;
- how the person communicates and what can support their decision making.

AT NUMBER 5

Max is in a residential rehabilitation facility following his stroke. Although he is making good progress, his speech is very difficult to follow and he is often confused. Samantha is aware that Max will have long-term care needs, and that because of investments that she and Max jointly own, they will be required to contribute towards the cost of his care once he comes home. Samantha visits her financial advisor to discuss releasing some money to cover these costs. The financial advisor tells her that Max will need to agree to this, and asks if he has the capacity to do so. Samantha doesn't know.

What evidence is there to suggest that a capacity assessment needs to be completed?

EXERCISE 5.3

- If an assessment is to be completed, who should do this?
- What would be the relevant information?
- What could the person conducting the capacity assessment do to facilitate communication?

Making best interests decisions

If a person is found to lack mental capacity in relation to a specific decision, then an evidence-based decision can be made in their 'best interests'. The term 'best interests' suggests that there will actually be one 'best' option, but the decisions we encounter in social work practice are often characterised by uncertainty, and rather than acting on best interests, we can feel that we are trying to identify the least worst option. MCA Principles 4 and 5 guide best interests decision making, and section 4 of the MCA sets out a checklist which must be followed in order to make a legally defensible best interests decision:

- Encourage participation.
- Identify all relevant circumstances.
- Find out the person's views.
- Avoid discrimination.
- Assess whether the person might regain capacity.
- Not be motivated by a desire to bring about the person's death.
- Consult others.
- Avoid restricting the person's rights.
- Take all of this into account.

Safeguarding adults

In 2000 the Department of Health's *No Secrets* policy guidance established that local authorities had lead responsibility for the Protection of Vulnerable Adults (POVA), and its key message was that 'safeguarding is everybody's business'. A consultation on the efficacy of *No Secrets* (Department of Health, 2009) made grim reading. People who had experienced POVA reported the process to be impersonal, disempowering and excluding; some felt that they had been diverted from the criminal justice system, with crime repackaged as abuse and the investigation led by social workers rather than the police (Department of Health, 2009). The language of POVA was difficult. Identifying people as *vulnerable* has long been contentious, with many people finding it a disabling term associated with deficit and stigma (Brown, 2011; Hollomotz, 2009; Hough, 2012), whilst *protection* further reinforces power differentials, implying helplessness and a need to defer to professionals. From this point, protection of vulnerable adults started to become safeguarding adults.

In 2010, the Local Government Association (LGA) and the Association of Directors of Adult Social Services (ADASS) began the Making Safeguarding Personal (MSP) initiative, funding research and piloting projects to reimagine adult safeguarding in a more person-centred way. The Care Act 2014 finally made the safeguarding of adults a statutory responsibility, and Chapter 14 of the statutory guidance (which replaced *No Secrets*) draws heavily from the MSP approach, directing that, as far as possible, the intended outcomes of safeguarding should be determined by the person at risk of abuse and neglect. Care Act Safeguarding duties apply to an adult who:

- has needs for care and support (whether or not the local authority is meeting any of those needs); and
- is experiencing, or at risk of, abuse or neglect; and

- as a result of those care and support needs is unable to protect themselves from either the risk of, or the experience of abuse or neglect (Department of Health and Social Care, 2018: paragraph 14.2).

Within the Care Act 2014, the person experiencing or at risk of abuse or neglect is simply referred to as *the adult*, but for clarity in practice we tend to refer to *the adult at risk*. It is important that we are not constrained in our view of what constitutes abuse or neglect, and look beyond single incidents or individuals to identify patterns of harm. The Care Act recognises ten categories of abuse:

- Physical abuse.
- Domestic violence.
- Sexual abuse.
- Psychological abuse.
- Financial or material abuse.
- Modern slavery.
- Discriminatory abuse.
- Organisational abuse.
- Neglect and acts of omission.
- Self-neglect.*

(*Self-neglect will not automatically result in a response through safeguarding; this will depend on the features of the individual situation.)

Figure 5.7 demonstrates the centrality of the person at risk in initial safeguarding information gathering.

Within the Care Act statutory guidance (Department of Health and Social Care, 2018), safeguarding's six underpinning principles are articulated as if voiced by the person at risk, to further aid us in taking a personalised approach:

1. **Empowerment** – Personalisation and the presumption of person-led decisions and informed consent: 'I am asked what I want as the outcomes from the safeguarding process and these directly inform what happens.'
2. **Prevention** – It is better to take action before harm occurs: 'I receive clear and simple information about what abuse is, how to recognise the signs and what I can do to seek help.'
3. **Proportionality** – Proportionate and least intrusive response appropriate to the risk presented: 'I am sure that the professionals will work for my best interests as I see them, and they will only get involved as much as I require.'
4. **Protection** – Support and representation for those in greatest need: 'I get help and support to report abuse. I get help to take part in the safeguarding process to the extent to which I want and to which I am able.'
5. **Partnership** – Local solutions through services working with their communities. Communities have a part to play in preventing, detecting and reporting neglect and abuse: 'I know that staff

treat any personal and sensitive information in confidence, only sharing what is helpful and necessary. I am confident that professionals will work together to get the best result for me.'

6. **Accountability** – Accountability and transparency in delivering safeguarding: 'I understand the role of everyone involved in my life.'

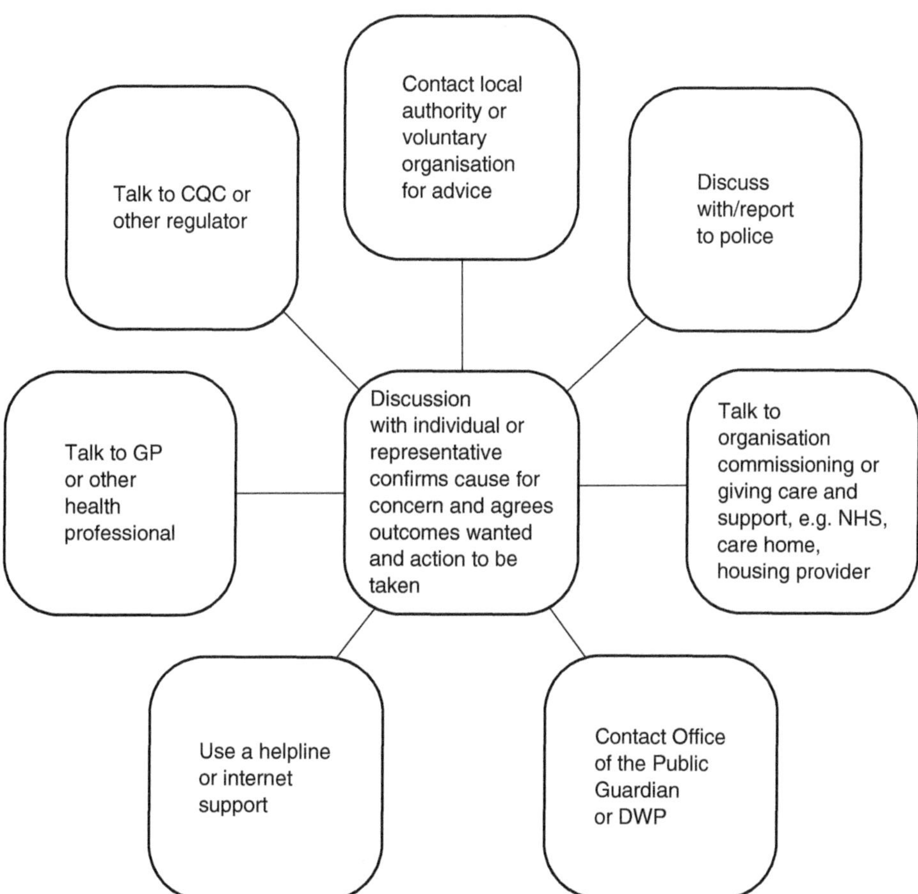

Figure 5.7 Initial safeguarding information gathering (Department of health and social care, 2018; reproduced under Open Government Licence v3.0)

SUMMARY

The context of social work with adults is shaped by notions of rights, autonomy and self-determination, but unfortunately, as we have documented in this chapter, people continue to experience inequality, stigma and exclusion – sometimes from within health and social care services. Although the Care Act 2014 has consolidated responsibilities that were previously located over a range of different acts, it is not a single legal framework; it must be used in conjunction with the Human Rights Act 1998 and the Mental Capacity Act 2005. The process of assessment with adults has many components, and identification of need does not necessarily result in eligibility for services; even when people *are* eligible for services, they may be expected to meet the costs themselves. As social workers, it is critical that we are aware of how people are oppressed on the basis of their difference from a perceived (but non-existent) norm by community, society, state and individual attitudes. It is our role to challenge this oppression and inequity through rights-based, personal practice that focuses on the outcomes people wish to attain for themselves, rather than on the assumptions of professionals or wider society.

6 PLANNING, REVIEWS, FLEXIBILITY AND SUPERVISION

Learning in this chapter relates to

PCF	KSS Adult Services	KSS Child & Family
1. Professionalism 2. Values & Ethics 3. Diversity & Equalities 4. Rights & Justice 5. Knowledge 6. Critical Reflection & Analysis 7. Skills & Interventions 8. Contexts & Organisations 9. Professional Leadership	2. The role of social workers working with adults 3. Person-centred practice 6. Effective assessments & outcome-based support planning 7. Direct work with individuals & families 8. Supervision, critical reflection & analysis	1. The role of child & family social work 5. Effective direct work with children & families 6. Child & family assessment 7. Analysis, decision making, planning & review 8. The law & the family justice system 10. The role of supervision & research

INTRODUCTION

Our assessments enable – or deny – access to social services, so they seek to support how we intervene in people's lives. Social services could not exist without professional judgements, but the judgement alone is merely an opinion. As social workers, we develop plans based on our assessments and through planning we are able to set goals, intervene and measure effectiveness. In this world of high accountability, planning (and the recording of plans) has taken central stage in our practice. In this chapter we focus on the principles of planning actions and explain how to incorporate outcomes, and we include separate sections on childcare and adult care plans. It may seem counterintuitive that we include reviewing and supervision in this chapter, before Part II of the book, which considers different interventions. Social work practice is not linear. Planning, reviewing and supervision are integrated and concurrent elements of our practice, and as social workers it is critical that we are flexible as well as process savvy.

PLANNING MADE SIMPLE

'Plan' is both a *noun* – 'a scheme or method of acting, doing, proceeding, making, etc., developed in advance' (e.g. 'the safeguarding plan'), and a *verb* – 'to arrange a method or scheme beforehand for any work, enterprise, or proceeding' (e.g. planning a meeting) (Dictionary.com). Common types of plan to think about are architectural drawings, or the instructions included with flat pack furniture. From this we understand that a plan is generally a list or diagram of stages detailing the timing and resources to be used to complete an objective, such as building a house or assembling a wardrobe. If you have ever tried to build a flat pack wardrobe, you will have reached a point where you stepped back and reviewed your progress. You may have noticed that sometimes the plans don't seem to work, and sometimes you will deviate from the sequence laid out in the instructions. A builder may follow the architect's plan but it will be frequently reviewed and altered – maybe a particular building material is unavailable or too expensive. Plans are guides. When the plan is executed it may turn out not to be the best fit after all, and therefore best laid plans should be open to scrutiny and flexible execution.

AT NUMBER 4

Olivia is planning a family visit with her two children, Matty and Georgia. The trip will take approximately two hours and Olivia has to plan the journey taking into consideration her children's very different needs. Both are vegetarians, but Matty is lactose intolerant and allergic to nuts. Georgia uses a wheelchair and the last family trip ended in disaster because the train did not have an available accessible toilet. Georgia is very concerned about the trip but she is excited about seeing her cousins.

EXERCISE 6.1

- What do you think Olivia has to consider when planning her trip?
- Do you think she has to make any additional arrangements?
- Why might it take longer for Olivia to plan her trip?
- How do you think she feels about having to make these plans?

PROFESSIONAL SOCIAL WORK PLANNING

Planning is embedded as a key skill for social work practitioners. Planning and reviewing feature across the PCF domains of critical reflection, intervention & skills, and professional leadership (BASW, 2015, 2018); the KSS for child and family social workers incorporate planning and reviewing in decision making (Department for Education, 2015a) while the KSS for social workers in adult services include effective assessments and outcome-based support planning and supervision, critical reflection and analysis (Department of Health, 2015). The planning component of our practice ensures we act systematically, as Wilson et al. state: ' ... reflecting and being in social work are intertwined, and the value of not rushing into action can be empowering' (2011: 343). In discussing formulating a plan, Parker refers to the negotiation process between agencies and the notion of *planning permission*, and writes:

> ... plans, like assessments, must be built on a developing relationship between you as a social worker, the other agencies and professionals who might be contributing to the plan and service users.(2017: 107)

Plans are not simply thrown together; instead they act as the overall focus of our work with people who use services. Social work plans come in many different shapes and forms and they have different names depending on:

- the agency and its legal requirements;
- the service user group and their capacity, vulnerability and rights to services;
- the purpose of the plan as an organisational response to identified needs/entitlements to services.

However, all plans contain similar elements, because they progress from the assessment (reflecting the assessed needs of the person), recording what is being done, why it is being done, when it will be done and by whom. In developing a plan, we use our negotiating skills to agree objectives and tasks with everyone involved. Practising ethically when arranging plans is vital as we seek to work collaboratively with people and not disregard their centrality to the process. The plan acts as a means to agree shared goals with people, and advises them about what it is they can expect. This sounds a little like a contract, and in fact contracts do feature within many plans. The plan should identify clear overall outcomes and clarify any actions attributed to participants and service providers, so that it acts as a mechanism for sharing information between all parties concerned. Essentially, the plan is a tool to help in the allocation of resources to meet the desired outcomes based on assessed needs. A plan simply will not work if it presumes that someone will act in accordance with it without this being negotiated, or if it includes a resource that cannot be provided. Through the plan, we are able to identify intended outcomes and indicate the monitoring and review process to ascertain if those outcomes are being achieved. Finally, the plan is a way of recording accountability and professional recommendations.

AUTHOR'S EXPERIENCE (PHIL)

As a newly qualified social worker, I was flummoxed by the very notion of developing a care plan. I was working with a family to assess their needs. At the time, I thought this was a very complex situation; there was some substance misuse, police involvement and financial difficulties. There were two children in the family and the parents were considering separation. I was confused about which direction I would take when working with this family. I felt more confident assessing their needs, or rather, I was happy to engage with the family and talk to them about their experiences and difficulties. Unfortunately, I wasn't really assessing, or forming a professional judgement, and did not develop any recognisable plan other than to visit the family.

In fairness to myself, practice has moved on since this time. Some years later, I was reviewing a number of childcare files for an independent fostering agency. I had been informed there were few childcare plans on file. An Ofsted inspection was imminent and this concerned me. To my relief I found that most of the files contained a childcare plan, but because children were placed by different local authorities who used different terms, many were not titled 'Childcare Plan'. Regardless of how they were titled, they were all care plans and contained the required information. They detailed the children's current situation, their assessed needs, desired objective and how to achieve that desired objective (Department for Education, 2015b). My years of practice experience had helped me to appreciate that a plan may take many forms, and identify what was and was not a plan.

OUTCOMES

Outcomes-focused practice has come to the fore over recent years. Outcomes are the results of an activity: consequences, impacts, effects, results and achievements. In our practice, outcomes are clear goals and targets to aim for when working with people, which are identified during planning and then reviewed later on to ascertain whether services and interventions have been effective. Outcome-focused approaches help clarify the purpose of practice, which often takes place in the midst of chaotic and confusing situations. They imply a time-limited, rather than an open-ended approach to intervention. Within larger-scale outcomes, such as maintaining a child in a foster placement, there is the flexibility to formulate smaller objectives and agree actions that may be needed to achieve the overall outcomes, e.g. agreeing the child's access to a sporting or recreational activity. The smaller, easier objective will go some way to achieve the more ambitious objective of maintaining the child's foster placement by being productively engaged in a recreational activity. Therefore, through objective forming we can embrace more creative and yet focused planning. Finally, through outcomes we are able to assess, plan and review our input with people and the community.

Wilson et al. suggest that outcomes can be classified in two ways: firstly, *final outcomes* – that are agreed to be significant in their own right, such as rehabilitation from hospital; and secondly, *process outcomes* – concerned with the way social work is delivered, e.g. the consultation with a child about foster care (Wilson et al., 2011: 242). Doel suggests outcomes and process are closely related and writes:

> Social work is a profession that is orientated towards process (how things are done, the quality), and it has had to come to grips with an increasing focus on outcome (what is the product, the quantity). (2012: 114)

Doel notes the tendency for *programme-based* practice whereby services are delivered through a specific programme, often with set results and by specifically trained practitioners who deliver the programme, such as parenting programmes. For Doel, these shorter-term, focused, outcomes-based programmes have tended to replace established social work methods. As we have shown, social work evolves, the emphasis changes and our practice shifts. Doel suggests the development of the managerialist approach to social work, following Thatcher's introduction of private sector management processes into the public sector, reflects the prioritisation of procedures and targets over professional values and standards, whereby 'Managerialist practice therefore values quantitative measures over qualitative ones' (Doel, 2012: 37).

There has been considerable work on outcomes and increased choice in adult social work through individualisation, responsibilisation and the marketisation of social services reflecting neo-liberal theory (e.g. see Clarke et al., 2007; Stevens et al., 2018). Research on the impact of personalisation and adult safeguarding practice by Stevens et al. (2018) considered the dangers of personalisation and the allocation of resources through direct payments and person-centred care which is concerned with choice and control for individuals (see Chapter 5). They concluded that a new balance 'may require reorientation of practice, as practitioners negotiate the potentially divergent requirements to promote autonomy, whilst remaining responsible for safeguarding' (Stevens et al., 2018: 18). This research highlights the different outcome perspectives social workers have to manage as part of contemporary practice.

As society changes, there is a danger that the social work profession moves unknowingly into new territory unprepared for the challenges we will inevitably encounter. Contemporary social work is primarily concerned with merging professionally based values with procedurally based organisational requirements. Naturally, the individual social worker and their values are central to this process of delivering people-based services to community members. Planning is crucial and plans have to be constructed on sound and robust assessments.

S.M.A.R.T. PLANNING

S.M.A.R.T. is a mnemonic acronym whereby each letter represents a word (**S**pecific, **M**easurable, **A**chievable, **R**ealistic and **T**imely). The concept of S.M.A.R.T. modelling derives from management and is originally associated with work by Peter Drucker and the process of managing objectives that are delivered sequentially within an organisational context (Drucker, 1954 [2007]).

More specifically, S.M.A.R.T. criteria were first written about by George Dolan (1981) in relation to management goals and objectives. Dolan offered S.M.A.R.T. as a mechanism for managers to write objectives because 'the process of writing objectives is a major source of anxiety that many individuals would like to live without' (Dolan, 1981: 35). S.M.A.R.T. has evolved and there are slight variations, e.g. Dolan refers to *assignable* rather than the more contemporary *achievable:*

Specific – aims and objectives, roles and tasks.

Measurable – outcomes and goals.

Achievable – goals and outcomes to enhance success and improve motivation.

Realistic and relevant – outcomes with a focus on core issues.

Timely and time limited – addressing current issues using a plan with a review date.

Not for the first time, management theories and models are seen to be complementary to social work practice. Although this may well be unpalatable to theorists and practitioners who favour a more radical or reformist approach to social work, it is hard to argue against social work gathering our knowledge from whichever source seems relevant. S.M.A.R.T. planning enables us to practise in a manner that combines our work-based commitments with the assessed needs of an individual, so long as we recognise the complexity of working with people and communities to maintain a person-centred, relationship-based approach.

AT NUMBER 4

Following the incident with Olivia's ex-partner (see Chapter 3), the social worker, though considering this relatively low priority, agreed with the team manager to make another visit. During this visit, Matty mentioned the ex-partner's name, which worried the social worker. Olivia told the social worker she loves her children but that she finds it difficult to cope with their needs. While Georgia has been allocated to the Children with Disabilities team, there has been little involvement from them. The social worker has some safeguarding concerns that Olivia is possibly still in contact with her ex-partner, but is more worried by her indicating she is not coping. She decides to contact the Children with Disabilities team manager, who agrees to allocate a team member to assess Georgia's needs. Olivia is relieved to have the opportunity to discuss her worries and is keen to have some support from social services.

EXERCISE 6.2

Consider some of the issues that an assessment may identify, such as isolation, poverty, parenting etc. Now use S.M.A.R.T. to develop a plan of work with Georgia and her family.

- **S**pecific – what are the aims and objectives, roles and tasks?
- **M**easurable – identify outcomes and goals.
- **A**chievable – negotiate goals and outcomes to enhance success and improve motivation.
- **R**ealistic and relevant – develop outcomes which focus on core issues.
- **T**imely and time limited – what are the timescales and how will the plan be reviewed?

THE SKILLED HELPER APPROACH

The *Skilled Helper* approach is based on work by Gerard Egan (2013), who built on Carl Rogers' person-centred counselling model. Rogers advocated for a self-actualisation approach to therapy by suggesting counsellors could better help their clients by encouraging them to focus on their current personal understanding of a situation, rather than on unconscious or external interpretations (Rogers, 1961 [2004]). Egan used this approach to look at high functioning helpers who are able to be attentive, show congruence, empathy and respect, and take a non-judgemental approach. Through three stages, Egan's model supports the skilled helper to enable the client (person) to concentrate on what is happening, what they want to happen and action plan.

The **Egan model** aims to support the helper in addressing three main questions:

1. Exploration – *'What is going on?'* – Helping clients explore their concerns and tell their stories.
2. Challenging – *'What do I want instead?'* – Helping clients design problem-managing outcomes and set goals.
3. Action planning – *'How might I get to what I want?'* – Planning the way forward (Egan, 2013).

Applying the Skilled Helper model to our practice can help us traverse the tricky road between professional assertiveness and organisational requirements, maintaining our focus on the person rather than agency or professional agendas. The Skilled Helper enables the person to remain central to the goal and objective setting, resulting in a person-centred plan. This model can be used in conjunction with S.M.A.R.T. criteria as the two approaches complement each other, S.M.A.R.T. being essentially more process driven, while the Skilled Helper model is relationship based.

EXERCISE 6.3

Reconsider Exercise 6.2 and the S.M.A.R.T. plan you devised. Now consider how you could use the Skilled Helper approach in your work with this family.

(Continued)

- Exploration – 'What is going on?' – Helping Olivia and her children explore their concerns and tell their stories.
- Challenging – 'What does Olivia want instead?' – Helping Olivia and her children to design problem-managing outcomes and set their goals.
- Action planning – 'How might Olivia get to what she wants?' – Planning the way forward for Olivia and her children.

Having completed these two exercises, how can S.M.A.R.T. and the Skilled Helper complement each other in your work with this family?

TYPES OF SOCIAL WORK PLANS

Childcare plans

There are a variety of plans social workers develop when working with children and their families. We may develop a plan to agree our initial assessment with the family, or we may instigate an Early Help assessment (formerly known as the Common Assessment Framework – see Chapter 4) or care leaving plans. Then there are many different agency and context plans involving particular work with children, young people and their families. In this section we focus on statutory childcare plans for children looked after by English local authorities.

The statutory guidance provided by the Department for Education (2015b) provides detailed instructions for care planning, process and timescales (see Figure 6.1). For a child to be looked after by the local authority, the social worker has a legal duty to ensure plans are made and that they are agreed and signed by those with parental responsibility (e.g. the parent or local authority when there is a Care Order). Statutory reviews are built within the planning process (see Figure 6.2).

Once a child is looked after by the local authority, there is then a statutory duty that the child's care plan is reviewed initially within the first 20 working days of being placed, with the second review within three months and thereafter every six months.

AT NUMBER 2

On Friday, Suzie receives a telephone call from the fostering placement manager asking if she and Alfie can look after a seven-year-old boy called David. She agrees, and later that evening a social worker brings David to their home. The social worker tells them that a colleague will deliver the 'paperwork' and clothing on Monday. Fortunately for David, Suzie and Alfie have some spare clothes that fit him and they buy him some underwear and toiletries. On Monday, they contact their supervising social worker who arranges to visit later on that day and asks if they have the correct forms. During the visit, their supervising social worker advises Suzie and Alfie that they should have the placement agreement signed by the parents. Alfie asks, 'What were we supposed to do, refuse to take him?'

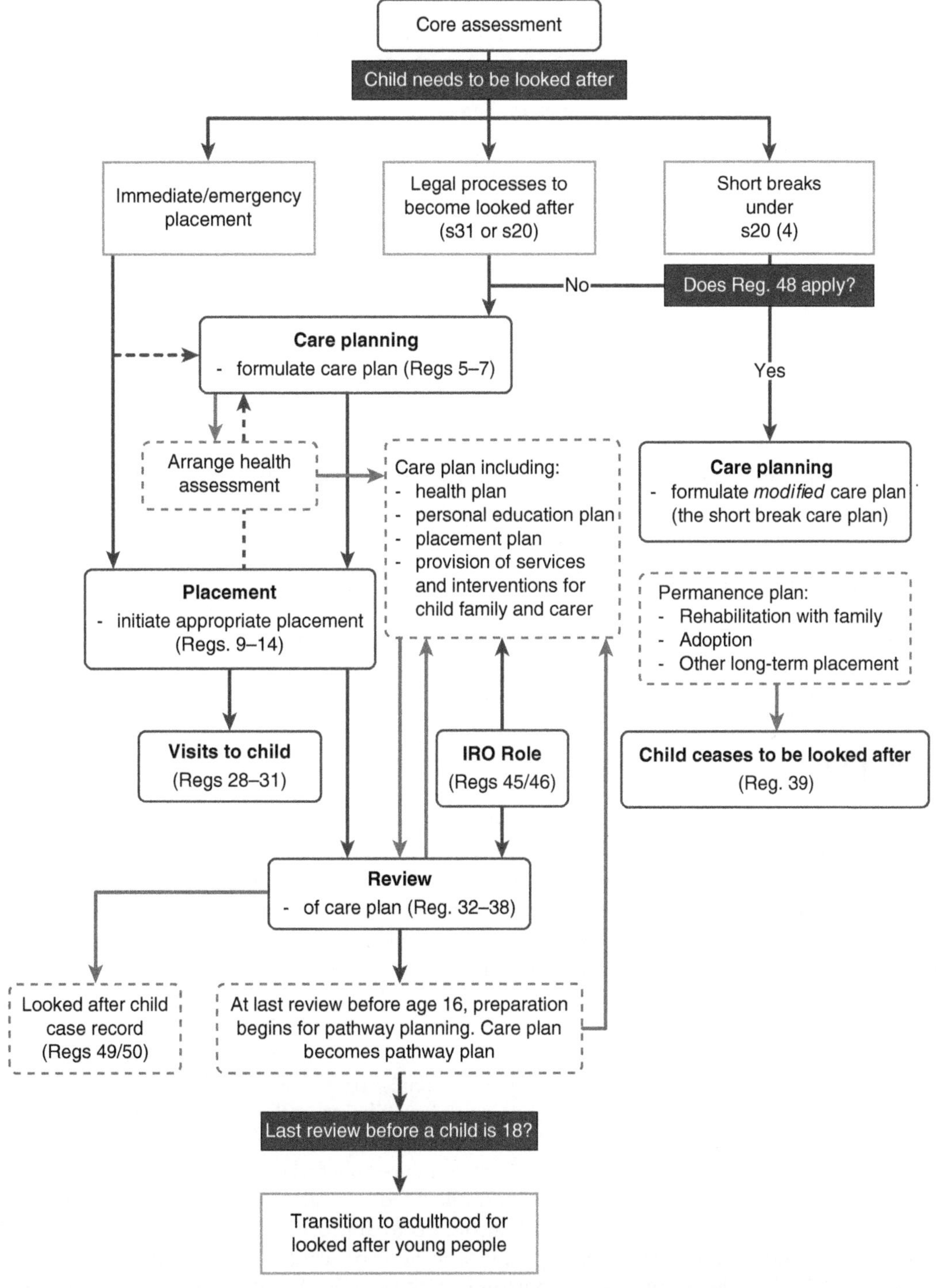

Figure 6.1 Overview of the care-planning, placement and review process (Department for Education, 2015b: 168; reproduced under Open Government Licence v3.0)

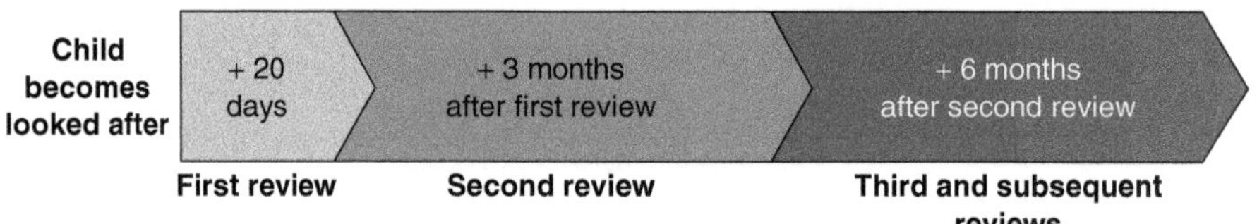

Figure 6.2 Maximum intervals between reviews (Department for Education, 2015b: 113; reproduced under Open Government Licence v3.0)

EXERCISE 6.4

- What type of 'paperwork' do you think applies to David?
- Why is it important to have the 'correct' paperwork?
- What is David's legal status and what about his parents?
- How would you go about making sure David's placement is legal and his parents are involved?

The care planning process for children ensures that legal rights and local authority duties are maintained. It is all too easy to prefer to postpone planning during emergencies and safeguarding. Placing children into foster care is stressful for practitioners, but must be more so for families and children. The planning process here ensures that our work, during very difficult times, is transparent and that we act ethically towards children and their families.

Adult plans

Following a needs assessment, if an adult is determined to be eligible for local authority support, then a care and support plan must be produced (Care Act 2014, s 24(1)), detailing the needs to be met how they will be met and how this links to the outcomes that the adult identified in the assessment process. The care and support plan should be person-centred and person-led, reflecting their wishes, aspirations and what is important to them (Department of Health and Social Care, 2018). Care and support plans must also include the indicative amount of money available to meet the person's needs (Care Act 2014, s 25(1)).

The Care Act 2014 rejects the professional gift model (Duffy, 2006) in favour of personalisation and self-directed support (see Chapter 5). Local authorities have resource allocation systems (RAS) which translate identified, eligible social care needs into an indicative amount of money available to be used to secure the person's wellbeing and identified outcomes. Once the person has an indicative resource allocation to work with, they can construct their own care and support plan with appropriate support. Some people feel confident to undertake their own care and support planning, perhaps with support from family or friends. Others do not, or are unable to because of their particular situation. Local authorities must provide appropriate help with care and support planning to people who need or want it, and in some areas this is provided in house, whilst in others it is outsourced. Stevens et al. (2018) consider the dangers of allocating resources through direct payments, suggesting that this may increase vulnerability to financial abuse or result in less robust care.

Money available to meet care and support needs can be used to purchase traditional care services or to fund solutions that are more creative. For example, someone whose arthritis has left them housebound and unable to cook for themself could use their personal budget to purchase domiciliary care to help with shopping and food preparation, or alternatively, they could use it to purchase a laptop and microwave, enabling them to shop for groceries online and reheat ready meals themself. The key consideration is the way that people want to spend their budget, and whether this is likely to meet their outcomes and assessed needs.

Completed plans require sign-off by the local authority to agree whether the proposed spend is an appropriate way to meet the identified needs. Regular reviews ensure that people have the opportunity to reflect on what is and isn't working and what needs to change. Think Local Act Personal (TLAP), a national strategic partnership of over 50 organisations committed to personalisation, has produced some excellent guidance on care and support planning to support the implementation of the Care Act 2014, including the Figure 6.3 model for developing person-centred outcomes.

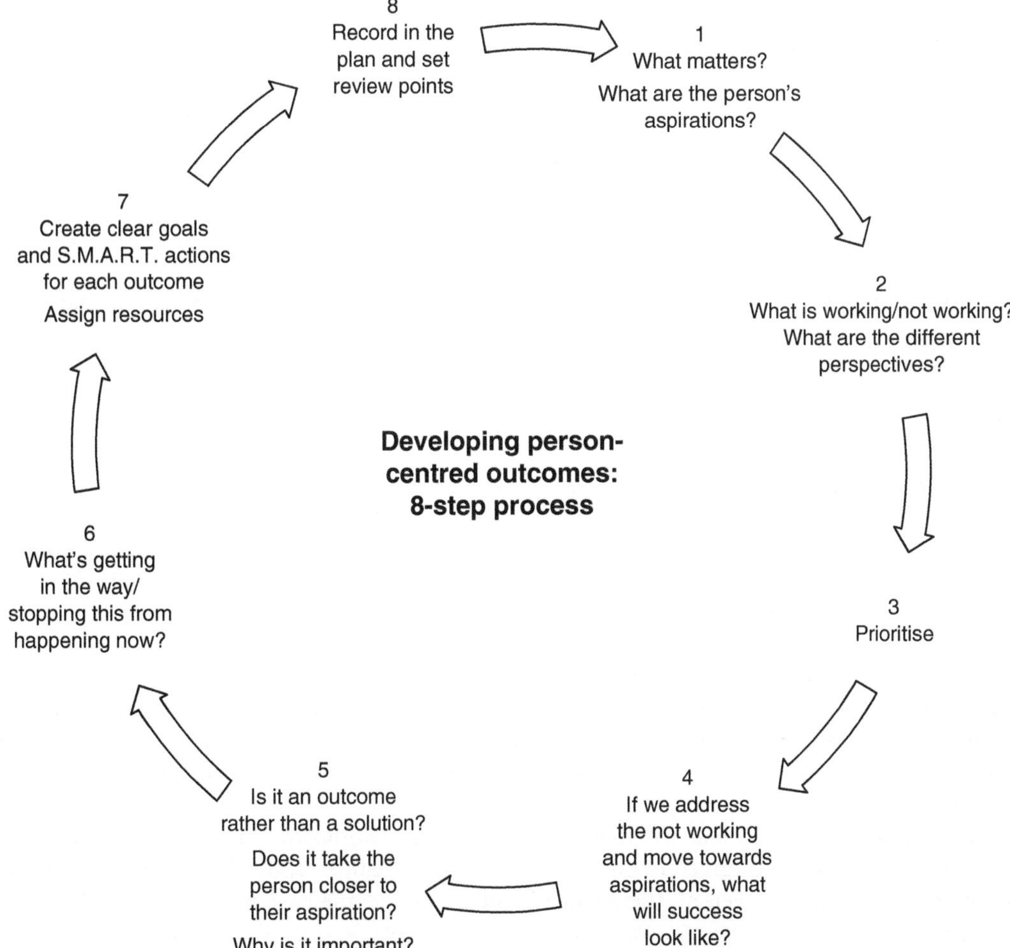

Figure 6.3 Developing person-centred outcomes: 8-step process (TLAP, 2014)

AT NUMBER 6

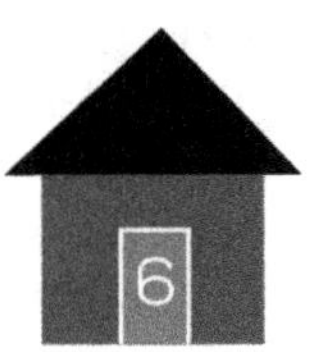

As a refugee, Adnan had a much interrupted education. Once he came into the care of the local authority, he was a bright student who made excellent progress. Adnan went to college to study for his GCSEs, but he lost a lot of weight and dropped out of college due to physical health problems. When Adnan's kidneys began to fail, it was discovered that he had an eating disorder. He worked well with a psychiatrist, psychologist and dietician, making slow but steady progress. He has been assessed under the Care Act 2014 and is eligible for a personal budget of approximately £1750 per year. Adnan identifies three long-term outcomes, which he would like to achieve:

1. To find his family.
2. To become a lawyer.
3. To maintain a healthy body weight so that his physical health does not impede his social relationships.

EXERCISE 6.5

You are the social worker supporting Adnan with his care and support planning.

- What shorter-term outcomes could work towards his three identified long-term outcomes?
- Work through the 8-step process (see Figure 6.3).

Negotiating plans

Throughout this chapter, we have reflected on social work planning with people and communities. Planning is a dynamic process, a skilled task and professionally driven. We have identified how plans form part of the PCF and KSS and the centrality of objectives in delivering services within a contemporary managerialist context. However, our practice has to be based on people skills. Social workers are neither fully autonomous nor bureaucratic. We work with people and within organisational and legislative contexts. Our skill-set is crucial when we manage and plan our workload within the competing complex environments we work in. As Parker explains plans 'are also "maps" based on prior and ongoing negotiations with those involved' (2017: 107).

Negotiation is a key element to effective planning. As Thompson writes, 'For a contract to work, its contents must be agreed by the people concerned' (2002: 200). For Thompson, the plan represents a contract between all the parties involved and as the case manager a social worker is generally responsible for negotiating with all stakeholders involved in the plan. To establish collaborative working with those who use social care, Rogers et al. (2017) offer key basic values of respect, acceptance, individuality, honesty and integrity, and equality. In discussing the contracting framework to social work practice, Beesley et al. (2018) make reference to Shell's (2006) negotiating techniques, applied in business, as useful skills for social workers to acquire, and they helpfully summarise the styles as avoiding, accommodating, compromising, collaborating and competing. Shell's work focuses on bargaining for a business advantage between reasonable people (Shell, 2006). Of the five styles Beesley et al. utilise from Shell, they suggest *collaborating* is closest to person-centred social work practice because it recognises the contribution of all parties in the negotiating process and particularly when the problem is of value to all concerned, such as social care. Research by Serbati (2017) on collaboration with parents during child protection in Italy refers to the participative and transformative evaluation as a method that aims to facilitate the successful involvement of people and professionals in the social care process.

The participatory and transformative evaluation model suggests there is not a linear, straightforward procession through the different stages of assessing, planning, intervening and monitoring, and movement through each cycle requires:

- reflection and negotiation: time for listening and reflection to understand participant perspectives before negotiating an agreed action;
- action: realisation of the negotiated tasks, monitoring and renegotiations and adjustments to produce change (Serbati, 2017).

In this model, negotiation is placed centre stage and afforded a significant role, with the explicit aim of promoting people's participation in social care services.

Negotiation involves not only the people who use services but also other professionals and service providers. Thompson (2002) suggests multidisciplinary collaboration involves avoiding stereotypes, understanding each other's roles, sensitivity towards diverse values and priorities, avoiding hierarchies and preciousness, and focusing on communication between the different parties. Specifically focusing on negotiation during multi-party decision making in social work, Dall and Caswell (2017) draw on Strauss's (1978) theory of negotiated order (this concerns the ways members of an organisation negotiate meaning and deliver the organisation's formal rules and guidelines; the continued negotiation by members then (re)produces the negotiated order of organisational activity. They suggest there are two patterns of *negotiation in talk*, which are *expanding* (interactions involving turn taking and closure) and *postponing* (where assessments are made irrelevant or avoided). Their research in Denmark concluded that both approaches are utilised by team members to negotiate the institutional order and the decisions made, whereby:

> ... resources form patterns of the negotiation of meaning between speakers in working teams, and they are given substance in the interaction by a sorting of potential meanings shaped by both the specific case at hand and the contexts negotiated. (Dall & Caswell, 2017: 495)

As we can see, there are many skills in negotiating plans, but please don't be daunted! Social workers deal with complex situations where there are many variables and competing demands, and because of this we often become extremely adept negotiators. However, as with the plan for the flat-pack furniture, it is critical that we remember to stand back and review how things are developing.

REVIEWING

A plan is a guide, an instruction that is based on our assessment of someone's needs. The plan is the *to do* manual which includes resources, tasks and timescales. A valid criticism of outcome-based practice is its emphasis on process and resource implications. We have referred several times in this chapter to management and business practices and models. Traditionally, such application does not fit well with many social workers, and we sympathise with this perspective. We are social workers who promote social justice and prioritise relationship-based, anti-oppressive practice. As practitioners, we caution against process-driven practice that prioritises organisational objectives at the expense of people. First and foremost, we seek to position people at the centre of public services aimed to meet community needs. Nevertheless, it is important to recognise the reality that contemporary social work practice often operates under a managerialist structure. Processes may be unavoidable, but *person-centred processes* can promote best practice.

EXERCISE 6.6

Consider an experience where you had to formulate a plan: this may relate to specific social work practice, while on placement or in work, or alternatively to your work or personal life. You could even use one of the residents' experiences we have provided throughout this book. Think about why you developed the plan and what you hoped to achieve.

- What were the basic elements of the plan?
- How effective was the plan in meeting your objectives?
- Did you review the plan? And if so how?
- Following your review, did you change or adapt the plan?

Plans should adapt to people, not the other way round. To make sure the plan is on track to meet assessed needs, and remains fit for purpose in light of any changing circumstances, it needs to be reviewed. In this section, we introduce reviewing as a part of the planning process. *The participative and transformative evaluation* (Serbati, 2017) model we introduced earlier incorporates monitoring, which is a central aspect of the social work process. This is just one contemporary model, most others – if not all – involve some form of evaluation and review. Thompson (2002) suggests the review is a stimulus for reassessment while Rogers et al. state, 'The opportunity to review and evaluate social work should be seen as an important opportunity to stop, think and learn' (2017: 178). Reviews are both formal through legislative guidance such as childcare planning (see Figure 6.3), and informal, through for instance discussion and personal reflection. The purpose of reviews is to gauge the progress and success or otherwise of a plan, and subsequently make any changes that are deemed to be required. A plan is only as good as its effect, and if it is ineffective, change the plan.

FLEXIBILITY

We have suggested social work is a magpie profession because we are not captivated by a single theory; rather we adopt different approaches that we apply in diverse contexts. In training social work students, it is common to refer to our 'tool bag', which is populated with theories, skills, approaches, models and knowledge. We do not apply one size fits all because we recognise people are diverse and we live in complex social environments. What seems sensible (common sense even) to one person can appear abnormal and unusual to another. There are many commonalities between people and at the same time much diversity. Just think about a cultural perspective, or the shared values of a religious group or political party. Even group members with many shared values are different. Reflecting on gender performance (Butler, 1990) and the spectrum between masculinity and femininity has led to speculation that there are as many genders as people inhabiting the planet. You may not agree with such an individualistic approach to gender, but it is generally accepted today that gender is much more fluid than it was understood to be several decades ago. The point is, people who use services are different, people who provide services are different, and agencies organise how they provide services differently.

Within all this complexity and diversity, process comes to the fore. Contemporary practice favours process and following procedures because this ensures transparency and some fairness in how services are delivered. But it's best not to get stuck on process; rather, let's see it as the oil in a giant machine – lubricating the efficiency of the machine and not the product itself. If the machine does not match the purpose, change the machine. To strive to meet the needs of people and communities we have to be mindful of being flexible. By flexible, we do not mean compliant. What we mean is compassionate flexibility, flexibility to address change, flexibility to recognise assessment and planning shortfalls, flexibility that promotes more robust practice. The plan and its objectives are designed to meet assessed needs. Through review and evaluation, the plan and its objectives are scrutinised and reflected on to assess progress. A critically reflective practitioner can adopt a flexible stand to take account of new information, changes in circumstances and new objectives. Through professional flexibility, the practitioner is able to develop defensible and emancipatory practice and not become embroiled in defensive and oppressive practice

SUPERVISION

Supervision is a key developmental tool that provides structured space for us to reflect on our assessments and professional judgements, and critically review our planning and interventions. Supervision takes many forms – group and individual, formal and informal, direct and indirect, mentoring and coaching. Williams and Rutter (2015) suggest that supervision relies on dialogues and questioning as a means to develop learning and knowledge, and that these become continuous conversations, which can help to create a workplace culture of learning. Critical questioning draws out not only assumptions and underlying thoughts, but also personal givens and accepted truths. Through effective supervision, practitioners can move beyond description to more meaningful analysis and evaluation. Bogo (2013) suggests that supervision has three, interrelated phases:

1. Observation of practice.
2. Reflective discussion.
3. Providing feedback, modelling and coaching.

It is generally agreed that good and effective supervision helps to promote practitioner effectiveness. Supervision is seen to work most effectively when it not only pays attention to task assistance, but also offers social and emotional support within the context of a positive relationship between social worker and supervisor. The often highly emotionally charged nature of social work can place particular demands on practitioners, and therefore it is important to provide opportunities for reflective supervision (Carpenter et al., 2012).

Supervision and practice review have been a consistent element of social work professionalism. Supervision has evolved to become more reflective, less clinical, and has moved away from rigid case management. The Social Work Reform Board (2012) recognised the central role of high-quality supervision in promoting best practice when supporting children, adults and families involved with social services, and recommended national standards for the supervision of social workers. Munro in her (2011) report also found supervision was integral to good practice. Fook categorises the process of gaining professional expertise and acknowledges how practice experience promotes professional confidence and knowledge (Fook, 2000; Fook and Gardner, 2007; Fook, 2016). Good supervision helps supervisees marry values, knowledge and skills in their professional practice.

AUTHOR'S EXPERIENCE (CAT)

As a newly qualified social worker, I worked in an integrated mental health team where my line manager was a Community Psychiatric Nurse. She undertook my case management supervision, but once a month I drove across town to receive social work supervision from the manager of a different team. I found the case management supervision from my manager really helpful. It focused on tasks and processes and I felt it helped me to do my job. For a long time, I struggled to see the point of my social work supervision; it was delivered by someone who didn't know my cases, and seemed to follow a much more abstract and less practical approach. After a while, I started to find reasons to cancel it.

One day my manager pulled me aside and told me she had noticed that I hadn't been going to my social work supervision. I told her that everyone in the team was really helpful, so I could access informal supervision from colleagues any time,

> and I got everything else I needed from my caseload supervision with her. I was quite surprised when she told me that what I was describing wasn't supervision, but instruction and advice. She suggested that I liked this, because it was immediately gratifying and provided me with solutions. She further suggested – very kindly! – that I didn't like the social work supervision because it challenged me to think about things that did not have easy answers. She told me that as a person from a different profession, she couldn't help me to establish my social work identity, but as my manager, she could insist that I stopped cancelling my social work supervision and she did. Later on in my career, I became responsible for the supervision of a large staff team. I always tried to provide supervision that was supportive but also challenged staff to critically explore their practice and their feelings. Whenever I felt that someone was approaching supervision superficially, I told the story of my first manager. ”

SUMMARY

In this chapter, we have contextualised plans as both organisational processes and essential practice tools to support our work with people. We have identified the legislative requirements and professional accountability in care planning with children and adults, and have introduced tools that can support planning, such as S.M.A.R.T. planning and Egan's Skilled Helper. Person-centred, collaboratively negotiated plans are time consuming to devise, but essential in promoting rights, social justice and achieving meaningful outcomes for people. Planning is integral to our practice and continues throughout the cycle of our involvement. We monitor and critically review interventions in supervision, and in collaboration with the person, to establish whether outcomes are being achieved or if the plan needs to change.

PART II

INTERVENTIONS: NOW LET'S GO AND HELP PEOPLE

7 INTERVENING AS A SOCIAL WORKER

Learning in this chapter relates to

PCF	KSS Adult Services	KSS Child & Family
1. Professionalism 5. Knowledge 7. Skills & Interventions	2. The role of social workers working with adults 3. Person-centred practice 7. Direct work with individuals & families	1. The role of child & family social work 5. Effective direct work with children & families 10. The role of supervision & research

INTRODUCTION

Having looked at assessments and planning, we now turn our focus towards social work interventions and how they relate to social work action. Intervening as a social worker requires practical elements such as communication and interpersonal skills, as well as professional knowledge of law and theories. This chapter forms the basis for successive chapters which focus on specific interventions in practice situations. In seeking to promote good practice when social workers intervene with individuals and groups, we argue that recognising individual and group identity and choice are important. At our core, we value relationship-based practice that sees those who use social services as people with a heart and soul and not as 'cases' to practise on. To this end, we include information on key professional skills and values for social work intervention. We recognise that social work practice can be challenging as well as rewarding, and reflect on how professional resilience and personal wellbeing enable better practice by maintaining a healthy and robust workforce, which is then best placed to offer much needed support to our communities and those who live in them.

WHAT IS INTERVENTION ABOUT?

Social workers intervene in people's lives; these people may seek our help, but often they don't. The basic dictionary definition of intervention is the interposition or interference of one state (person, group etc.) in the affairs of another (Dictionary.com). More specifically, Thompson writes about '"intervention", by which I mean the various tasks people workers become involved in with a view to making a difference in someone's life in a positive and constructive way' (Thompson, 2002: 161). For Thompson, therefore, the task of social work is to intervene in people's lives to promote positive change. This interpretation is recognised by many practitioners and theorists, and whilst it is laudable, it suggests practice is much more straightforward than we know it to be. Karen Healy reflects on a dynamic approach to social work practice, stating 'our professional purpose is shaped by our field of practice and is informed by three key sources: service user needs and expectations; institutional requirements; and our professional practice base' (Healy, 2012: 4). This is reminiscent of Halmos' (1978) foundational trinity of social work practice which we introduced in Chapter 1.

Healy's model recognises that social work practice (our intervention in people's lives) is both conceptual and practical, and that a sense of purpose during professional activity and intervention has to be constructed by the practitioner. She contends that the practitioner constructs this sense of purpose from a range of sources that are often contradictory, and suggests critical reflection assists the practitioner in constructing this professional purpose. Healy (2014) details five different groupings of contemporary theories for social work practice and these are:

- systems theories, such as systemic practice and ecological social systems;
- problem-solving theories, such as task-centred practice;
- strengths and solution-focused theories;
- modern critical social work theories, such as radical social work and anti-oppressive practice;
- postmodern social work theories, such as narrative therapy.

Whilst we have not structured this book on Healy's typology of social work theories, we feel they are useful to help students and practitioners understand the relationships between different theories and professional approaches. Adams et al. posit that practitioners cannot assume their practice and agency are not problematic, and therefore must be self-critical (Adams et al., 2002). We can achieve this by reflecting on the perspectives of others and assessing how our interventions affect their actions.

SKILLS THAT HELP US TO INTERVENE SUCCESSFULLY

People skills

As social workers, we rely a great deal on our ability to relate to different people, in different situations, which we often refer to as our 'people skills'. Social work is about the relationships we develop, and effective people skills promote positive relationships. People skills are often dismissed as basic and inherent, and are therefore taken for granted or overlooked, but our profession recognises their critical importance. People skills are the combination of our emotional intelligence and our communicative abilities, underpinned by our values. Hennessy (2011) proposes that practitioners can integrate *self* and *practice* by envisioning their unique self at the core, with their professional values, skills and theory on the outside. Jordan (2017) considers the potential for humour in our practice, suggesting it can be a tool to help establish positive relationships (Jordan, 2017). Hingley-Jones and Ruch (2016) acknowledge the difficult but crucial task of social work practice during a time when austerity policy reduces public service spending, concluding:

> In the increasingly unequal social context that is currently being configured by the politics of austerity, social workers face the daily challenge of retaining a depressive state of mind that is able to offer hope in difficult circumstances. Long may we stumble along our relationship-based way. (Hingley-Jones & Ruch, 2016: 246)

Emotional intelligence

Emotional intelligence (EI) is concerned with recognising our own feelings and considering those of others; it can be thought of as the ability to monitor emotions, both our own and other people's. It has been suggested that understanding emotions and the ability to mentalise them intellectually is a key facet of social work practice (Rogers et al., 2017). However, emotional intelligence is theoretically contested and there are various ways to understand it. EI was initially popularised in the 1990s by Daniel Goleman, who identified its five main constructs as being self-awareness, self-regulation, social skills, empathy and motivation (Goleman, 1998). Since then, EI is generally considered to have three main models.

Emotional intelligence models

- *Ability model* – emotions are viewed as helpful sources of information to understand and navigate the social environment. This process involves four main abilities, which are perceiving emotions, using emotions, understanding emotions and managing emotions. This model is concerned with the ability to understand and interpret another person's behaviour and emotional wellbeing (Salovey & Grewal, 2005; Mayer et al., 2012).
- *Trait model* – EI is seen as a personality trait so that an individual has a self-perception of their emotional abilities (Petrides & Furnham, 2000). Trait theory, in general, is concerned with aspects of personality such as empathy, and their measurement. Rogers et al. suggest personality traits like empathy are transferable to social work practice because empathy is about understanding the feelings of others (Rogers et al., 2017).
- *Mixed model* – generally now associated with Goleman, this model integrates ability and trait-based behaviours, essentially proposing that individuals are born with the potential to learn EI and go on to learn and develop EI capabilities.

EI is theoretically contested, with the accuracy of tools designed to measure EI particularly disputed, but the implication that emotions and behaviours can be understood by others clearly relates to social work practice. Ingram (2013) promotes an EI model for social work, reflecting on the possible relationship between elements of EI, such as empathy and emotional regulation, with social work practice that seeks to use the views and perspectives of people who use services.

As we have seen, EI relates to an awareness of own emotions as well as those of others. Concerning professional practice, Beesley et al. (2018) suggest that reflection develops EI and resilience, and they state that by 'developing your [social worker] communication skills through reflection and audit, you will inevitably develop your emotional intelligence' (Beesley et al., 2018: 26). We discuss resilience later on in this chapter, but for now note how Beesley et al. indicate that positive relationships between communication, reflection and emotional intelligence help develop enhanced practice and resilience skills, which can reduce practitioner stress. It seems EI has the potential to promote professional resilience and improved collaboration by practitioners with people.

Communication skills

Communication skills are a core aspect of social work practice (see Lishman, 2009; Thompson, 2011; Koprowska, 2014; Beesley et al., 2018). Beesley et al. explain that in 'order to engage service users, you [the social worker] will have developed your skills in relation to initial engagement, listening, empathy, clarification and challenging' (2018: 174). We communicate in different ways, with people in diverse situations. Many of the people we work with do not communicate in the same primary way that we do, e.g. young children, people who communicate non-verbally and others whose first language is not English.

AT NUMBER 6

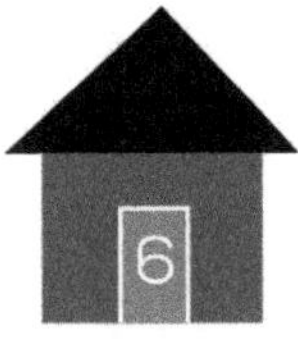

When Adnan arrived in the UK, he knew little about the country, language and services. He had made a very hazardous journey to escape the war in Syria and had experienced many hardships. Arriving in the UK as an unaccompanied asylum-seeking child (UASC), Adnan was placed with foster carers. When he left care, Adnan settled into the shared house with Sally and Liam and received some support from the leaving care team. Adnan found it difficult to sleep, was very worried about the people he had left behind and grieved for his parents. One day while out shopping he became very distressed and could not move. A passer-by spoke to him, but this made Adnan more worried and distressed. Adnan's GP referred him to a health project, where he had an initial appointment with a social worker. Although Adnan had a decent grasp of English, he found it difficult to articulate his feelings in a second language. He felt that the social worker seemed uninterested, and made a lot of generalised assumptions about him based on the experiences of other refugees she had worked with. He told the social worker that she didn't understand him. When he attended his next appointment, she had arranged for an interpreter; this was not what Adnan had meant. He found the interpreter did not translate everything he said, and the conversation was mainly between the translator and the social worker. Adnan did not return to the project.

EXERCISE 7.1

- What were the barriers to effective communication with Adnan?
- What do social workers need to consider to communicate effectively through an interpreter?

Social workers are not expected to be fluent in multiple languages or communication methods. We can draw from the expertise of others, such as translators or speech and language therapists to augment our communication. Koprowska (2014) explains that communication comes naturally, but communication skills do not. Communication is interactive, taking place within a relationship and a context. Developing and using communication skills in a practice context can be an empowering process through the active engagement and involvement of people (Fook, 2016). Communication theory helps us to be aware of how language and communication are understood, and specifically structuralism and post-structuralism relate to communication in that:

> *Structuralism* – the structural approach to linguistics originating from Ferdinand de Saussure, following the posthumous publication in 1916 of Saussure's *Course in General Linguistics*. Structuralism broadly argues that all human activity and its products are constructed rather than natural and meaning is therefore derived through language. Furthermore, language can be understood as a self-defining system or structure.
>
> *Post-structuralism* – Jacques Derrida deconstructed structuralism and Saussurian linguistics (based on work by Ferdinand de Saussure, 1857–1913) through removing communication (spoken and written) from a single truth or singular meanings, and moving towards multiple understandings and diversity of meanings. Language and social norms are representations of the world and as such are socially constructed, and Derrida's binary logic categorised normative and abnormal conceptual understanding whereby personal social identity is defined through a negative connotation. In this way, a person is heterosexual by not being homosexual (Derrida & Bass, 1995).

Communication is varied and skills include listening (including active listening), proximity (spacing and environment), discussion, body language, gesturing and clarifying. Silence itself is an important skill for our social work tool bag. Verbally articulating meaning is only a limited aspect of communication. Metacommunication refers to non-verbal cues, such as body language, and paralanguage refers more specifically to pitch and the nuanced expression of emotional meanings through gestures, nodding and so on (Koprowska, 2014). Koprowska comments on the importance of first impressions when working with people. In preparing for a social work intervention, the venue has to be considered. There are certain safeguarding instances when an unannounced home visit may be appropriate, but we will have prepared for this visit in advance. It is more usual to advise people we are intending to meet with them and here we can use a range of techniques, such as a letter, a telephone call and e-mail. This communication all occurs before any personal contact and each personal contact will require its own planning and methods of communication. We then have to consider the communication variables with different groups and individuals and develop a professional communication strategy.

AUTHOR'S EXPERIENCE (CAT)

I was very apprehensive about assessing the mental capacity of a man who had no verbal communication. He was living in a residential home following a stroke, and two different members of his family both felt that they should manage his finances for him. The starting point was to find out whether he had the mental capacity to decide for himself what he wanted to happen. I really didn't know how I would conduct the assessment, and I telephoned the care home to find out about the man's communication methods so that I could make a referral to the Speech and Language Therapy (SALT) team. I was surprised when the care home manager suggested that this was unnecessary and offered to assist me with my assessment by showing me how the staff at the home communicated with the man by using photographs. When I visited, I found that although the stroke had left the man unable to verbalise or manipulate a pen to write, he could communicate very clearly. He could dip his chin to signify yes, and make a sound in his throat to signify no. His face was extremely expressive, and from it I could understand when he found something funny, or was impatient when I misunderstood him. Using photograph albums, he was able to clearly show me how he felt about different family members and indicate who he wanted to manage his finances (and those members he did not!). I did not need specialist skills to complete my assessment and establish the man's capacity, I simply needed to adapt my expectations and tune into different elements of communication.

Engaging others

Unsuccessful social work assessments or interventions are often attributed to 'failiure to engage'. This suggests that the blame or fault lies with the person, rather than the social worker. We exercise choice over whether or not we engage with a dentist or car mechanic, but many people do not have a choice about social work involvement. A parent may feel hugely conflicted about engaging with someone who they fear may 'take their children away'. As social workers, the responsibility for engagement is ours, and we must find ways to achieve it, even when it is difficult. We can enact this tokenistically, by sending a letter offering an appointment, which we can then use as evidence of our efforts to engage someone and say, when they don't respond, that they failed to engage. Alternatively, we can act more ethically and really make every effort to engage with people we work with and take professional pride on being able to engage well and effectively.

AT NUMBER 5

Samantha's GP recognises that Samantha undertakes a significant caring role with Max, and believes that this is a contributory factor to both her drinking and low mood. She suggests that Samantha contacts adult services to request a carer assessment. Samantha rings the council and is put through to their screening service. After a brief telephone conversation, she is told that a carer's self-assessment form will be sent out for her to complete. When the form arrives Max sees it and becomes very upset. He says that Samantha obviously finds caring for him to be a burden, and suggests that she would be better off leaving him. She assures Max that this is not the case at all, and throws the form in the bin.

EXERCISE 7.2

What were the barriers to Samantha engaging with the carer's assessment?

Caring and compassionate practice

Many people cite their desire to help others as their motivation to become a social worker, but little direct focus is given to compassion in social work training programmes (Stickle, 2016). Social work practice benefits from being both caring, as a matter of course, and compassionate – however, as professionals, we are in danger of rejecting this motivation as naive or too unsophisticated because we seek professional competence. Swindell (2014) argues that she wants to be not only a culturally competent social worker, which she defines as practising ethically and effectively with diverse people and groups, but also one who practises authentically. She recognises that acting competently is essential – the alternative is incompetence – but also advocates for compassionate practice, which is about being helpful to others and sympathetically conscious of any distress they are feeling. She concludes by calling for compassionate competence in social work, 'an ethically, successful integration and transformation of knowledge, skills, attitudes, behaviours, and policies to sympathetically alleviate suffering' (Swindell, 2014: 2). Others reference meditation and mindfulness when discussing compassionate practice (e.g. see Stickle, 2016), and reflect on philosophical views and notions of spirituality. Stickle (2016) recognises that a compassionate approach helps us to work with people more acceptingly, while Crowder and Sears (2017) suggest that incorporating mindfulness into our practice can promote self-compassion and professional resilience.

Understanding identity

We construct identity. The notion of 'the teenager' emerged during the 1950s with the advent of commercially produced music and research on stages of human development. It is now a recognised identity stage related to hormonal growth and emotional development, but was unrecognisable before the twentieth century. Did teenagers exist before they were known as teenagers, or did our understanding of adolescence result from social recognition of a life course stage of development? Social constructionism influences social work practice by recognising diversity in the place of universal truth.

EXERCISE 7.3

Think about the groups with which you identify – these may be real or virtual. For instance:

- Phil is a man, a social worker, a dad, a partner, a lecturer, a grandad, an author.
- Cat is a daughter and a mother, a lecturer and a student.

Now consider:

- How are you a member of this group?
- What are the identity issues associated with this group?
- How much do you identify yourself in line with this group?
- Are you a member of other groups – i.e. do you have multiple identities?
- What is your personal identity?

Our identity relates to who we are, who we see ourselves as and how others identify us – essentially our identities are systemic relationships. This relates to gender, ethnicity, race, sexuality, culture, religion, philosophy, disability, music, fashion, interests, family, friends, and many, many more. As social workers we must strive to recognise and appreciate how multiple identities shape the individuality of the people we work with, and use reflexivity and self-awareness to recognise our own identity. For instance, Daly (2016) writes about her concern that social workers may absorb negative societal perceptions of Irish Travellers. She proposes that social workers should adopt an anti-oppressive stance of curiosity to enable them to learn about the historic marginalisation of Irish Travellers and model their cultural and social identity to recognise the strengths of the community.

Evidence-based interventions

We introduced evidence-based practice in Chapter 1, and it seems very obvious to suggest social work practitioners should use evidence in selecting intervention approaches. Unfortunately, we know that many of our students put their books down when they qualify and go into very busy practice environments, and then struggle to find the space to pick them back up again. Howe (2009) talks about how many theories and approaches compete and cancel each other out, explaining that we 'could go around in circles describing how each theory in turn is intent on shooting another until there is no theory left standing' (Howe, 2009: 197). By conceptualising research evidence to guide practice, social workers and people using services can work together to identify what works best and under what conditions. The gathering and utilisation of evidence through research leads to a dynamic and responsive profession (Healy, 2012), as well as innovative practices that can be shared professionally. With new research comes new evidence on the effectiveness of particular social work practices, theories and approaches, and generally speaking, research on approaches with proven success will be more widely disseminated and benefit a greater number of people.

Practice which values evidence from research does not necessitate that as social workers we become researchers or undertake research ourselves. We can utilise research from a wide range of academic disciplines, and access it from a number of sources. The internet has emerged as a fantastic tool to gather research evidence, and specialist electronic databases have purposefully been established to disseminate research to practitioners, such as the Social Care Institute for Excellence (SCIE) and Research in Practice (RiP)/Research in Practice for Adults (RiPfA). The distribution of knowledge to professionals has become a significant objective for many organisations. One of the rationales for local Teaching Partnerships has been the opportunity to pool knowledge and share resources between different local authorities, higher education institutions and third sector agencies, as well as community members and people who use services who are often referred to in this context as 'experts by experience'.

RESILIENCE AND PERSONAL WELLBEING

Our professionalism, and construction of professional identity, evolve in ever-changing environments of social need and public services. Throughout all of these changes, we need a positive sense of self as we practise professionally. We regularly assess the resilience or resiliency capacity of individuals we work with; however, it is also important to consider our own resilience and personal wellbeing. In the past decade, resilience has become something of a buzzword in social work. Its basic definition has two components – firstly, it relates to recovery and toughness, and secondly, to the ability for an object or substance to have elasticity and spring back into shape. In social work practice, we strongly associate resilience with the ability to bounce back and recover from adversity. Rogers et al. (2017) summarise our understanding of resilience as an exploration of three interrelated factors: risk, vulnerability, and protective factors.

AUTHOR'S EXPERIENCE (PHIL)

I was involved in developing training on the effects of secondary trauma on foster carers and social workers supporting children and young people experiencing post-traumatic stress disorder. Developing this training helped me understand

(Continued)

how our work with people who have experienced trauma can personally affect us. In order to develop my own resilience, I began to practise meditation. I recognise that meditation is not for everyone, but I find it very calming and feel that it resources me to better manage stressful situations.

Once whilst on my way to a home visit, my car broke down on a very busy road blocking traffic and causing irritation to many drivers. Ordinarily, this situation would have caused me a great deal of anxiety, stress and embarrassment. Even though I knew on a cognitive level that the only way the situation could be rectified was by contacting breakdown services and waiting for them to arrive, I would have felt responsible for all of the people I was holding up and worried about what they were thinking of me. I would have felt that I was letting down the family who were expecting me, and appearing unprofessional. However, I was able to use meditative skills and techniques to consciously relax, centre myself and let go of my unhelpful thoughts. I responded much more calmly, and rationally to this situation, which meant that by the time I arrived (albeit later than expected) for my home visit, I was able to be present and effective, rather than preoccupied with what had just happened to me.

”

It is important that we consider our own welfare and professional resilience, and students starting their social work training are quickly introduced to concepts like burnout, compassion fatigue, and secondary trauma. Crowder and Sears suggest that mindfulness-based stress reduction interventions can help build a more resilient professional population, and they found, in their small Canadian study, that mindfulness promoted wellbeing in social workers (Crowder & Sears, 2017).

SUMMARY

Assessments and interventions are entwined and they are not easily separated during social work practice. Intervention is a dynamic process requiring people skills, which are a combination of our self and our professionalism. It is our responsibility to find creative ways to engage, communicate and intervene with people, and we strongly suggest that caring and compassionate practice is key to this. It is also important that we afford ourselves similar care and compassion, by recognising the impact that the very difficult situations we work in can have on our wellbeing, and considering ways to promote our resilience.

8 RELATIONSHIPS, SYSTEMS AND COMPLEXITY

Learning in this chapter relates to

PCF	KSS Adult Services	KSS Child & Family
5. Knowledge 6. Critical Reflection & Analysis 7. Skills & Interventions	2. The role of social workers working with adults 3. Person-centred practice 7. Direct work with individuals & families 8. Supervision, critical reflection & analysis	1. The role of child & family social work 5. Effective direct work with children & families 6. Child & family assessment 7. Analysis, decision making, planning & review

INTRODUCTION

Social work is a relationship-based profession, and in this chapter we focus on relationships and some different theoretical perspectives on systems. We start by introducing the notion of systems, then focus on relationships in professional practice, different theoretical perspectives and definitions of system theories, and provide information on general systems theory, family therapy, ecological systems theory and attachments. Moving on from these more generally applied system theories, we expand to include sections on complexity, chaos and intersectionality. This chapter is a practice-orientated summary of systems approaches and reflects on the importance of co-production with people and their families. We introduce contemporary ideas about practice with localised networks and systems, and how they help build social capital and resilience, as well as more long-standing ideas from systemic intervention practice. Drawing on family therapy, as well as other systems theory-based interventions, we detail how to use practice tools such as genograms and ecomaps. Firstly, though, we introduce the notion of systems and their relevance to social work practice.

INTRODUCING SYSTEMS

We have found that our students often experience the new, complicated, technical terminology associated with system theories as a barrier to their understanding. Language is important, and it must be accessible. We can understand the basic premise of systems theory by thinking about how we commonly use the word 'system', e.g. central heating system, solar system, digestive system. From these everyday examples, it is easy to understand that systems involve connection, interaction and relationships between multiple parts to form a complex or unitary whole. Systems can be social, environmental, mechanical and biological. In this way, we can see how most of our social work theories and approaches are in fact some form of systems theory. Take for example Maslow's hierarchy of needs (1970 [1954]), which represents the categorising of human needs and their relationships with individuals.

Appreciating system theories enables social workers to make sense and assess people and their environments. As social workers we ourselves represent several systems, e.g. the *professional* and the *personal,* and we interact with the systems of the people we work with. The relationships and variations between multiple systems are possibly too large to quantify, but an awareness of the relational nature of social work helps us understand the impact of our professional role and the different perspectives of people connected to our practice.

RELATIONSHIPS AND PROFESSIONAL PRACTICE

Many services are provided without the establishment of any significant relationship. For example, you are unlikely to have more than a cursory relationship with your telephone provider, your car mechanic or your postal worker. Social work is a compassionate profession, so therefore it seems very obvious that it is dependent on relationships that are far more than cursory. However, in previous chapters we have identified how the combination of managerialism, technology, responsibilism and an economic backdrop of austerity has impacted on the way we interact with people who use our services. As Tuck-Chee Phung explains:

> Given the increasing bureaucratisation and the pervading dominance of the rational-technical approach of social services, where processes and outcomes are often subjected to public and political scrutiny, social work is increasingly challenged to hold on to its ethical and humanistic values in practice. (2018: 269)

Relationship-based social work has emerged in response to the apparent trend for the bureaucratisation of our practice. It is concerned with how social workers can form meaningful and purposeful relationships with people using services which appreciate and respect individuality. Relationship-based models of practice recognise that the relationships we form have a beginning, middle and end; exist during crisis and uncertainty; are influenced by organisational culture; and are theory based rather than intuitive. Relationship-based practice is also a response to heroic and rescue-based social work, which we explored in Chapter 4. It recognises that people are experts on themselves and their situations and have their own strengths and resources, rather than privileging professional expertise. Ruch et al. argue that:

> … for Relationship-based practice to take hold, there needs to be a significant shift in how individuals are perceived. The realisation that people are not simply commodities within a market system, or objects that can be reduced to a computer record, but are unique individuals with complex intersubjective experiences need to be reclaimed. (Ruch et al., 2010: 26)

AUTHOR'S EXPERIENCE (CAT)

As a recently qualified social worker, I was asked to work with a woman who was well known to mental health services and had substance abuse issues, a chaotic lifestyle and frequently took overdoses. Her diagnosis was unclear, and there were many unhelpful narratives about whether she was 'genuinely' mentally unwell: she was described to me as 'a nightmare'. I'm afraid that I wasn't very critical and accepted these narratives at face value. I now recognise that this coloured the way I approached working with her, before I had even met her (this is an example of framing bias; see Chapter 3). I tried to set up a raft of different services and interventions that I thought would support the woman, but she wouldn't engage with any of them. She took a number of overdoses, which terrified me. I felt I was trying so hard to help her, but she was doing nothing to help herself. One day I took a call from her GP, who told me he was very worried about her and asked me why I wasn't doing more for her. I furiously rattled off a list of every service I had referred her to, every appointment she had failed to keep, every home visit when she hadn't opened the door. He was quite surprised, and told me she had not mentioned any of these. I put the phone down and complained to my colleague that I didn't know if I could go on working with this woman, she was so manipulative!

My colleague was much wiser and more experienced than me. She stopped what she was doing and talked things through with me. She – very gently – helped me to see that I had thrown an overwhelming amount of interventions at the woman without really understanding either her or her situation. I was very attuned to my own fears and frustrations about how badly things were going, but I wasn't considering how the woman felt. She told me that 'It all starts with the relationship. Build that before you do anything else.' This conversation was a genuinely life-changing moment for me, which had more impact on my social work practice than anything else.

In their book on relationship-based practice with adults, Dix et al. (2018) introduce the mnemonic acronym IDEAS (influence, delivery, expertise, alliance and support) model of relationship-based social work (see Figure 8.1).

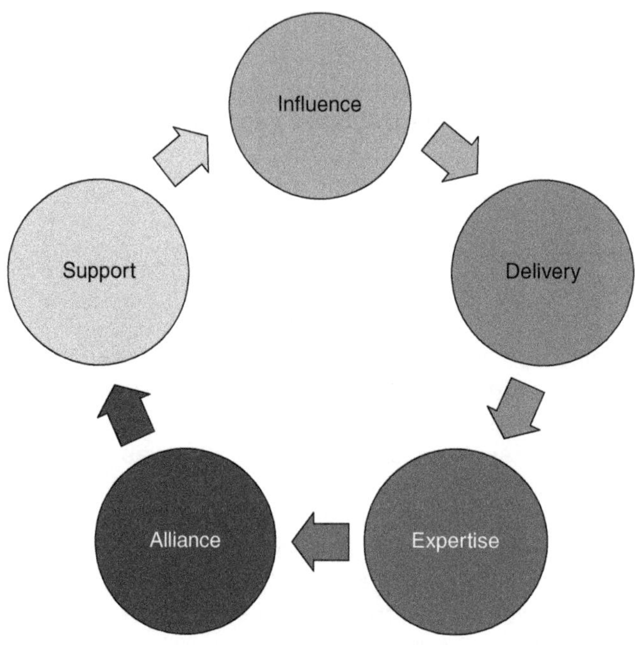

Figure 8.1 The IDEAS model of relationship-based social work

Influence – awareness of the power differentials in our relationships with people who use services and carers.

Delivery – what we actually 'do' as social workers. Working within clear frameworks and processes, relevant to our particular area of social work practice.

Expertise – knowledge of theory in relation to our area of practice and understanding of how we can to translate this into practice, acknowledging the importance of 'practice wisdom'.

Alliance – viewing our relationships with the people who use services, carers and other professionals as a mechanism for change.

Support – relationship-based social work practice can only be effective when organisational cultures support it (Dix et al., 2018).

Relationship-based social work may appear as common sense to a compassionate profession. However, as Ruch et al. (2010) and Dix et al. (2018), amongst others, explain relationship-based social work is person centred and culturally different from contemporarily technocratic and austere approaches that seek to bureaucratise and organise the delivery of social care services.

THEORISING SYSTEMS

In this section, we reflect on those social system theories that are routinely applied in social work practice.

Social systems theory

Closely associated with Talcott Parsons in the 1950s, social systems theory is historically dated but remains influential. Generally and historically, family and social systems have been seen as functionalist and fairly static organisms. The nuclear family concept developed during industrialising society and represented a more or less linear evolution of family type, which defined masculinity and femininity along gendered parenting and relationship roles. Parsons (1951) noted that families had evolved, moving away from larger, extended families towards a nuclear composition of a mother, father and children. For Parsons, the nuclear family was a natural development within capitalism and the growth of an urban bourgeoisie or middle class. He posited that industrialisation meant that men moved away from agricultural-based employment in the countryside to urbanised industrial areas near centres of mass production, such as factories, and their wives and children migrated with them. This process of urbanisation produced socialised individuals operating within interconnecting social systems and acting in accordance with the rules of society that defined relationship norms (Parsons, 1951).

In general systems theory the emphasis is on the relationship between societal components rather than any intrinsic differences, and the relationships (connections) between different components are recognised as linear (straightforward) and natural. However, this fairly static nature of family relationships and social systems was questioned by Luhmann and his work on general systems theory. Luhmann argued there is some capacity for self-organisation and reproduction within subsystems, and therefore social systems evolve and are not wholly static, which highlights the variance within social systems (Luhmann, 1995). In contrast to Parsons' single nuclear family model, Pfau-Effinger (2004) identified that the nuclear family model is only one of at least five different family models emerging during industrialisation in Western Europe. While the concept of normalising roles within relationships and families remains influential (Butler, 1990), few people actually believe these roles are inflexible at the personal level.

AUTHOR'S EXPERIENCE (PHIL)

Whenever I deliver training on *working with men as carers,* someone always explains that they understand gendered family roles but that 'my family is different'. I have delivered this training to many groups of social workers, students, parents, foster carers, other professionals and at several conferences over the last decade. Nearly everyone who has attended this training has said that they understand different mothering and fathering roles prevalent in society but almost unanimously go on to describe how their family is somehow different. It now seems to me that at the societal, macro level, roles are still understood to somehow involve breadwinning fathers and home caring mothers (just as Parsons explained), but at the personal, micro level we go on to negotiate many different roles in the families we live in. Naturally, these family-based roles involve same and different sex couple relationships, and single-headed families, families with

(Continued)

and without children as well as nuclear and extended families. In fact, there is an infinitely rich diversity to families and how they function. When we assess individuals, it's worth considering how we, as professionals, identify the diversity within family types and the different roles people negotiate and experience, and do not assume the gendered roles ascribed by society. ”

Family therapy and systemic therapy

Family therapy and systemic therapy were pioneered by Murray Bowen. He believed that the family is a system of interconnected and interdependent individuals, which forms an emotional and physical unit. Individuals, therefore, cannot be understood in isolation from one another, only as a part of their family (Kerr & Bowen, 1988). According to Bowen, a family is a system in which each member has an allocated role to play, with rules to regulate family members. Members of the family system are expected to respond to each other in certain ways according to their allocated role within the family and these responses are developed through relationship agreements. Within the boundaries of the family system, family members present behavioural patterns that relate to other family members' behaviours in predictable ways (Bowen, 1990). The maintenance of predictable patterns of behaviour within a family results in internal family balance (equilibrium or homeostasis). However, if behaviours deviate (consciously or unconsciously) from these predictable and negotiated behavioural patterns, this may lead to family dysfunction.

AT NUMBER 3

Maureen has always taken responsibility for driving the children to and from activities, because Claire's hours of work mean that she doesn't get home till after 7pm. Maureen has had surgery to correct a problem with her knee cartilage, and can't drive for six weeks. Claire asks for some flexibility at work so that she can get the children to some of their activities, and her boss reluctantly agrees. Claire feels stressed and concerned that she might be being criticised by her boss and colleagues for leaving work early. Maureen feels guilty because she has struggled to come to terms with being made redundant, and now her operation is threatening the stability of Claire's career. The children feel frustrated that they are missing out on some of their regular activities, but also concerned that Claire and Maureen do not seem their normal selves. Everyone in the family is unhappy.

Maureen's knee operation has affected every member of the family in different but interrelated ways. The family dynamics have changed, and the former state of balance (equilibrium) within the family has been upset. The family's new behavioural patterns may lead to dysfunction if these continue for more than a short period of time.

EXERCISE 8.1

What could help Claire, Maureen and their children restore balance (equilibrium) to their family dynamic whilst Maureen is recovering?

Murray Bowen

Murray Bowen (1913–1990) was an American professor in psychiatry at the Georgetown University. Bowen devised eight interlocking components of family systems theory, which are:

1. *Levels of differentiation of self* – families and social groups affect how people think, feel and act, but individuals vary in their susceptibility to 'group think'. Also, groups vary in the amount of pressure they exert for conformity.
2. *The nuclear family emotional process* – this concept describes four relationship patterns which Bowen suggests govern where problems develop in a family, and these are: anxiety; marital conflict; dysfunction in one spouse; and impairment of one or more children.
3. *Family projection process* – describes the way parents transmit their emotional problems to a child. The relationship problems that most negatively affect a child's life are: a heightened need for attention and approval; difficulty dealing with expectations; the tendency to blame oneself or others; feeling responsible for others' happiness; and acting impulsively to relieve the anxiety of the moment, rather than tolerating anxiety and acting thoughtfully.
4. *Multigenerational transmission process* – the way people relate to one another creates differences, which are transmitted across generations.
5. *Sibling position* – people who grow up in the same sibling position have important, common characteristics.
6. *Triangles* – a triangle is a three-person relationship system. It is considered the triangle is the 'molecule' of larger emotional systems, as it is the smallest stable relationship system. Marital therapy uses the triangle to provide a neutral third party capable of relating well to both sides of a conflict.
7. *Emotional cut-off* – individuals sometimes manage their unresolved emotional issues with family members by reducing or totally cutting off emotional contact with them. This does not resolve the situation and risks making new relationships too important.
8. *Societal emotional process* – describes how the emotional system governs behaviour on a societal level, similar to that within a family, which promotes both progressive and regressive periods in a society (The Bowen Center, n.d.).

Hills (2013) explains that the dominant professional model of individualistic practice places constraints on working with families, because:

> The families we work with haven't found their solutions, so they cannot be functional. Best not to touch the severe dysfunctionality of the whole family system; we'll just treat the individuals. Nothing could be further from the truth. (Hills, 2013: 10)

Family and systemic therapy shuns work with individuals, and instead seeks to bring the members of the family together to consider what is happening in their family system and navigate towards solutions. This is difficult, and both families and practitioners can be resistant to the approach. Change is viewed in terms of interaction between family members, and the importance of psychological wellbeing through family relationships is emphasised.

Ecological systems theory

We explored ecological social systems theory in Chapter 4, which is mostly associated with the Russian-born American psychologist Urie Bronfenbrenner. Bronfenbrenner has had a significant influence on childhood development services – both in the United States of America, where he is attributed with being the father of the 'Head Start' programme (Cornell University, 2005), and in the UK through the 'Common Assessment Framework' (Jack, 1997, 2000; Calder, 2003; Gill & Jack, 2007). Bronfenbrenner's ecological systems theory (see Figure 8.2) seeks to explain the developing person, or child, within an environmental context of nested systems that are similar to a set of Russian dolls (Bronfenbrenner, 1977).

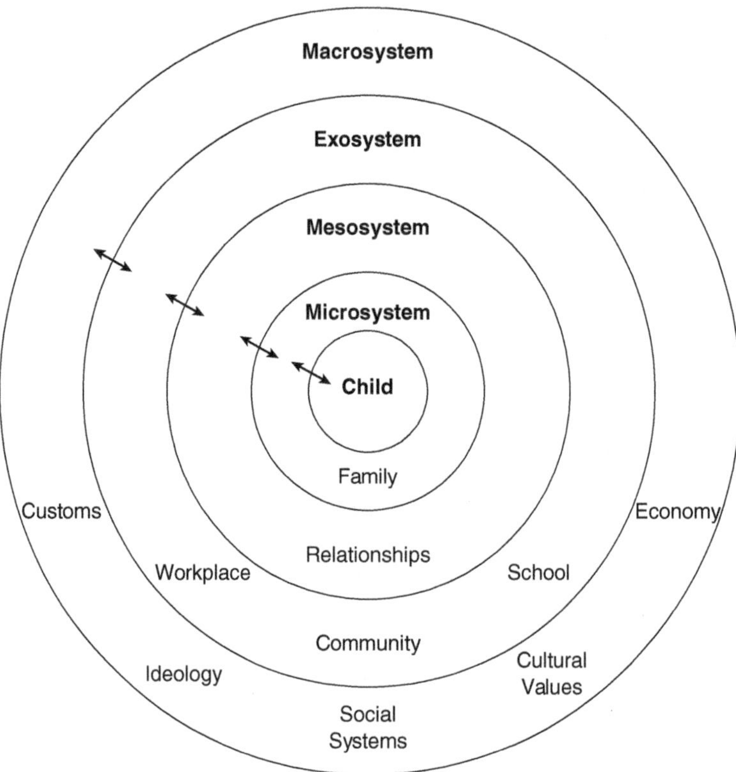

Figure 8.2 Ecological social systems

Bronfenbrenner argued that the nature of social relationships, along with the child's developing psychological comprehension, is strongly influenced by the primary dyadic maternal relationship. He drew attention to the importance of a positive maternal relationship and presupposed that within this both parties should – at least ideally – undergo periods of growth (Bronfenbrenner, 1979). The contemporary application of this theory has inserted the parent/carer relationship with the child rather than assume the maternal relationship.

Attachments

The field of attachments was developed by John Bowlby through his study of maternal influence among 'delinquent' young males. Attachment behaviour is presented as an evolutionary response (with associated behavioural styles) by humans to ensure close and affectionate bonds between caregiver and infant (Bowlby 1997). Attachment theory is concerned with the strategies, such as crying or smiling, a child may use to gain the attention of their caregiver to relieve discomfort, or 'Put simply, attachment behaviour is activated whenever young children feel distressed and insecure and need to get into close proximity with their main caregiver' (Howe, 1999: 13).

The resulting response by the adult caregiver helps the child make sense of the world and promotes child development and the child's internal working model (or self-perception). There is little argument about the importance of adults in the care of children. Mary Ainsworth (Ainsworth & Marvin, 1995) developed the mother–infant strange test, involving the observation of infant behaviour following withdrawal of the mother for 10 minutes, to assess the levels and patterns of attachment in children.

Attachment patterns

Ainsworth initially identified three attachment patterns through the mother–infant strange test and incorporated disorganised attachments following work by Main and Solomon:

- *Secure:* Secure attachment occurs when the carer is available, sensitive and responsive to the child.
- *Avoidant*: Child feels the caregiver rejects attention-seeking behaviour and becomes more self-reliant.
- *Ambivalent:* Child becomes uncertain how to seek caregiver's attention due to the caregiver responding only sporadically and unpredictably.
- *Disorganised:* Children present disorganised, and apparently unpredictable, attachments when the caregiver is frightening and rejecting. (Note that Main and Solomon, who were students of Ainsworth, identified the disorganised attachment pattern through their work on the Adult Attachment Interview; see Main & Solomon, 1990.)

Attachment theory has become central to childcare social work practice, where understanding how an infant bonds/attaches – or does not – with an adult caregiver is a vital component of assessment. Attachment strategies continue across the whole course of a person's life, so our understanding of attachment theory is helpful for practice with adults as well as children. Our childhood attachment strategies influence our ability to regulate our emotions in relationships in adulthood. This may result in an adult who was abused as a child not realising when they are in an abusive relationship, or normalising abuse because they find safety in its familiarity (Baim, 2016).

Social learning

How we learn has long been the focus of academic attention, producing important theories such as social and experiential learning (Bandura, 1978; Kolb, 1984). Russian psychologist Ivan Pavlov's work on classical conditioning had an enormous impact on learning theory. Pavlov conducted an experiment with dogs whereby every time the dogs were fed a bell was rung. After a short while the dogs became conditioned to associate the bell with food, and so even when they were not given food, if they heard a bell, they would salivate. Pavlov's work directly influenced the behaviourist Burrhus Skinner, whose animal-based research into learning theory suggested that when an action is rewarded it continues to be repeated.

Albert Bandura conducted experiments into patterns of aggression in young children. He proposed that humans are responsive (at least partly) to external stimuli and therefore behaviour is learnt socially. Within the framework of social learning theory, repertoires of aggressive behaviour are socially learnt through three principle sources: family, community and mass media (Bandura, 1978). Bandura argued most people are anti-violence but go on to accept violence within contexts, particularly where it is explained through moral justification rather than impulsivity (Bandura, 1978). For example, a person who considers themself a pacifist may well applaud someone intervening in a fight, even though they used violence to stop the aggressor.

EXERCISE 8.2

Consider the theories we have introduced in the previous section.

- How are they all systems theories?
- How does each one relate to social work practice?
- Identify one limitation for each of the theoretical perspectives.

SYSTEMS THAT ARE DIFFICULT TO UNDERSTAND

The theoretical models we have considered so far in this chapter are relatively accessible, and it is easy to see how they may apply to common practice situations. In this section we reflect on more complex theoretical perspectives, which are also applicable to social work practice.

Complexity and chaos

Social systems are not static; they evolve over time. Our contemporary understandings of social systems are much more complex and chaotic than Parsons' functionalist perspective. Complexity and chaos theory originated in the natural sciences and computer technology, emerging in response to difficult to understand and disorderly systems. They identify non-linear relationship patterns that have previously been undetectable. Hudson has transferred complexity thinking to social work practice to help appreciate the complex relationships of people involved with social workers in North America (Hudson, 2000, 2010).

At a superficial level, complex social systems – for example families which are regarded as highly dysfunctional – appear disordered and impossible to pattern. In fact they are not as random as is often assumed, if we shift the way we try to understand them. Distorted noise in a microphone creates an apparently chaotic sound, but actually, if we stop comparing it to non-distorted sound, we can see that it is predictable. Predictable patterns exist in complex social systems, but they are much harder to detect because they are non-linear (Harvey & Reed, 1996). When we seek to understand very complex families and relationships, we tend to unhelpfully compare them to more 'normal', 'usual' or 'expected' patterns of behaviour, and then classify them as chaotic or inexplicable when they are not a good fit. Applying complexity and chaos theory to social systems requires that we disregard our existing frameworks of reference and view those systems on their own terms.

There has been some focus on complexity and safeguarding children (e.g. see Green & McDermott, 2010; Saltiel, 2013). Satiel suggests there is an element of uncertainty surrounding social workers' decision making in child protection situations concerning complex, unconventional and chaotic families. He argues that an appreciation of the non-conventional way people actively negotiate their family roles could be a useful way of understanding this complexity, and provide social workers with a valuable tool for understanding the situations about which they must make decisions (Saltiel, 2013).

Intersectionality

The term 'intersectionality' was first used by Kimberle Crenshaw (1989) in relation to black women and disability in the USA (Crenshaw, 1989), and then developed to recognise the inadequacy of using single social inequalities, such as gender or disability, to understand the extent of disadvantage and the marginalisation of separate groups by appreciating how social inequalities intersect to create new ways of oppression (Yuval-Davis, 2006). Conceptualising intersectionality is a far more complex approach than using approaches that reduce individuals to a single social inequality only, such as sexuality or race. Intersectionality can help to overcome the tendency for competing and hegemonic inequalities, e.g. race or disability, as fluidity in social structuring is better understood through the application of diverse inequalities embracing both race and disability. Mattsson suggests that intersectionality is a usable tool for critical reflection, and to challenge oppression and inequality because it focuses on the interplay and complexity between gender, sexuality, class and race (Mattsson, 2014).

THE FAMILY SYSTEM

The system that we are most concerned with as social workers is the family. The actual nature of experienced family life varies enormously, and sadly not all family experiences are positive. Families are diverse in their construction and the way in which they negotiate roles. When we are intervening as social workers, it is vital that we seek to understand individuals and families within their social and familial context, rather than applying assumptions derived from our own experiences or societal expectations.

Gender and gendered roles

Parsons devised his nuclear family at a time when gender was viewed as static and binary. Gender roles were very prescribed and therefore his social systems theory was premised on a breadwinning father and a homemaking mother. In the contemporary age we understand gender much more fluidly; however, gender stereotypes persist. We use the term 'gendered roles' in recognition that roles are ascribed to individuals through stereotyping and notions of traditionally accepted rules of behaviour that normalise different roles for men and women. These roles are not necessarily accepted by the individual, and social workers should seek to assess individuals and not stereotyped versions. Judith Butler focused on subverting gender by reflecting on performance and performativity, to argue that individuals are located on a spectrum between masculinity and femininity (Butler, 1990). Conceptualising gender performance and performativity has been transferred to social work (Green & Featherstone, 2014).

AT NUMBER 3

Maureen was in her first year of university when she fell pregnant with Harry. She intended to resume her studies after Harry was born, but before she knew it she was pregnant again with Sam, and with two small children university seemed impossible. Maureen loved her kids but did not enjoy being a full-time mum. She and her partner Richie talked things through and agreed that Maureen would get a job and Richie would stay at home and look after the boys. Maureen's mother told her that she was selfish, and her place was with her boys who needed their mother. Richie found that when he took the boys to toddler group, he was usually the only man, and everyone made a big fuss of him.

Maureen and Richie split up amicably a few years later, and Maureen is now in a relationship with Claire. Maureen, Harry and Sam live with Claire and her son Asif. All of the boys still have regular contact with their dads. One day Harry is playing at a friend's house, and his friend's dad asks him what it's like having two mums. Harry explains that he hasn't got two mums, and the man says 'oh, which one's the dad, then?'

EXERCISE 8.3

What gender stereotypes, assumptions and gender roles are present in Maureen's, Richie's and Harry's experiences above?

Social capital

Economically, the term 'capital' relates to assets, and the accumulation of assets has sociologically been applied to human and social conditions. Human capital is the development of assets and production inherent within individuals, and was initially related to the education process and the intergenerational transmission of earnings, assets and consumption from parents to their children (Becker & Tomes, 1986; Becker, 1993). In relation to social interaction, social capital (Putnam, 2000) is the ability of an individual to secure benefits through membership of social networks and other social structures, along with the networks of social relations characterised by norms of trust and reciprocity (Ravenera, 2007). Furstenberg and Kaplan acknowledge that the measurement of social capital within families can be difficult, though they speculate that interpersonal family relationships and negotiating skills are important in defining family roles (Furstenberg & Kaplan, 2007). Hawkins and Maurer have reflected on the usefulness of social capital during social work assessments, and suggest it is a helpful concept as an analytical and theoretical model for micro and macro practice (Hawkins & Maurer, 2012).

Families of choice

The family of choice concept is intended to capture the commitment of chosen, rather than fixed and assigned relationships and ties of intimacy (Ribbens et al., 2011). Kath Weston originated the idea of families of choice in 1991, when she noticed that gay men and lesbian women were increasingly extending the meaning of family beyond the biological family, which is the source of traditional support and intimacy. She argued that when friends provide the intimacy and support, which traditionally family members are expected to provide, then the family extends by choice (Weston, 1991). The development of families of choice within the LGBTQ+ community has resulted in some reflection on what the same-sex family represents. The shared narrative of LGBTQ+ relationships is based upon an understanding of the limitations of an institutionalised heterosexism, with gendered constructs dependent upon sexual differences. Within the LGBTQ+ community, the network of friendship has been an observed social phenomenon, along with relationships negotiated within positions of mutuality and the reinventing of intimate life within the sphere of choice. The resulting perception of greater choice and openness in relationships, along with the aim to break away from heterosexually structured differences, has led to a feeling of openness towards relationship possibilities within the non-heterosexual community (Weeks et al., 2007). Anthony Giddens argues that choice

also transforms heterosexual relationships in modern society because intimacy within relationships evolves where forms of control based on social assumptions of male dominance are less easily maintained (Giddens, 1992; Giddens & Pierson, 1998).

Family practice and displays

David Morgan (1996) argues that families are not concrete structures because they are created through everyday practices that are fluid and take place in social contexts. Family participation is represented by activities within families where the emphasis is on the social actor recreating his or her world within the context of the family, and performing gender (West & Zimmerman, 1987) and family practices (Morgan, 1996) in everyday routines which overlap and intersect with other practices based on class, age, gender, ethnicity and culture. The display of these family practices (Finch, 2007) emphasises the social construction of these activities as they are both conveyed and understood by others, internally and externally to the family, and are understood to define roles within families. The doing and displaying of family in everyday routines has been transferred to fostering families during daily routines to show an ethic of care (Rees et al., 2012) and in the creation of adoption kinship (Jones & Hackett, 2011).

SYSTEMIC TOOLS TO SUPPORT PRACTICE

Thinking systemically helps us to move beyond locating a problem within an individual and begin to understand the impact of experience, identity, networks, and relationships with community and state. Systemic models are increasingly popular in social work, and in this section we look at systemic tools that can support our practice. Genograms, ecomaps, lifelines, life road maps and timelines all present creative ways we can collaborate and co-produce with people who use services to collect, organise and represent information. They don't fit neatly into pro formas of computerised recording systems, but they often provide a much more effective and relationship-based means of understanding family systems.

Family scripts

John Byng-Hall was a pioneer of family therapy in the UK who first proposed the idea of family scripts (Byng-Hall, 1985). He proposed that families unconsciously interact by repeating circular sequences and attachment relationships – in other words, family scenarios with a common script. The family script provides stability and ready guidance for action, saving the need for repeated negotiation of roles and behaviours. The family script casts family members in roles within the family system, e.g. good/bad (think of the 'golden child' or the 'wrong 'un'), aggressive/gentle (perhaps the disciplinarian – 'wait till your father gets home!', or the 'soft touch') etc.

> ... family dramas or family scenes are part and parcel of family life. Script is one element of the metaphor of theatre, itself deeply embedded in our culture – 'all the world is a stage'. (Byng-Hall 1985: 1)

As newcomers to the family system, social workers do not know the family script, so we can objectively 'read' the family script and see patterns of behaviour of which the family are unaware. By bringing new information to the family, we can help them to move away from the script and approach situations more flexibly in order to successfully adapt to challenges. Once you become adept at spotting family scripts, you can start to see them in other systems, e.g. scripted behaviours at work or school.

EXERCISE 8.4

Consider your own family.

- Can you think of any behaviours or interactions that are repeated over and over?
- Can you identify the roles that family members are cast in?

Genograms

Genograms are visual tools that help us understand and explore family composition. Most readers will be familiar with family trees, which trace the lineage. Although genograms share many similarities with family trees, they can tell us much more than who is who. Typically, genograms capture family information over three generations, using symbols to represent individuals, and lines connecting the individuals to demonstrate their relationship to each other (see Figure 8.3).

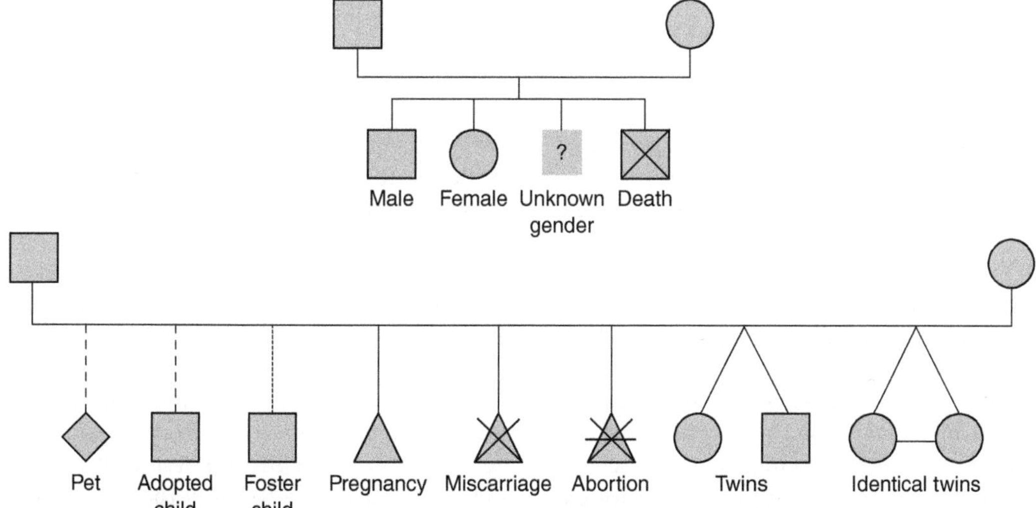

Figure 8.3 Genogram symbols

McGoldrick et al. popularised the use of genograms in social work practice in the 1960s (McGoldrick et al., 2008). Once completed, genograms present an easily absorbed and understandable visual record of the structure of a family system (Dyke, 2016); however, the process of constructing a genogram can be even more valuable than the end product. Hills (2013) describes how constructing and co-producing a genogram together with an individual or family can be:

> … [a] joint odyssey of discovery from the flow of feedback of experience. Following the therapist's interested curiosity, family members begin to discover different aspects of the family story and awareness of one another and their shared situation. (Hills, 2013: 12)

Genograms, therefore, should not be viewed simply as tool for professionals to understand family composition, but as a systemic intervention, which can enable families and individuals to gain a new understanding of themselves and their situations.

EXERCISE 8.5

Try creating a genogram of three generations of your own family.

- Reflect on what you learnt from this task, e.g. did you notice any gaps – people you don't know about? What does this tell you?
- Were there any family members who you would rather not include, or any friends who are so close that you consider them family? What does this tell you about the nature of family?

Ecomaps

Ecomaps (sometimes known as ecograms) are closely related to Bronfenbrenner's ecological systems theory, and were developed by Professor Anne Hartman (1978) as part of her systems approach to social work (see Figure 8.4). Championing systemic practice, Hartman said:

> If social workers are to avoid reductionism and scientism, if they are to translate a systems orientation into practice, they must learn to 'think systems' or to develop … new and more complex ways of imprinting reality. (Hartman, 1978, cited in Dyke, 2016: 40)

Whereas genograms focus on family, ecomaps are much broader in scope, and consider the relationships and influences (positive and negative) between individuals, families and their ecological environment, including their social and support networks. Different styles of line can indicate the different qualities of a relationship, and arrows are used to show the direction in which an effect occurs.

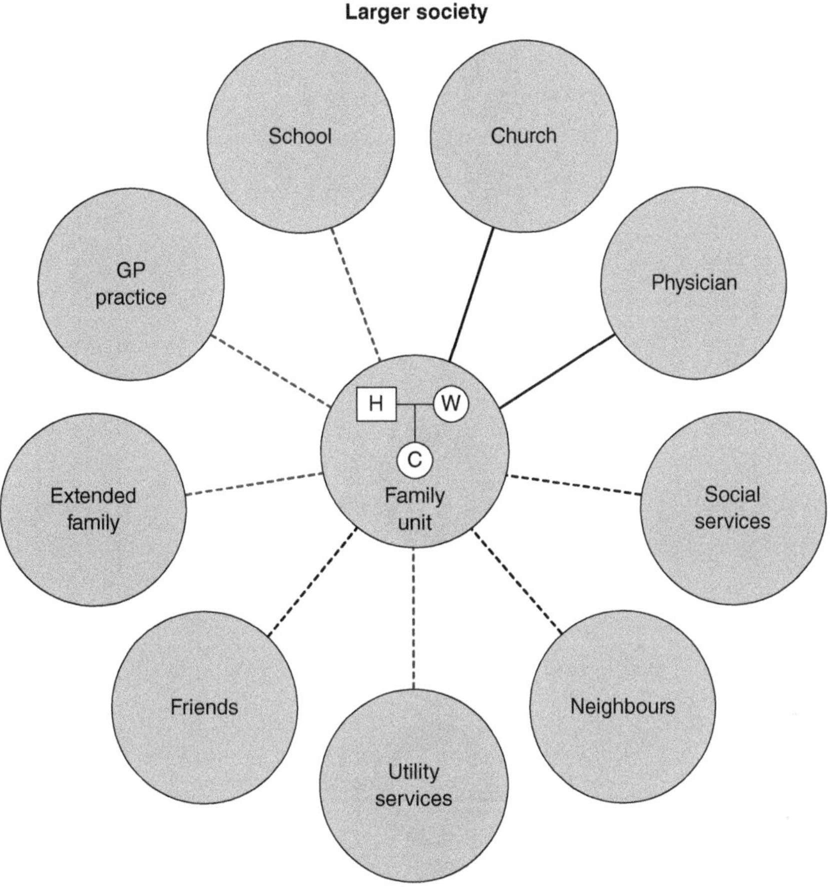

Figure 8.4 Ecomaps

Lifelines, life road maps and timelines

Lifelines, life road maps and timelines are names that are used interchangeably to describe visual, systemic tools which create a chronological narrative (Hennessey, 2011). They support social work assessments and interventions by enabling us to work with individuals and families to identify significant events, relationships and feelings, and to understand how the past influences the present. They can explore the whole life course, or focus on a particular period. Lifelines, life road maps and timelines present tremendous creative possibilities, and so they are a great way to engage children and adults who enjoy drawing or graphics representations. We like to complete them with our students on wallpaper, which they can spread out and work on from left to right, capturing key events from birth to the present through drawings and text. We then encourage them to go back and add more detail, such as the feelings a key event prompted and who/what supported them at that time. Finally, we ask the students to draw lines to link past events to future events on which they had an impact.

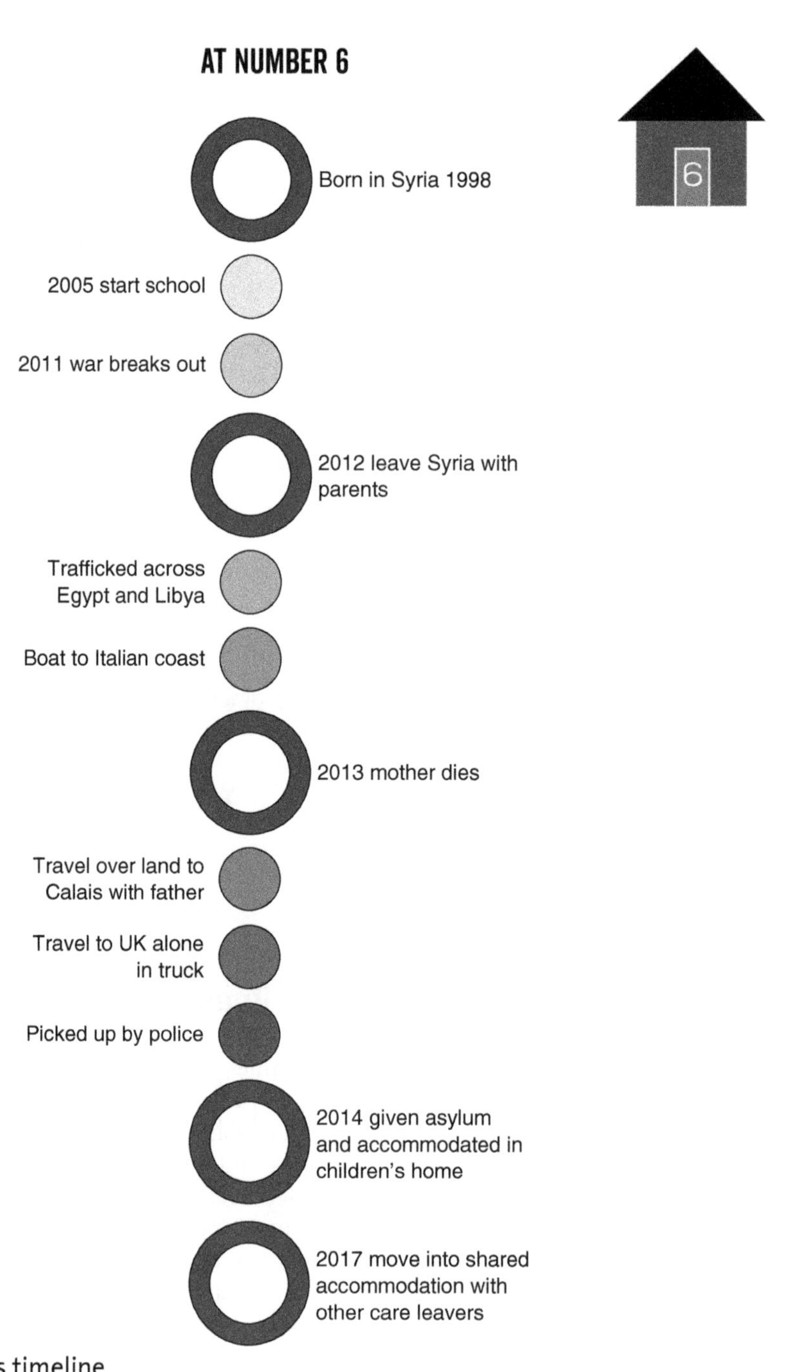

Figure 8.5 Adnan's timeline

This is a powerful diagrammatic and visual tool, which highlights important life events. Through Adnan's timeline (see Figure 8.5) we visually see how his life has changed and realise the traumatic difficulties he has encountered. Through the co-production of this lifeline both Adnan and his social worker collaborate to understand his emotional needs as well as his strength and resilience in overcoming the adversities of his traumatic experiences.

SUMMARY

In this chapter we have introduced and reflected on individuals within their social environments, recognising that these are in fact multiple, interconnected systems. People are social entities and our environments, whatever the context, have a large influence on our identity, relationships and behaviour. We have reflected on the relational nature of social work and introduced more generally applied systems theories, such as ecological social systems and attachment theory. Developing on these more generally applicable social system perspectives, we have looked at more difficult to understand theories that seek to explain multiple levels of oppression and complexity. More specifically, we have discussed approaches that seek to explain how roles within families are negotiated through tradition and choice. Finally, we have identified systemic tools, which we can use to enhance the way we gather information, form understanding and intervene with people as part of social work practice.

9 INTERVENING DURING A CRISIS

Learning in this chapter relates to

PCF	KSS Adult Services	KSS Child & Family
3. Diversity & Equalities 5. Knowledge 7. Skills & Interventions	2. The role of social workers working with adults 3. Person-centred practice 4. Safeguarding 6. Effective assessments & outcome-based support planning 7. Direct work with individuals & families	1. The role of child & family social work 5. Effective direct work with children & families 6. Child & family assessment 7. Analysis, decision making, planning & review

INTRODUCTION

This chapter explores the nature and stages of crisis and considers social work responsibilities and responses. We will consider practitioners' agency during crisis management, and facilitate the understanding of choice and options when professionally intervening during crises. 'Crisis' is a highly emotive word which conjures up ideas of urgency, risks and danger. Personally, we tend to experience crises infrequently, but as social workers we very regularly find ourselves working with people during crises, which are deeply felt and cause great anxiety. Many people associate social work crises with safeguarding, but crisis intervention responds to many different situations.

WHOSE CRISIS?

Professionally, we conceptualise crisis in a fluid and dynamic sense, recognising that it is not dependant on a particular situation, event or response. What is a crisis for one individual is a minor inconvenience for another. Consider not being able to find your car keys before leaving home to go to work. Is this a crisis? It is certainly an acutely stressful situation, but it can be fairly quickly resolved in any number of ways – finding the keys, using a spare set, taking the bus to work. However, any interpretation of the crisis has to consider the particular situation. What is at stake? How equipped is the person to manage the stress of the situation? Have other difficult situations occurred recently so that the cumulative effect means that losing your keys is a final straw? The unfolding events and personal responses to *small crises* or inconveniences indicate the level of crisis a person is experiencing – and our interpretation may indicate that an individual is not successfully coping with a crisis.

EXERCISE 9.1

For a moment sit back and consider some form of crisis you have experienced.

- When did you notice this was a crisis?
- What was it about it that made you identify it as a crisis?
- How did you feel about the situation?
- What did you do?
- Looking back, what if anything could you have done differently?

DEFINING A CRISIS

A crisis is understood as an upset in a steady state. Roberts defines it as:

> An acute disruption of psychological homeostasis in which one's usual coping mechanisms fail and there exists evidence of distress and functional impairment. The subjective reaction to a stressful life experience that compromises the individual's stability and ability to cope or function. (2005: 778)

Therefore, a crisis leads to an acute psychological and possibly physical reaction. It is a subjective experience; one person's crisis is another person's recreation (think about falling from a height or bungee jumping). Crises are not isolated events – no one truly lives in isolation and we're more likely to live within what are often complex social environments. Therefore one person's crisis is likely to have an impact on their social connections, their family, work, relationships etc. (McGinnis, 2013). This is often when and how social work practitioners become involved with a person's crisis. Hart explains that it 'should be noted that stress, or a stressful situation, is not necessarily a crisis; however, it may develop into a crisis' (2018: 282). Essentially a crisis is partly in the subjective perception of the person experiencing it, but there are certain key features, which are:

- a precipitating event or result of long-term stress;
- individually or collectively experienced distress (a personal crisis, family crisis);

- a sense of loss (actual or anticipated);
- feeling out of control; unexpected events; disruption;
- uncertain future and distress may continue over time.

AT NUMBER 1

Mary experienced a crisis following the death of her partner after forty-two years of marriage.

AT NUMBER 2

Alfie experienced a crisis when told he was at risk of being made redundant.

AT NUMBER 3

Maureen experienced a crisis when she fell pregnant unexpectedly during her first year at university.

EXERCISE 9.2

We have described the precipitating event for each person's crisis.

Identify how each person is likely to be experiencing the other key features of crisis that we have set out above.

Hart (2018) classifies two types of crisis: *maturational* – those linked to a person's transition between developmental stages, and *situational* – those that occur when individuals experience uncontrollable experiences. Crises are therefore determined by the personal responses of an individual to specific stressful events. A crisis only develops when an individual perceives that a specific event or events are so significant and threatening after unsuccessfully using their usual coping strategies that they are not able to use alternative strategies to rectify the crisis. A crisis that comes to our attention as social workers usually means that a person is not coping, and without some support it may escalate and become out of control, possibly creating safeguarding concerns. Crisis intervention involves a social worker working in partnership with a person based on their assessed needs and capabilities.

UNDERSTANDING CRISIS

Crises can occur suddenly, and be unpredictable, but crisis theory recognises that they are a normal part of life. Erikson's developmental psychology (Erikson, 1968) suggests that personal development is as a result of individuals adapting to overcome crises, so that *what doesn't kill us makes us stronger*. Therefore, a crisis can be seen as a developmental opportunity as well as a process. Person-centred approaches and Gestalt therapy have influenced crisis intervention by focusing on the 'here and now' and opportunities for personal growth due to crisis (Parker, 2017).

In 1944, Lindemann studied the survivors of a fire and identified five related reactions: somatic distress, a preoccupation with the deceased, guilt, a hostile reaction, and the loss of patterns of conduct (cited in Parker, 2017). Social work has moved away from a *just get on with it* attitude towards understanding crisis as part of a process, and attitudes to loss, bereavement and crisis have changed over time. We understand that individuals who experience significant loss may regress to childhood experiences of stress (Payne, 2005), requiring support with historical issues as well as the current crisis. In the 1980s, Claudia Jewett identified that children living in foster care experience bereavement in response to separation from their birth families. Averting crisis in the home situation by placing children in foster care can therefore create a different crisis (Jewett, 1994).

CRISIS INTERVENTION

We have defined crisis as being highly subjective, but a recognisable human process that most people have experienced at some time in their lives. Social work interventions mostly occur when an individual's attempts to manage crises through their available mechanisms are unsuccessful and they are unable to access or construct an alternative response. Crises can be exacerbated by unsuitable attempts at resolution, e.g. someone who resorts to alcohol when encountering an emotional problem may achieve some temporary respite, but the risks ultimately worsen the underlying problem rather than resolving it. Situations may also escalate when a current crisis reactivates an earlier, unresolved crisis. Social workers are often called upon to intervene with individuals and help them in coping with their crises.

AUTHOR'S EXPERIENCE (PHIL)

While working in Out of Hours (OOH) emergency I would often receive telephone calls from foster carers concerning a missing child or young person. At first glance, a child or young person missing from their foster placement seems to be a real crisis and possibly a safeguarding situation. However, these were most often not a crisis as such and rarely triggered safeguarding. Most of the young people or

(Continued)

children had simply stayed out later than usual or had not returned by the agreed time. The foster carers were rarely seriously concerned, but their instructions were to contact the OOH social worker whenever a young person was *missing*. They also had to inform the police who would visit the foster home, quite often early the next morning, to find the young person having returned. Some young people would even telephone the police themselves after staying out later than agreed, because they knew they'd be taken back home to the foster carers.

Going even further back in my career, I can recall how as a newly qualified social worker I panicked when a young person was declared missing. I felt somehow responsible, and sure that he was in grave danger, but a much more experienced colleague explained that the boy often went missing, mostly going back to his family or friends.

Are these crises? They were certainly concerning, but perhaps they also represented normal adolescent behaviour which to some extent could be expected? I have had similar experiences as a father with my own teenage children. In my experience, foster carers can lose patience when a young person persistently goes *missing* by staying out later than agreed, and then the young person may end up moving from the placement. This therefore is a practice scenario warranting crisis intervention with the young person.

Crisis intervention is a practice response, which is time limited and seeks to assist individuals, families and groups adjust to the crisis (Hepworth et al., 2010). While there is no one model for crisis intervention, in general such interventions look to interrupt crisis and restore equilibrium by helping people readjust through practical tasks (Hart, 2018). Crisis intervention is not restricted to individuals, for example during social group work with child survivors of sudden disasters using guided artwork activities (Abbas & Sulman, 2016). In general, crisis intervention can be specifically segregated into different stages, which are the beginning, action and termination phases. While we will focus on these three general phases in the next section, there are other, more specific versions of crisis intervention that include more stages.

Various definitions of different stages of crisis intervention

Hepworth et al. (2010) have identified the six stages to crisis intervention as being the following:

1. Define the problem.
2. Ensure client safety.
3. Provide support.
4. Examine alternatives.
5. Make plans.
6. Obtain commitment.

McGinnis (2013) has identified six tasks which are:

1. Assess risk harm.
2. Gather important information relevant to the *here and now*; in the case of a new client ascertain supports.
3. Attend to feelings and provide reassurance.
4. Outline the use of a crisis intervention timeframe.
5. Set realistic goals.
6. Define individual tasks in achieving goals.

Roberts (1991) has defined a seven-stage intervention model as including:

1. Plan and conduct crisis biopsychosocial assessment.
2. Establish rapport and collaborative relationship.
3. Identify dimensions of presenting problems.
4. Explore feelings and emotions.
5. Generate and explore alternatives.
6. Develop and formulate action plan.
7. Follow up plan and agreement.

Parker (2007) has devised a crisis intervention flow diagram when reflecting on practice with people with dementia and their carers:

1. Does the referral situation constitute a crisis?
2. Whose crisis?
3. Agree on the wants, wishes and needs of significant persons.
4. Check:
    i. Legal and statutory duties
    ii. Availability of local resources and services
    iii. Values – personal, professional and service user.
5. Negotiate an initial agreement.
6. Coordinate services and implement an initial plan of care.
7. Review, renegotiate and formulate the care plan.

Working with people during a crisis can be challenging and demanding for practitioners. Crisis itself implies risk, which in turn fosters emotional concern from many practitioners. We encounter diverse needs and people who have a wide range of different coping mechanisms. We need to employ a wide range of skills, beginning with basic research skills.

AT NUMBER 6

Liam moved into foster care from the residential home because it was felt he would settle down when living with a family. At first he seemed quite happy and appeared to want to settle down but missed his friends. Then, after a few weeks

(Continued)

in placement, he stopped out later than was agreed and was picked up by the police in a local park and was very drunk. Liam was angry and said he should be allowed to stay out, particularly as 'no one cares for me'. Over the next few weeks he stopped out regularly, and his carers became very concerned when he returned with fresh bruising to his face. Undaunted he went out the next day and did not return for a few days. His behaviour is causing concern.

EXERCISE 9.3

- Do you think Liam considers himself in crisis. Why?
- Do you think Liam's foster carers consider this a crisis? Why?
- Do you think Liam's social worker considers this a crisis. Why?

Managing crises can be difficult for practitioners and current work is emerging on the use of immersive technology in simulation exercises for student social workers and practitioners, which may have application for practice during crisis (e.g. see Bogo et al., 2014; Dodds et al., 2018). Working during crisis intervention requires practitioners to develop strategic planning and the ability to provide individualised, person-centred support.

APPLYING CRISIS INTERVENTION IN PRACTICE

The application of crisis intervention is meant to be time limited and to enable the person to adopt and develop coping strategies to overcome the crisis. As we have discussed, crises are highly personalised and person specific, and thus our practice has to be tailored to meet each individual's need (Roberts, 2005). In this section, we utilise three overlapping stages relating to crisis intervention practice: beginning, action and termination (McGinnis, 2013). We feel these three stages help us to focus on the practice and not get bogged down in the theoretical detail. Naturally, we recognise the importance of theory to practice, but identifying these three stages, and the respective components in each, clarifies the process involved in crisis intervention.

Beginning phase

McGinnis suggests that the beginning phase may last longer than two weeks. Those practitioners versed in crisis work during safeguarding may well baulk at the luxury of a two-week introduction period. They may well argue that the assessment of risk and speedy action take priority when a child's wellbeing is at risk. However, crisis intervention does not exclusively relate to safeguarding. This does not negate undertaking a risk assessment, which should take into account the cause of the crisis, the severity of the situation and levels of risk (Hart, 2018). During a safeguarding situation, it may be deemed appropriate to work with parents to identify their crisis and how they can develop coping strategies. It may also apply to the child who has moved from the parental home to live with extended family, connected persons or in foster care; crisis intervention can help the child adapt to the change of living environment. Alternatively, crisis intervention could support an extended family member to care for the child. So while crisis intervention does not relate necessarily to safeguarding practice, there is scope to apply this approach during aspects of safeguarding work, but it has to relate to the person's perceived crisis and not the practitioner's understanding of the crisis leading to safeguarding.

It is important to mention that people often take longer to process information during crises and therefore, as McGinnis points out, the beginning phase may take up to two weeks and lead to concrete goals. During this process the practitioner could use S.M.A.R.T. planning (see Chapter 6) to set realistic goals. It is not realistic to expect the parent during safeguarding concerns to transform into a showcase parent, and our practice may well lead to family separation. Childhood family separation through children's social care involvement does not resolve the child's experienced problems. Yes, foster care keeps the child safe, but we must expect more from our practice and consider identity, emotional wellbeing, maturation and the child's self-efficacy. Our professional practice must be more than safeguarding in the *here and now* and should promote longer-term coping strategies through managing crisis. So, a two-week beginning process is not too much time considering the person's lifespan. During this beginning phase using S.M.A.R.T. planning, the practitioner can assess any risks, gather information, and attend to the person's feelings, as well as reassure them about roles and objectives. The beginning phase requires a lot of energy and enthusiasm to 'short out' the crisis. Identifying the specific nature of the crisis itself may take some time.

AUTHOR'S EXPERIENCE (PHIL)

At first I found the transition moving into a fostering and adoption team from a children and families team a little difficult. I had been more used to dealing with safeguarding issues, which in many ways were very useful experiences for me to take to fostering and adoption work. The pace of my new role was different, less frenetic even. However, I found I was more autonomous and worked closely with foster carers, children and young people to help them manage many crises that were not safeguarding. One time I worked with a parent to facilitate the return of her son to the foster placement. She was in crisis resulting from her personal circumstances and this was affecting her relationship with her son. I arranged several sessions and over two weeks took time to develop the beginning stage for them to get to know me. I simply felt this was important, and during this time we worked on agreeing the crisis, possible solutions and action plan.

As we have noted, crises may be extraordinary and unexpected events but they do not occur in isolation. An emotional breakdown may only be recognised when a person attends their GP, but the breakdown will not have materialised instantaneously, it will have occurred over some time and be due to some problems. The crisis point and actual crisis may be distinct. During this phase, the practitioner will identify the crisis with the person and help them set realistic goals and tasks to achieve those goals:

> ... only if we have engaged with the client in attending to their present narrative and skilfully facilitated them to move to a position where they can begin to identify priority need in their situation, can we begin to formulate goals. (McGinnis, 2013: 45)

By collaborating with a professional, the person is able to feel supported, and through goal and task setting, they should become more confident in their own ability to manage the crisis. Having completed the beginning phase, the next step is to focus on the action phase.

AT NUMBER 3

Maureen's knee surgery is not successful and leaves her in a lot of pain. She is prescribed painkillers, which are highly addictive. When Maureen's GP refuses to increase her dosage, she starts buying medication over the internet, which is very expensive. Maureen is ashamed of her dependency and doesn't want Claire to know about it. She takes out a high interest loan and after a short while misses payments. The high interest rates mean that Maureen's debt increases very rapidly. She is unable to sleep because of worry. She loses weight and takes more and more pain medication. She cancels some direct debits so that she has money to pay the loan, resulting in a court summons for non-payment of council tax. The children notice that there is no Wi-Fi, and when Claire checks she discovers it has been terminated because of non-payment. Claire confronts Maureen, who breaks down and confesses everything. Claire tells Maureen she has to get help immediately or leave. Maureen self-refers to the drug and alcohol treatment service. When she attends for her initial appointment, she is in a state of extreme distress and reports that she has stopped all of her pain medication.

EXERCISE 9.4

You are the social worker in the drug and alcohol treatment team working with Maureen. In supporting her to resolve her crisis, what need would you address first?

Action phase

The action phase is about achieving or working towards the tasks and goals identified during the beginning phase. The agreed tasks, which should look something like an action plan list, should detail who does what and when. So for instance, if the agreed goals are to address health issues, access community facilities and have contact with family members, the tasks may be to book an appointment with the GP, identify local community groups, select a community facility to attend and arrange to speak to family members. With the tasks agreed, the action phase should include regular meetings to briefly review the intervening period. In our examples the first two goals appear quite straightforward, and feeling healthier and active by accessing community facilities will help the person progress along the plan. The more problematic goal of contacting estranged family members may cause a barrier. It is therefore important during a review to reframe the goals/tasks not achieved. This third goal may be too much for the person or may actually not be a goal at this stage. Perhaps the goal is to address personal feelings towards family members and circumstances. The tasks can be redefined and we could consider emotional feeling towards family and the possible impact on the individual as we progress along the plan. We may negotiate a change to the plan and reframe the task to access some counselling sessions through the GP.

The plan is only as good as its implementation and therefore we must attend to any new information and developments. No one's life ever remains static; the state of crisis is due to the person not being able to cope with a situation. During crisis intervention, life does not stand still. It is likely that new information will emerge, but how relevant is it to the crisis intervention itself? Our aim is to help promote independence and for the person to develop successful and transferable coping strategies. After all, during this action stage we need to ensure the end is still being focused on and that the process of negotiation, action and modification enables the individual in crisis to move ahead.

Termination phase

As we have emphasised, this phase is focused on from the beginning and is concerned with the desired end result. Within the action plan, the termination and end session should be detailed and diarised as a final session between the practitioner and the person using the service. The final session should be clearly identified as the ending event. While this may be the final stage in this particular intervention:

> ... this is not to say that the client and worker will have managed all the issues, rather that through the process of negotiation, action and modification – and doubtless some frustration – essential building blocks for moving ahead should be in place. (McGinnis, 2013: 47)

The intervention has been undertaken in collaboration with the aim of reducing the professional's participation in the person's life as the person becomes more resourced to manage their own situation. The final meeting will review progress, evaluate outcomes, and can help to identify longer-term goals, which the person can achieve without professional help. Finally, the ending event will seek to ensure that the support and coping mechanisms, which have helped during the action phase, remain in place. A successful crisis intervention can develop a person's confidence in their own ability to generate appropriate solutions, and seek out new and accessible sources of support, without recourse to social work input.

AUTHOR'S EXPERIENCE (CAT)

As an Approved Mental Health Professional (AMHP), I frequently worked with people experiencing mental health crises. AMHPs coordinate assessments under the Mental Health Act 1983, and if the statutory criteria are met can complete an application for the person to be detained in hospital (commonly referred to as being sectioned). Detaining someone under the Mental Health Act infringes their

(Continued)

right to liberty under Article 5 the Human Rights Act 1998, and the key task of the AMHP is to identify whether the crisis can be managed through a less restrictive alternative. The process of determining whether someone should be detained in hospital for assessment or treatment of their mental health is prescribed by statute, and AMHPs have legal powers and duties. However, in carrying out this very specialist role within a specific legal framework, AMHPs are performing a crisis intervention, which has beginning, activation and termination phases, and utilising their professional skills, knowledge and values.

”

SKILLS IN MANAGING CRISIS INTERVENTION

It seems almost needless to say that practitioners require communication and negotiation skills when applying crisis intervention. However, Parker cautions that while:

> A crisis presents an opportunity for social workers to influence positively the coping capacities of others ... crisis intervention, if handled inappropriately, may also distort reality and lead to maladaptive coping strategies. (2017: 168)

Many people appear motivated for change during a crisis, because their personal defences are often lowered. Working during crisis involves many practitioner skills. Parker (2017) in fact emphasises that this particular approach requires almost all of our social work skills, particularly advocacy, negotiating, communication, empathy, and being able to appropriately challenge a person in a non-threatening manner. Assessment skills are key to crisis intervention to understand the possible risk, capacity and motivation for change, as well as being able to reassess changing circumstances.

LIMITATIONS OF CRISIS INTERVENTION

There are a number of limitations to crisis intervention. A very straightforward limitation is its possible association with safeguarding. While teaching crisis intervention one student asked 'How does this relate to safeguarding?' and seemed surprised that it was not a lecture on safeguarding. On another level, safeguarding may result from earlier crises and modern practice tends to react to safeguarding and rights-based needs rather than to an earlier stage in the person's life. Another limitation is the difficulty in devising a structured approach to deal with crises, which are very different between people. Basically, people cope with loss and crisis in very different ways and at different speeds. Therefore, an approach based on a model with a specific route through crisis does not fit well with the diverse ways people deal with crisis, loss and challenging experiences (Wilson et al., 2011). A final limitation is that crisis intervention focuses on the individual, and while not necessarily pathologising that individual, this approach seems to ignore structural factors such as poor quality housing or poverty.

SUMMARY

In this chapter we have focused on crisis intervention, offering a definition of crisis and noting that it is a very subjective experience. Social workers can play a pivotal role during a crisis, but we have also noted that sometimes social work decisions to resolve one type of crisis can generate another. We have charted the development of crisis intervention in social work, highlighting that whilst that intervention is not necessarily safeguarding, the two often overlap. There are various different approaches to crisis intervention and we have concentrated on the practical, i.e. application, by focusing on the beginning, action and termination phases to crisis intervention.

10 TASK-CENTRED INTERVENTIONS

Learning in this chapter relates to

PCF	KSS Adult Services	KSS Child & Family
1. Professionalism 2. Values & Ethics 5. Knowledge 7. Skills & Interventions	2. The role of social workers working with adults 3. Person-centred practice 6. Effective assessments & outcome-based support planning 7. Direct work with individuals & families	1. The role of child & family social work 5. Effective direct work with children & families 6. Child & family assessment 7. Analysis, decision making, planning & review

INTRODUCTION

In this chapter, we focus on task-centred interventions in social work practice, which engage people in identifying goals and co-producing time-limited interventions. We consider how the approach developed in response to concerns that traditional social work casework lacked focus and fostered dependency. We explore the concept of recovery, and consider how we construct our professional approach, reflecting on the power imbalance between social workers and people who use services. We then explore each of the interlinking stages of task-centred practice in some detail, offering guidance on how to collaboratively identify problems, establish clear and specific goals, develop structured, task-orientated contracts and evaluate outcomes.

THE DEVELOPMENT OF TASK-CENTRED INTERVENTIONS

Uniquely amongst social work interventions, task-centred practice was designed within the social work profession, for the social work profession (McColgan, 2013). This may well be why it is often cited by social workers as their preferred approach. A task-centred approach does not mean that the social worker sets the person a list of tasks to do, or vice versa; it is concerned with enabling people to identify their own goals and negotiating with them how these will be met. The method was initially developed in the 1960s by Bill Reid, in response to concerns about traditional casework approaches potential to be both resource intensive and disempowering. Reid and Shyne explored alternative practice approaches and suggested that brief, focused interventions may be more effective (Reid & Shyne, 1969). They developed a social work approach comprising time-limited but intensely focused interventions, centred on purposeful, allocated actions, and named it 'task-centred practice'. McColgan writes:

> They [Reid and Shyne] found that when clients were working on agreed problems identified by service users themselves, the short-term focus on agreed goals and actions resulted in more effective outcomes. (2013: 66)

Reid subsequently worked with Epstein to devise a seven-point list of problems which they felt social workers could successfully work through with people by applying a task-centred approach (Reid later added an eighth).

Seven/eight point typologies of problems

1. Interpersonal conflict.
2. Dissatisfaction in social relations.
3. Relations with formal organisations.
4. Role performance.
5. Social transition.
6. Reactive emotional distress.
7. Inadequate resources (Reid & Epstein, 1972).
8. Psychological/behavioural problems (Reid, 1978).

Recovery

In developing task-centred practice, Reid was responding to a growing dissatisfaction that open-ended, psychodynamic casework approaches resulted in social workers continually intervening in people's lives over long periods without clear focus or defined aims. People were being maintained by social work, rather than supported or empowered to move forwards. When we intervene in people's lives, what *we* do is conceptualised and understood as social work. How do we conceptualise and understand what the person or family is doing within this process? Webber and Joubert (2015) suggest that the process people and families go through in restoring rights, roles and responsibilities lost through social problems is *recovery*.

Recovery is a concept central to social models of illness and disability, which grew primarily from the mental health community (Slade, 2009). Recovery rarely receives much focus as a theory informing social work practice during social work training. This may well be because as a relatively new concept, recovery is generally under-theorised (Weber and Joubert, 2015) and the evidence base that does exist does not specifically speak to social work practice (Tew, 2013). Although not specific to social work, we believe that the recovery model is very congruent with our values and discourses – it also recognises the impact of structural oppression, and social and environmental factors, and values personalisation, self-determination and wellbeing.

The complex situations and problems social workers become involved with can seem entrenched and intractable. This can cause social workers to believe that things are hopeless and develop low expectations for the people they are working with (Webber and Joubert, 2015). Whilst working with people experiencing issues such as crisis, mental health difficulties, relationship breakdown, social isolation or abuse, we need to maintain hope and expectations that they deserve and can achieve quality of life. The recovery model empowers people by allowing them to define what recovery means to them, creating outcomes that are unique and contextualised within their individual experience, rather than defined by services (Webber and Joubert, 2015). Borg and Davidson (2008) recognise that recovery in everyday life may be feeling normal again by taking the kids to school or returning to work, finding effective coping strategies or being good to oneself by finding time for activities that help. Recovery is a process; an underlying issue may never be fully resolved, but the person can recover in an ongoing sense. Davidson highlights that 'The role of professionals is seen in recovery literature as that of a companion or fellow traveller rather than an expert' (2005: 32).

AUTHOR'S EXPERIENCE (CAT)

I worked with a woman who, following a great deal of unresolved trauma, made a very violent attempt to end her life. Although she survived, her health and relationships were forever changed, and this further traumatised her and created many social issues. It was very hard for the woman to have hope or believe in her ability to move forward. I worked with her very intensively over a long period, establishing trust and developing a strong, effective relationship. Slowly things got better. Over time, my involvement gradually reduced. One day my supervisor reviewed my caseload and asked why I had not ended my involvement with the woman. I explained that her risks had been so high, her needs so complex, and engaging her had been so difficult, that I felt that I needed to stay involved to monitor so that if her situation deteriorated I could provide support quickly. My supervisor asked me, did my doctor monitor me when I was well, in case I became ill again? Of course, I said no. She helped me to see that in remaining involved with this woman once the active need for my involvement had passed, I was encouraging a dependency on me, rather than enabling the woman to recognise her own strengths, resources and capabilities. I was not allowing her to move on and recognise some of her issues as resolved.

Task-centred practice

A fairly simple way to conceive of task-centred practice is through building blocks, one on each other, or as steps detailing stages to the final goal (Parker, 2017). Task-centred interventions are time-limited, problem-solving approaches with clearly defined tasks. Problems are prioritised and people are encouraged to build on their resources by achieving the agreed goals. Task-centred practice and crisis intervention are closely related, with both incorporating learning theory, and intended to be brief, problem-solving interventions – in fact, task-centred practice often informs crisis intervention. There are many different models of task-centred practice, but Marsh and Doel (2015) envisage three basic and connecting phases, which are exploring problems; agreeing the goal – written agreement; and planning and implementing tasks. These three phases are preceded by the social worker's entrance into an often uncharted situation where the purpose is unclear, and succeeded by an exit stage, which concludes this particular intervention cycle (Doel, 2002; Marsh & Doel, 2005).

APPLYING THE APPROACH TO PRACTICE

Task-centred approaches are applied in a highly structured manner. Humphrey (2018) proposes five distinct, sequential – though overlapping – stages: problem exploration, identifying priority problems and agreeing goals, agreeing required tasks, carrying out and achieving the tasks, and finally endings and evaluation. Marsh and Doel (2005) suggest that the movement from problem to goal setting involves incremental steps away from the problem towards the goals.

Engaging people

Task-centred interventions are principled; they rely on the particular way we work with people. Rogers et al. explain that 'task-centred social work practice is as much – if not more – about the way we work with people to resolve problems than what the task or problem is' (2017: 234). Task-centred practice focuses on negotiation and agreement, and the engagement process is crucial in establishing the foundation of the relationship between practitioner and person, which will be fundamental to the efficacy of the intervention. As social workers, we must be able to positively engage with people and instil trust and confidence in our professional abilities

(Hepworth et al., 2010). We often notice that when our students return to university after a practice placement, they have acquired a new, highly abbreviated and jargonistic language. Adopting the language of a team or service can be an important part of understanding and integrating to it; however, it excludes those who are outside of it and reinforces a status/power differential. Successful engagement in social work practice is characterised by clarity in language, communication and interpersonal skills (Koprowska, 2014) which seeks to empower and respect personal choice and wellbeing. Marsh and Doel (2005) emphasise the importance of social workers using accessible language to enable the person to focus on wants rather than needs.

Problem exploration

In simple terms, this involves working with the person to identify the things that they find problematic and would like to change. Healy (2014) suggests that the purpose of the first session is to agree a shared understanding of the problems and begin to concentrate on the intervention through tasks and goals. Similarly Rogers et al. (2017) suggest that the initial stage is to identify and negotiate the problems/tasks to be addressed. This stage is very much about the practitioner helping/enabling the person to explore and define problems so that a shared understanding is constructed. It can be tempting to take over and analyse the presenting problem; however, this stage establishes the person-centred model of the intervention and should follow the person's pace and agenda from the start. Humphrey suggests that practitioners can use fairly simple techniques to help the person extricate themselves from seemingly enmeshed problems with no apparent solution. In such situations, the individual may find it too difficult to identify a problem or feel overwhelmed and unable to recognise a significant problem. Humphrey suggests that practitioners may find it useful to advise using a bullet-point diary to jot down issues and feelings, or using a mobile phone to record thoughts and feelings as part of the exploration process (Humphrey, 2018).

Prioritising problems and agreeing goals

Agreeing goals requires the identification of priority problems: 'The service user should be encouraged and supported to rank the range of problems in order of priority – that is, which problems are most important for them to resolve' (Humphrey, 2018: 318). During this stage, it is useful to consider with the person:

> What is the problem? – What is wrong?

and

> What is the goal? – What is wanted?

The problem and the goal can become conflated, e.g. in Phil's experience below, school attendance was superficially both a problem and a goal. The exploratory process of identifying priority problems is critical, and must not be rushed or based upon assumptions. It helps the person to become more self-aware of the issues they are experiencing. It can be a cathartic process, which becomes a coping strategy the person can replicate in the future to become more self-sufficient. As problems are explored and better understood, the social worker motivates the individual to categorise and prioritise their individual problem in line with their perceptions (Naleppa & Reid, 2003).

AUTHOR'S EXPERIENCE (PHIL)

A young person was refusing to attend school. The foster carer explained that she felt this was non-negotiable – the young person must attend school or she would have to withdraw the fostering placement. I met the young person and foster carer separately to ascertain the issues and plan goals. I established that the foster carer wanted to continue with the placement, and the young person felt it was continuing to meet her needs. The young person disclosed some difficulties with a friend were making her want to avoid school. The two immediate problems I identified were school relationships for the young person, and school attendance for the carer. Although each had a different perspective, the overall goal for both parties was school attendance. The young person saw school as a social outlet, while the carer felt it represented the young person's future prospects. We agreed the basic shared goal of attending school and moved on to negotiate tasks and timeframes to achieve this.

Once problems have been identified, explored and prioritised, the next stage is to focus on goal setting. Goals should relate to the problem, be specific and clear, feasible and desirable (Marsh & Doel, 2005), and it is easy to see that we can use S.M.A.R.T. criteria here. Humphrey (2018) suggests that the convention is that task-centred intervention should generally not exceed three months. Within this general timeframe for the overall intervention, each element will need to have its own timescale. Parker explains that once a course of action is agreed on, 'An important way of recording this is to negotiate a written agreement specifying exactly what will be done, who will do what, and when and how they will do it' (2017: 155). Timescales are generally acceptable as being practical in task-centred work; however, the use of contracts is a little more contentious.

Contracts are associated with contested areas of social work practice, such as managing parent and child contact or participation in a safeguarding assessment. In such situations, although the contracts are often not legally binding, they may be used to demonstrate the possible non-compliance of a person to a court or decision-making panel. When we think of contracts as authoritarian and disempowering agency tools, it seems counterintuitive to include them in a task-centred approach. The purpose of contracts in task-centred practice is not to evidence participation or manage behaviour, but to negotiate the nature of the intervention, and commit to goals and tasks, roles and timescales. The contract commits the social worker/agency as well as the person. A clearly structured contract based on the person's agenda can be an effective means to empower, provided that it is used openly and transparently. Quite simply, if the person does not 'own' the contract and view it as their document, then it is not fit for purpose in this type of practice.

AT NUMBER 6

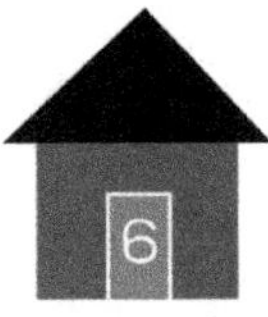

Sally's attitude towards social services is fairly ambivalent. She has known some good social workers, but then her daughter was placed into foster care and there is now a plan for her to be adopted, which has understandably really upset Sally. Sally thinks her leaving care social worker seems all right, but she doesn't trust her. She gets upset when this social worker suggests they agree a contract, because the last one led to her daughter being taken from her. The worker is patient and over four weeks helps Sally to identify her most pressing problem as her isolation due to her emotional distress at the pending adoption and lack of family contact. They agree a goal, which is for Sally to see her brother, who lives in London, and identify several tasks – to check her benefit entitlement, seek advice about the adoption process, identify her family members and contact her brother. This all seems a little daunting, and because she has begun to trust the social worker agrees a contract detailing who will do what, how it will be done and when it will be done.

EXERCISE 10.1

- Why do you think Sally is more responsive to this social worker?
- How do you think a contract will benefit Sally to meet her goal?
- What do you think should be included in the contract?

Agreeing required tasks

This is the central stage of this particular approach, where tasks are identified, negotiated and agreed in order to respond to the identified problems and work towards the agreed goals. The tasks need to be clear, connected to a goal and achievable. Say, for example, the identified problem is a young person overspending their limited income on fast food due to social isolation and boredom. An agreed goal may be to generate more funds, and buying a lottery ticket is an achievable task connected to this goal, but winning the lottery is not – it's about luck! A different agreed goal may be membership of a recreational group aimed at reducing social isolation, raising confidence and promoting active participation in activities. Negotiating tasks could involve identifying any surplus income or ways to cut expenditure, seeking out a recreational activity, sourcing transport to that activity, and joining an activity group. This all seems very simple, but it is not for many people; consider how difficult it may be to devise such a strategy if you have a learning disability, or have been the victim of violence. The skilled helper will focus on the person's abilities to help identify and negotiate agreed tasks:

> The practitioner must be particularly attuned to the process during this stage as the identification of appropriate tasks is absolutely crucial in enabling the service user to build confidence, independence and a sense of confidence. (Humphrey, 2018: 321)

Carrying out and achieving the tasks

Having agreed and negotiated a structure and a person-centred intervention, the next stage is to implement the planned tasks. This implementation stage is crucial in enabling lasting change for the individual. The process so far has ensured their active participation in the development of a plan they own and value as worthwhile. The process is very valuable; it is an enabling and learning activity that can be transferable. After all, task-centred practice was envisaged by Reid to reduce never-ending and poorly focused casework, which fostered dependency and had little success. During this stage, progress is monitored and any variations may lead to some adaptation of the plan, which should not be applied religiously. Rather, this approach is highly focused on the individual to promote their own plan of action.

Ending and evaluation

The stage at which the overall intervention will end is agreed in the contract and focused on from the beginning of the process. Alongside termination of the particular planned intervention, this stage incorporates a review and evaluation of the plan/contract, determining its success as well as the individual's progress in working in a task-centred fashion. Finally, the social worker can review and evaluate their role and performance during this particular intervention, perhaps using formal work-based or clinical supervision.

AT NUMBER 3

Maureen's social worker from the drug and alcohol treatment team used a task-centred approach to help Maureen identify, explore, prioritise and negotiate tasks to address her situation. Maureen was sceptical at first; everything had gone wrong and her situation was totally overwhelming. She found the contract that she co-produced with the social worker helped her to break things down into small tasks, rather than focus on huge problems. This made everything seem more achievable, and although the work was hard, Maureen got satisfaction from seeing her incremental progress. At the end of the agreed intervention period, she reviewed the goals with her social worker:

1. Overcome her painkiller addiction.

Maureen was on a reducing prescription and regularly attending Narcotics Anonymous. She was no longer buying medication over the internet.

2. Maintain her relationship with Claire.

Maureen, Claire and the children were still living together. Claire still found it hard to trust Maureen, and the couple were sleeping in separate rooms.

3. Address the debt.

Maureen had accessed debt counselling and received support to prioritise her debt and set up payment plans.

EXERCISE 10.2

- Is Maureen's situation resolved?
- Has the task-centred approach been effective? If so why?

SUMMARY

Task-centred approaches are used commonly in social work practice, although they are often employed in abbreviated ways, rather than following the full structure that we have set out in this chapter. Task-centred practice is underpinned by a commitment to empowerment and self-directed outcomes. If the central elements of collaboratively identifying goals and negotiating and co-producing tasks that work towards these are lost, then the model is reduced to professionals allocating people to-do lists. Task-centred practice developed from a sense that social work lacked focus and fostered dependency, so when we use this approach, it is critical that we ensure that it is empowering rather than oppressive.

11 STRENGTHS AND SOLUTION-FOCUSED INTERVENTIONS

Learning in this chapter relates to

PCF	KSS Adult Services	KSS Child & Family
2. Values & Ethics 4. Rights & Justice 5. Knowledge 7. Skills & Interventions	2. The role of social workers working with adults 3. Person-centred practice 4. Safeguarding 6. Effective assessments & outcome-based support planning 7. Direct work with individuals & families 8. Supervision, critical reflection & analysis	1. The role of child & family social work 2. Child development 5. Effective direct work with children & families 6. Child & family assessment 7. Analysis, decision making, planning & review 9. Professional ethics 10. The role of supervision & research

INTRODUCTION

Strengths-based approaches recognise that all people have the potential expertise to resolve personal and social issues, but some may need to collaborate with others in order to unlock this. Strengths-based approaches offer social workers the opportunity to be catalysts of change, working in empowering ways to promote people's agency and capitalise on their existing strengths. Solution-focused practice is a strengths perspective, which focuses particularly on resolution through optimism (Healy, 2014; Rogers et al., 2017). Combining the identification of strengths with the generation of solutions is a feature of many strengths-based interventions, e.g. the Signs of Safety child protection model (Turnell & Edwards, 1999). Focusing on strengths and solutions, rather than current or historic problems, empowers people by encouraging hope and suggesting ways forward. For social workers it can be enormously liberating to find *exceptions,* rather than becoming saturated with difficulties. This chapter describes how strengths and solution-focused approaches evolved, and then considers a range of different tools and techniques that can be employed in social work practice.

ORIGINS OF STRENGTHS-BASED APPROACHES

Traditionally, social work casework has taken a psychoanalytical approach to explore the history and development of a person's current difficulties in order to understand how to help them move forward. In contrast, strengths-based approaches seek to separate the problem from the person and look towards a resolution (Healy, 2012). Strengths-based approaches originated in North America, and a key influence was Bertha Capen Reynolds, an American social worker with the Maritime Union during the 1940s (Healy, 2014). Bertha was critical of the professionalisation of social work and its reliance on diagnosing and exploring social problems. She advocated for wellbeing through inclusivity and politicisation, and suggested that rather than problematising and pathologising people, practitioners should reflect on their accomplishments and strengths. Strengths-based approaches are underpinned by the philosophy that everyone has strengths and resources, and therefore rather than inputting entirely new mechanisms, practitioners should become attuned to the person's unique characteristics, skills and support systems, and amplify these. Simply put, a strengths-based approach seeks to identify what is going well, and do more of it.

Healy highlights how 'the strengths perspective insight that social work is based on a deficit model resonates with social workers across many countries' (2014: 165). In the UK, strengths perspectives have been adopted in childcare social work through the Signs of Safety model (Turnell & Edwards, 1999), and in adult care through initiatives like 'Think Local Act Personal' (TLAP, 2018). The Department of Health recognises the influence of strength-based practice in adult social care, and its connection to the professional values and ethos of social work:

> A strengths-based social work approach to working with adults is not yet a fully formed set of ideas and the evidence base for some more recent models is still emerging. However, strengths-based practice is not a new concept and reflects the core principles at the heart of the social work profession. (Department of Health, 2017: 6)

Coulshed and Orme concur:

> ... this approach is seen to resonate with social work, drawing on the values of both individualisation and empowerment. It starts from the premise that there is always something working in people's lives and that service users have underutilized resources to deal with problems. (2012: 164)

PRINCIPLES OF STRENGTHS-BASED PRACTICE

Saleeby (2013) identifies six basic principles of strengths-based practice, which affirm the potential for strengths and resources available to individuals both personally and within their social and community networks:

1. All people have strengths, capacities and resources.
2. Adversity, though potentially harmful, may be the source of strengths.
3. Don't assume limitations of people and communities.
4. Collaboration is best.
5. Environments (e.g. communities and families) are abundant with resources.
6. Social work is concerned with care and hope.

AT NUMBER 6

Sally was four years old when she came to the attention of social services. Her mother, Anna, had addiction problems and was arrested for seriously assaulting a teacher. Sally was initially placed in foster care, then following a social work assessment and a court order, placed for adoption with a couple who already had two children. The care plan appeared to be very successful; all the outcomes were being met, and Sally appeared to have settled into living with her new family. However, before the adoption order was granted the couple split up and therefore withdrew from the adoption. Sally was told she would have to move into a foster home because she 'hadn't settled'. She didn't understand this, because she had felt very settled, and was very upset to be leaving.

After moving from the adopters, the next foster family asked for Sally to move because they felt unable to cope with her behaviour. She experienced a number of placement changes over the years, living with different foster carers and occasionally in a residential home, and was described as 'hard to place'. She eventually settled down with a single carer who had adopted two other children. Sally asked if she could adopt her too. The foster carer explained she would love to, but adopting her would end the income she earned through fostering.

Throughout these years of different placements, Sally had occasional and intermittent contact with Anna. Sally has told her social worker she loves Anna, but knows she can't live with her because 'she won't be able to cope with me – no one else can'. Sally is devastated now that her own baby is being placed for adoption, and wonders if her life would have been different if she had been adopted. No one ever told her that the people who planned to adopt her split up; she has always believed that she did something wrong.

EXERCISE 11.1

Reflect on Sally's childhood experience and consider how decisions were made about her care plan. Try to identify any intended outcomes for Sally and compare these with the actual outcomes.

What strengths does Sally have which could help her in her current situation?

Origins of solution-focused approaches

Building on the concept of strengths, brief solution-focused therapy emerged from the Milwaukee Brief Family Therapy Centre through work by Steve de Shazer and Insoo Kim Berg (de Shazer, 1982; Sklare, 1997). They observed psychotherapy sessions and noted that they tended to consist of a predetermined number of sessions (a 'course' of therapy) which followed a deficit-based approach of problem exploration. De Shazer and Berg set about devising a strengths-based, time-bound approach, which would last only as long as needed, and focus on goals without necessarily exploring the history of problems (de Shazer, 1991). A central component of their early work considered the role of the therapist in creating a conversation, which could help people to talk about their preferred future, rather than looking back.

APPLYING SOLUTION-FOCUSED PRACTICE

Solution-focused practice helps us to promote change because focusing on solutions rather than problems creates optimism, and identifying personal assets and achievements creates an expectation of further success (Healy, 2014). The practitioner relinquishes any claims to expertise and strives to establish shared recognition with the person that no problem, however pervasive or difficult, is constantly experienced. Two questions arise from this stance:

1. Why and when does this issue become a problem?
2. What stops the problem from being ever-present?

Helping the person to respond to these questions enables them to find their own, already formed, coping strategies and solutions by identifying *exceptions,* when their behaviour and actions have produced desired outcomes (Shennan, 2014). The solution-focused brief therapy (SFBT) approach offers the practitioner a range of potential tools to use:

> Whilst the SFBT model offers a specific approach, the range of techniques contained within the solution-focused practitioner's toolkit has much to offer social work practice. (Rogers et al., 2017: 194)

Shennan (2014) sums up the solution-focused process in three elements:

- Starting with what the client wants.
- Describing what is wanted in detail.
- Describing progress towards the desired future.

A strong aspect of solution-focused practice is its practical application:

> ... since its earliest days, solution-focused practice has always been a pragmatic approach that is best grasped by seeing it done and by doing it. (Gollins et al., 2016: 11)

This pragmatic approach is helpful in our practice because it frees practitioners from adopting a particularly onerous therapeutically or process-laden approach. Social work is theory-driven but is a practically applied profession. Many students and practitioners who have received training in applying a solution-focused approach are immediately impressed by its practice potential, but others argue it has limitations when confronted by risk.

AUTHOR'S EXPERIENCE (PHIL)

A student social worker accompanied me on a visit to a foster carer, and afterwards asked, 'What did you do? You did nothing.' I felt a little challenged by this comment. I had worked with these carers for some time. During the visit, the carer told me about difficulties they had experienced the previous week with a young person they were looking after. We discussed how he had felt at the time (pretty stressed), and how he felt now (all right). I validated him for finding a good solution, which had resolved the problem, and everyone was happy – except for the student. She told me that her parents fostered, and would have contacted their social worker for support with such an issue as soon as it arose. I explained that the carers knew they could contact me if they required my support, but said I was pleased that they had found their own solution and not deemed this necessary.

When the student successfully completed her placement and was about to leave, I rather nervously enquired what she thought of my practice. She surprised me and said, 'I didn't particularly like you to begin with, I thought you were a skiver.' Well, I had asked! She then went on, 'I realised you do work hard, by helping and allowing carers and children find their own solutions.' She told me that her mother was a very experienced carer, but did not dare to act without consulting her supervising social worker. In the end, I think she appreciated my strengths-based and solution-focused approach.

Shennan (2014) makes some helpful suggestions about how to construct solution-focused questions:

- Get straight to the point and be focused – *seek to create an immediate focus for the conversation.*
- Include the client's words when constructing questions – *try to use the client's words when constructing questions.*
- Use plurals as a general rule and then ask 'what else?' – *It's useful to think of plurals and to help the client to extend their self-awareness as they make progress.*
- Direct the person's attention to their life outside the session – *solution-focused practitioners concentrate on the client's life outside of the session.*
- Allow yourself to amend questions, while in the process of asking them – *rather than asking the same question, seek to find the most useful/straightforward question.*
- Move from the general to the specific – *aim to move from a general question, such as 'how are you' to a specific question such as 'can you explain how you felt about…'.*
- Keep it simple and minimal – *focus on the client's answers rather than the practitioner's perspective.*
- Ask how the person gets through, not into, problems – *focus on the person's solutions and not problems.*

Exceptions and instances

Exceptions, instances or micro-solutions are occasions when the problem the person has experienced was absent. Shennan describes how in creating their brief solution-focused approach, Steve de Shazer and Insoo Kim Berg took the 'simple yet revolutionary step of finding exceptions to the problems instead and helping them to happen more often' (Shennan, 2014: 75). In Shennen's version of solution-focused practice, *instances* is used instead of exceptions. Essentially exceptions (or instances) identify what is working in the person's life. We all experience them, but most of the time we pay little attention to them, and tend to be fixated on the things which do not go so well. You may find pleasure reading, gardening, driving, running etc., and notice that during this time you do not focus on any problems or problematic memories. This is an exception on which you can build.

Identifying exceptions means they can be replicated. Exceptions are categorised into two basic types:

- The *deliberate exception* – for which the person is/was responsible. Something the person did or did not do which alleviated the problem. Deliberate exceptions represent the seeds of possible solutions.
- *Spontaneous exceptions* – for which the person is not responsible. These spontaneous exceptions may have resulted from another person's actions or have happened by chance. Spontaneous exceptions may be important particularly when they are predictable, e.g. the exception may be due to a friend's visit refocusing the person away from their problem. This could be predictable, and when exceptions are predictable, the activity can be reproduced to repeat the exception (Parton & O'Byrne, 2000).

AT NUMBER 4

Olivia has been feeling down since the ending of her relationship and her children have been getting on her nerves. She decided to contact the social worker from the Children with Disabilities team who had been involved with Georgia in the past. The team primarily concentrates on safeguarding issues. Olivia explained she was finding life difficult, and while the social worker did not feel there were any current safeguarding concerns, she did consider the deteriorating situation to be a risk, and organised an appointment with Olivia in a couple of weeks. With the appointment arranged, Olivia found that her mood changed and she felt less irritable and worried. As the appointment neared, she felt a little silly and decided it would be better to cancel it. She rang the social worker who asked what had changed. Olivia explained that she didn't really know, but she just felt less pessimistic generally, and where she had previously dreaded the children returning home from school, now she looked forward to it.

EXERCISE 11.2

Why do you think Olivia's mood changed and how would you have reacted as the social worker?

STRENGTHS-BASED AND SOLUTION-FOCUSED TOOLS FOR PRACTICE

Strengths-based and solution-focused approaches are attractive to social workers because they speak directly to our core social work values of empowerment, anti-oppressive practice, and respecting and valuing diversity and unique experience. They are also very accessible, because many derive from solution-focused brief therapy (SFBT), a strengths-based approach that was deliberately designed as a practice method, and is therefore not overwhelmingly theoretically driven. In this section, we provide an overview of the range of highly useful tools and techniques available to social workers.

Motivational interviewing

We have talked a great deal already about the need for social workers to actively and creatively engage with people to achieve change. Prochaska and DiClemente's Stages of Change Model (1983) describes five stages that people go through on their way to change (see Figure 11.1).

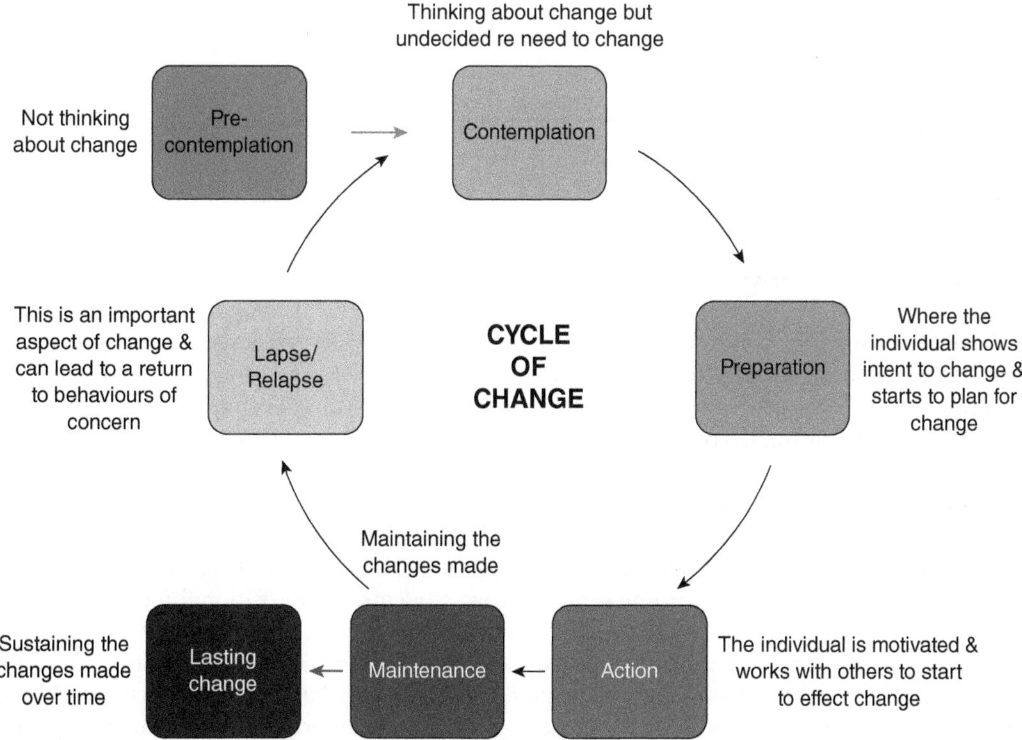

Figure 11.1 The Stages of Change Model

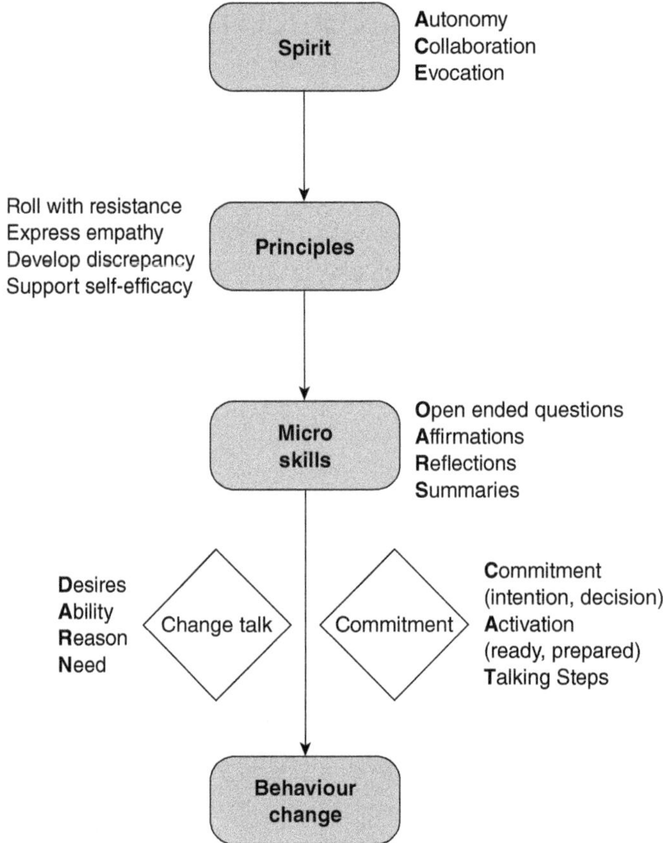

Figure 11.2 The MI Framework

Motivational Interviewing (MI) is an intervention model that views resistance as a normal response to ambivalence (see Figure 11.2). Change is scary, and if the person does not clearly understand the need for it or the potential benefits, then they are extremely unlikely to engage in it. Rather than externally motivating change through coercion, persuasion, confrontation or ultimatum (e.g. the threatened loss of family or home), MI seeks to elicit motivation from within the person, through a conversation which identifies values and goals. Miller and Rollnick (2013) describe it as a collaborative conversation style for strengthening a person's motivation to change. It is often used when working with addictions, though it has been suggested MI could successfully be applied in a wide range of social work settings because it relates to professional values of co-production and relationship-based practice (Watson, 2011).

A North American study on training social work students in motivational interviewing conducted by Greeno et al. (2017) concluded that an understanding of MI promoted empathic behaviours as well as a belief in the strengths of people using services. Hohman et al. (2015) refer to MI as an evidence-based communication method employed to encourage change. In their student-based study, they concluded that teaching MI to social work students significantly raised their skill set. The research evidence appears to promote the validity of applying MI to practice, at least because it affects practitioners' and students' skills and promotes a more positive value base.

The Three Houses

The Three Houses tool was designed in 2003 by Weld and Greening in New Zealand as a practical tool for social workers to gather children and their families' perspectives (Weld, 2008). By using three separate houses (see Figure 11.3) the practitioner can help children and their families to explore their lives and focus on danger and harm, safety factors and their hopes and dreams. This tool also provides a visually accessible means to help parents recognise their strengths, hopes, dreams, and vulnerabilities, and to identify a future of possibility which helps to build greater safety. The version of the tool that is applied with children is shown in Figure 11.3

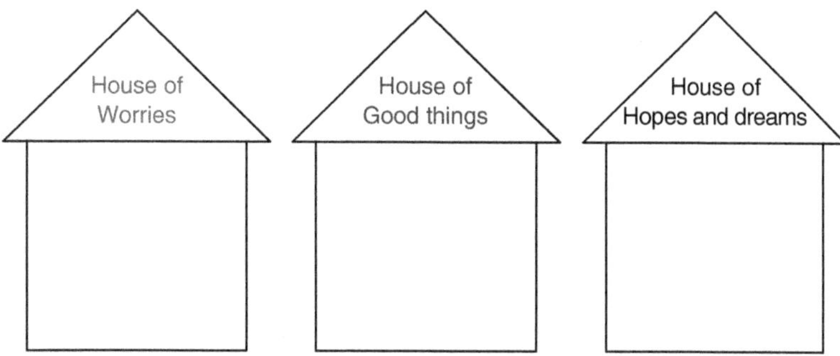

Figure 11.3 The Three Houses approach

The Three Houses has been widely used by different approaches, for instance Signs of Safety (see below) during assessment, the USA Safety-Organized Practice framework for day-to-day child welfare casework and Munro (2011) recommended it as a practical tool in her review of child protection.

Signs of Safety

Signs of Safety (SoS) was created in Western Australia during the 1990s by Turnell and Edwards (1999) in their work on child protection. It draws upon techniques from Solution Focused Brief Therapy and is based on the use of strengths-based interview techniques. The model seeks to foster a shared focus during child protection work through working collaboratively and in partnership with families and children. Working collaboratively through SoS, risk assessments and action plans are co-produced, focusing on the family's strengths, resources and networks to increase safety and reduce risk and danger. The SoS model has continued to evolve since the 1990s and has been adopted in many English local authorities as well as internationally to respond to practice situations (Turnell, 2012), so that:

> [there is] no single prescribed right way to apply the approach. Each time a child protection worker uses the Signs of Safety model in the field and then describes his/her endeavours, the approach continues to evolve. (Signs of Safety, n.d.)

The Department of Education evaluation by Baginsky et al. (2017) of SoS child protection practice in English local authorities explains SoS risk assessment and planning are based on:

1. Working relationships.
2. Stance of critical inquiry, fostering critical thinking.
3. Locating grand aspirations in everyday practice.

The objective of SoS is to be able to identify and quantify the strengths and risks in child protection. Through applying SoS, the Government of Western Australia and the English Department of Education (Baginsky, 2017) sets out three questions to be considered:

1. What are we worried about?
2. What's working well?
3. What needs to happen?

Having considered these three questions, professionals and parents use a scale of 0–10 to scale the current situation.

Children are central to child protection, and hence SoS adopts various different tools to gather opinions from children, including the Three Houses Tool, Wizards and Fairies Tool, Safety House Tool, and Words and Pictures.

AT NUMBER 2

Childcare services became involved with Jasmine and Jamie following a police referral concerning domestic violence and the arrest of their mother's partner. Education professionals had concerns and after medical reports indicated substance misuse, the mother acknowledged she was using heroin. Childcare services convened an SoS meeting to reflect on the children's welfare. Prior to the meeting, a social worker worked directly with Jasmine and Jamie to ascertain their perspectives and views. Adopting a Three Houses approach, the social worker observed that both children loved their mother and dreamt of living with her in a big house. They had different worries, with Jamie concerned about his mother's well-being whilst Jasmine was far more worried about her own welfare. The SoS identified strengths were that: maternal love was not in doubt, and there was some family support. However, there were considerable concerns around relationships, adult violence, substance misuse, parenting capacity and debt. The family support was insufficient to allay these concerns, and it was agreed with the mother that the children would be accommodated to allow her to seek help for her substance misuse, and social workers to complete assessments of parenting capacity and the children's needs. Jasmine and Jamie were placed in foster care with Alfie and Suzie.

EXERCISE 11.3

What are the strengths and limitations of applying the three SoS questions (what worries, what's working and what needs to happen) with this family?

The SoS model does not have a set period of intervention; it can be used in a single session or for longer-term work. Whilst the model is most widely used in child protection, its application in practice extends beyond this. SoS offers an ethically attractive position by promoting parental engagement through focusing on future safety, recognising potential parental competence, and it includes the parents – along with the children – in the decision-making process.

APPRECIATIVE INQUIRY

Appreciative inquiry is a strengths-based, solution-focused model originating in the business world, which seeks to harness the potential of people and engage them in self-determined change. Perceptions that problem-solving approaches may be hampering organisational change and innovation led to the development of appreciative inquiry at Case Western Reserve University (Cooperrider & Srivastva, 1987). Bushe claims that it has 'revolutionized the field of organization development and was a precursor to the rise of positive organization studies and the strengths based movement in American management' (2013: 41). Cooperrider and Srivastva (1987) describe their model as inquiry into the art of the possible (see Figure 11.4). Premised on the assumption that in every system, and for every person, something works, this approach begins with appreciation by asking people to describe and explain those moments that activate their competencies and energies, e.g. by asking the question 'What is the best thing that has happened to you today?'

Appreciative inquiry asks the following questions:

- What works?
- What are the circumstances that enable this?
- What possibilities are there to build on this?
- What if we could make these circumstances the norm rather than the exception?

The knowledge created through appreciative inquiry can then be used, applied and validated in action. There are five principles to appreciative inquiry, which are:

1. The constructionist principle – recognition that we co-create stories and truths together with our words.
2. The poetic principle – we will find what we choose to look for, i.e. the good, the bad and whatever we focus on we will magnify.
3. The simultaneity principle – change begins when we ask a question. Our questions determine the direction of the outcome.
4. The anticipatory principle – we create mental pictures of the future, which influence what happens.
5. The positive principle – focusing on positives creates upward spirals.

Appreciative inquiry has been applied by practitioners in a variety of social work contexts. Gomez et al. (2014) argue that appreciative inquiry reflects social work's historical guiding principles of social justice and empowerment as it is 'a system of questions characterized by a questioning attitude that looks for the potential of the person' (Gómez et al., 2014: 115). They contend that an appreciative approach applied with a psychosocial inquiry may make the performance of social workers more effective. Reflecting on what works can create new

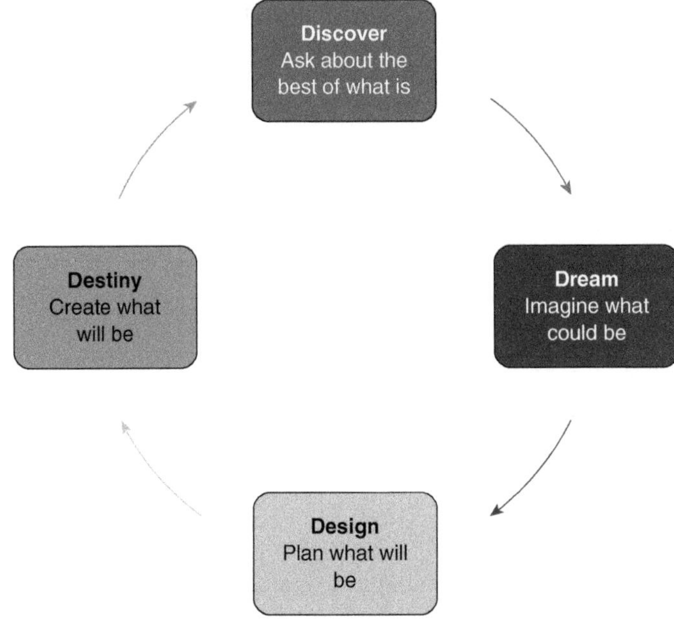

Figure 11.4 Cycle of appreciative inquiry

narratives, which appreciate accomplishments and strengths, and identify and activate dormant skills. They also identify that appreciative inquiry is rooted in constructivist and postmodern philosophical approaches, building on existing, well-established theories and employing interactive language to construct positive narratives that can empower the people who use social care services (Gómez et al., 2014). These new stories suggest possibilities, which extend into actions that people can transfer to other, more problematic areas of their lives.

It has been suggested that appreciative inquiry can promote social work knowledge and research by reflecting on examples of good practice in supporting student practice learning (Bellinger & Elliott, 2011). Bellinger and Elliott consider appreciative inquiry a robust research methodology, with the potential for research activity to promote a cultural shift as well as achieve positive change. Research in Practice for Adults (RiPfA) published an adult safeguarding tool incorporating appreciative inquiry to help make professional decisions and formulate action plans (Elliott, 2015), and a similar tool has been produced for child protection (Martins, 2014). Both of these RiP tools identify that the basic elements of appreciative inquiry are to:

- explore essential features of participants' experience of existing best practice;
- collectively develop a shared vision of most desirable practice for the future;
- work together to develop, design and create this practice, with changes occurring from the very first question asked.

Through appreciative inquiry, Elliott (2015) and Martins (2014) suggest that social services could experience structural change away from a deficit organisational model focused on practice mistakes to refocus on what works well. They also suggest that appreciative inquiry can help to ensure that the perspectives of children and families are incorporated within service improvements (Martins, 2014). Appreciative inquiry has been adopted by many local authorities and social work teams. For example, in West Sussex County Council a team of practitioners write down their successes, and place these in a 'Jar of Joys' to see their good work filling it up, and catalogue examples they can draw on to assist in other situations (Watkins, 2017).

VIDEO INTERACTION GUIDANCE (VIG)

Video Interaction Guidance (VIG) is a strengths-based intervention involving reflection on recorded video clips of positive interactions. During VIG, people are supported to watch selected clips of 'better than usual' interactions, and then engage in a collaborative, mediated dialogue, which reflects on their successes:

> Video interaction guidance is an intervention where the client is guided to reflect on video clips of their own successful interventions. The process begins by helping the family or professional to negotiate their own goals. Asking them what it is they want to change helps to ensure that they are engaged on the process. Adult-child interactions are then filmed and edited, to produce a short film that focuses on the positive. (Association for Video Interaction Guidance UK, n.d.)

VIG is specifically a programme of parent counselling that uses video to help parents/adults become more attuned and responsive to their child's verbal and non-verbal communication. In the UK, the Association of Video Interaction Guidance UK (AVIGuk) provides specialist accredited training. VIG has been successfully applied by the NSPCC in situations when there were initial child neglect concerns, with parents finding it a positive experience that left them more able to understand their children (Whalley & Williams, 2015). A study on the implementation of VIG in an autism support agency found that staff were initially reticent as they believed it would be critical of their practice, but once they experienced VIG, their feedback was extremely positive (Hall et al., 2016). The same study, however, also found that organisational cultures were not receptive to creative interventions; implementation of learning through VIG requires management support, and is not a quick fix solution.

AUTHOR'S EXPERIENCE (PHIL)

While attending a support group for men caring for autistic children, a father talked about his partner's experience of VIG. He was very enthusiastic and explained that watching examples of her positive interactions with her autistic son had reassured her that she was able to communicate with him. The father told me that the VIG practitioner had helped his partner to identify her strengths, where previously she had only seen her shortcomings, and this had increased her confidence and enabled her to build on the successful interactions with her son.

THE THREE CONVERSATIONS

This model was developed by Partners4Change (Partners4Change, n.d.), a social care consultancy firm that works with local authorities to deliver personalisation. Their aim was to create an alternative to traditional, pro-forma based assessment and care planning, which would facilitate a more collaborative approach between social workers and people who require social care services. Partners4Change explained that 'The 3 conversations model is a great way of delivering on the demands and opportunities of the Care Act 2014' (Partners4Change, n.d.). The three conversations are as follows.

Conversation 1 – Most initial situations

How can I connect you to things that will help you get on with your life – based on your assets and strengths, and those of your family and neighbourhood? What do you want to do? What can I connect you to?

Conversation 2 – Applicable to people who are at risk

What needs to change to make you safe? How do I help to make that happen? What offers do I have at my disposal – including small amounts of money and my knowledge of the community – to support you? How can I pull these together in an 'emergency plan' and stay with you to make sure it works?

Conversation 3 – What is a fair personal budget and where do the sources of funding come from?

What does a good life look like? How can I help you use your resources to support your chosen life? Who do you want to be involved in good support planning?

This model is a collaborative and strengths-based approach, which seeks to value people who use services and empower them to make informed choice about the services they receive.

> The 'three conversations model' provides a set of tools to enable our committed, principled and skilled workforce to have conversations based on what people want to tell us, not what we want to ask them. It makes us see them as people (not clients, service users or even customers), reminding us they are often part of a family neighbourhood and community. (Partners4Change, 2016)

A *Community Care* article reported on Cambridgeshire's integrated learning disability team's adoption of the Three Conversations, and positively concluded that 'no one [in the team] wants to go back to the way we were working before' (Kirin, 2016).

AT NUMBER 1

Mary's long-term unstable diabetes caused peripheral artery disease (PAD) which was tremendously painful and began to affect her mobility. Eventually Mary had to give up the job she loved running the community centre's cafe.

EXERCISE 11.4

Which of the three conversations would apply if you were working with Mary? Why?

FAMILY GROUP CONFERENCING

Family group conferencing was developed in New Zealand during work with members of the Maori community (Ashley & Nixon, 2007; Harris & White, 2013) and has since been adopted internationally in over 20 countries. The approach has many applications in child welfare situations, and is frequently used by the NSPCC and the Children and Family Court Advisory and Support Service (CAFCAS) to resolve disputes following parental separation (NSPCC, 2009b). More recently, it has begun to be applied in adult contexts, including mental health (de Jong and Schout, 2011) and adult safeguarding, where Hobbs and Alonzi (2013) suggest that it can promote choice and control alongside protection from abuse and harm.

Family Group Conferencing is a voluntary, family-led, decision-making approach. The conference takes place on neutral ground and is facilitated by a trained practitioner, providing a safe and controlled environment for people whose relationships may be quite strained, in which they are empowered to take control of their situations (ADASS, 2011; Cass, 2011). This approach enables a child's or adult's family, friends and community members – and if appropriate, the child or adult – to use their pooled knowledge and experience to identify risks and formulate strategies (Hobbs and Alonzi, 2013), e.g. by highlighting strengths and assets not readily identifiable to professionals. Professionals involved with the family attend the first half of the conference, and then they and the facilitator withdraw, giving the family ownership of the decisions made (Pennell and Anderson, 2005). The family creates a plan, and provided it is safe, are supported by the professionals to implement it.

Brief solution-focused formula first session task

This exercise was devised by de Shazer and Molnar when working with a family who were saturated in difficulty and could only vaguely describe their situation. They told the family members:

> Between now and next time we meet, we want you to observe, so that you can tell us next time, what happens in your (life, marriage, family or relationship) that you want to continue to have happen. (de Shazer and Molnar, 1984, in Shennan, 2014: 77)

This exercise represents an appreciative inquiry, and it helped the family turn their situation around by being able to concretely describe positive changes and behaviours. The exercise was successfully applied when working with other families and individuals too. Critically, de Shazer and his team observed that this positive change occurred *before* therapeutic sessions:

> 'A client who, in a first session, had been describing a problem as deep-rooted and seemingly intractable mentioned, almost as an afterthought, improvements in the three days leading up to the session. (Shennan, 2014: 77)

This task is clearly an important one in the evolution of solution-focused brief therapy, because it helped de Shazer and his colleagues identify people as their own self-experts who already possess the solutions to their problems. The therapist's task is to facilitate the location of these solutions through finding exceptions or micro-solutions to be replicated. This is a very straightforward exercise, which social workers can use to help people think about their lives and relationships.

The miracle question

This key solution-focused technique is also simple to apply in social work practice. The miracle question is expressed along the lines of:

> Imagine yourself in bed tonight and while you are asleep a miracle happens and all your problems have magically gone away. Because you are asleep you are not aware of this miracle and do not know all your problems have gone. When you wake up what will be the first signs for you that the miracle has happened?

The aim of this exercise is to encourage the person to imagine a brighter, more positive future. The exercise seeks to identify problems and then creates the scenario of sleeping and miracle to magic the problem away – the main question is, What solved the problem? This miracle question helps the person imagine the world without the problem, a life without therapy, and acts as a process of goal setting and finding solutions. While this remains a useful question to help focus someone on solution finding, Shennan (2014) points out it is now used less frequently by solution-focused practitioners because many people are able to make the shift to a desired tomorrow without recourse to a miracle question. However, he also points out that it remains a useful technique to employ when a person finds this shift to thinking about a brighter future difficult. We suggest that for many social work practitioners this question is a useful tool which we may only rarely use, but one which can be refreshing and may act as a good starting point when working with a particularly stressed person.

AT NUMBER 5

When Samantha attends a carer support group, the social worker asked her to imagine a miracle while she is asleep that makes all of her worries disappear. He then asked Samantha what had changed once she woke from her sleep. Samantha said Max was healthy. Since the carer's group, Samantha has thought a lot about the miracle question and feels guilty because she lied. She did not imagine Max was healthy, she had in fact imagined she was living with someone she could share her life with who was not Max. While on the surface their relationship had appeared happy, Max had actually been very controlling and on occasion violent. Samantha often fantasised about leaving Max, but didn't because she worried about how this would affect Tyra. Now, after Max's stroke, she feels she can't ever leave him.

EXERCISE 11.5

We may well expect positive scenarios and feel solution-focused practice is straightforward when in fact it is not.

How do you think a solution-focused approach can help Samantha?

AUTHOR'S EXPERIENCE (CAT)

The miracle question is a tool I used a great deal in my practice with people who were experiencing thoughts of suicide. Solution-focused tools are very helpful at times when people are completely consumed by the difficulty of their lives and find it almost impossible to have hope. Although it is critical to recognise and validate how a person is currently feeling, exploring their precipitating problems is rarely helpful. It is likely that ruminating on their problems will have contributed to their current feelings of hopelessness. Sensitively using the miracle question can help the person step outside of their problems – albeit only briefly – and imagine a hypothetical recovery. The miracle question does not provide a miracle solution, but it can be a key tool in a positive engagement that helps someone feel less alone, and in realising that there may be alternative solutions.

Scaling questions

This is another very practical and versatile tool for social work practitioners. Scaling questions can be used in a wide range of scenarios. Quite simply you ask the person to put their scale on a problem, such as:

> 'On a scale of one to ten, ten being very high, how much does this situation upset you?'

You can rephrase the question scenario to for instance:

> 'How do you feel?' or 'How do you manage?'

The list is quite expansive and you can apply different numerical scales, e.g. 1–3.

A useful comparison can be drawn when the same scaling question is asked twice over a period of time. For instance, it could be asked at each contact and if there is any variation, the social worker can ask the person why they think this is. Although it is a cliché, things do usually improve over time. Using scaling questions can enable people to recognise this as they see yesterday's 9 become today's 6 and tomorrow's 2. The social worker has not directly improved the situation; the person has found ways of tolerating or adjusting to it. However, using comparative scaling questions helps the person articulate their progress, and the social worker can then support them to identify how they have coped.

AUTHOR'S EXPERIENCE (PHIL)

I attended a solution-focused teaching session as part of a post-qualifying social work module. I immediately saw the potential of using this approach and some of its techniques with foster carers and young people. To be honest, I became almost messianic about solution-focused brief therapy! My visits to foster carers became much more fulfilling when they were focused on strengths and solutions rather than problems. When a foster carer telephoned to advise me a child's placement had broken down, I used a scaling question to ask how bad the situation was and she exclaimed that it was 11 out of 10 and the child had to move NOW. I calmly arranged a visit for the next day and she told me she would hang on until then. When I arrived at her house the next day, the carer's perspective had changed, and she seemed to have almost forgotten she had requested the child to move. When I brought it up, she told me she wanted the child to stay. I asked her to scale how she felt about the situation now, and she told me not to be daft, everything was all right. The situation had shifted from 11 to less than zero overnight because the carer had created her own solution. The child remained in the placement until she was old enough to live independently, and then nominated the carer for an award.

SUMMARY

Strengths perspectives emerged to counter deficit-based models of intervention, which tend to pathologise individuals. We have given an overview of multiple time-limited and cost-effective strengths-based techniques, many of which social workers can employ without the need for specific training. Strengths-based practice shifts power and agency from the professional to the individual. By working in a less directive and more facilitative way, we can empower people to recognise and activate their own strengths, resources and strategies. Creative solutions to issues are generated, and this positive, self-generated resolution engenders greater confidence and self-reliance, reducing the future need for professional involvement. Social workers can feel uneasy about stepping back from their traditional leadership role, but it is important that we question these feelings. Strengths-based approaches have application even in situations where the stakes are high, although they may well need to be an element of the intervention rather than its main focus.

12 WORKING WITH GROUPS AND GROUP WORK

Learning in this chapter relates to

PCF	KSS Adult Services	KSS Child & Family
5. Knowledge 6. Critical Reflection & Analysis 7. Skills & Interventions 9. Professional Leadership	2. The role of social workers working with adults 3. Person-centred practice 7. Direct work with individuals & families 10. Professional ethics & leadership	1. The role of child & family social work 5. Effective direct work with children & families 7. Analysis, decision making, planning & review

INTRODUCTION

Social work has made a marked shift away from traditional group work, but in this chapter we suggest that awareness of theoretical perspectives and skills in working with groups is very much relevant to contemporary practice. Awareness of how to work with groups is important, even when not undertaking group work, because social workers operate within multiple groups – families, multidisciplinary teams, group supervisions. Working within groups and teams involves negotiation; therefore, we seek to support students and practitioners to develop confidence and competence in working with groups by detailing group-working skills and providing guidance on different techniques. Finally, we consider the rationale for using group work skills, informally and formally, during professional practice.

HISTORY OF GROUP WORK

The development of what we know as group work originated during the nineteenth century through the emergence of youth work and settlement work in North America. Andrews (2001) reflects on three particular periods of group work in North America; firstly, the formation of a group work association in the 1930s; secondly, the merger into the National Association of Social Workers during the 1950s; and thirdly, the rebirth of group work during the 1970s. In the United States group work became increasingly associated with the professionalisation of social work between the 1930s (Hansan, 2011) and 1950s when it was popularised by characters such as Gertrude Wilson and Gisela Konopka (Andrews, 2001). In the UK, group work was championed during the 1960s by youth and community work as an element of community development and community functioning, and became associated with social action and the collectivist approach through the *social group worker.* During this time, group work was seen as a purposeful activity that involved a process which considered the individual in the group, the group as a whole and the larger community. Andrews suggests that it 'was not until its affiliation with social work that it [group work] became defined as a method of social work practice' (2001: 48).

Indeed Andrews, amongst others, argues that group work tends to be a specialism within social work. In North America, group work vied with casework, which was more widely practised. Group work, which was less popular amongst practitioners, sought validity by assimilating elements of casework, and became less concerned with social action and more focused on clinical practice. During the generic trend in social work, specialisms like group work practice meant that group work practitioners experienced a loss of identity as they were subsumed into social work in general (Andrews, 2001). Andrews suggests that many social work programmes do not include in-depth training on group work, though she argues there has been an upturn in practitioners using group work skills and concludes that:

> While 'social group worker' is seldom the term applied to a professional position, many social workers (often with no training in philosophy and practice of the group work process) spend a substantial amount of their jobs facilitating groups. (2001: 63)

A review of the literature on traditional group work education in social work suggests that students are not being provided with the knowledge, skills and evidence of group work practice (LaRocque, 2017).

AUTHOR'S EXPERIENCE (PHIL)

As an experienced practitioner and trainer, but new lecturer, I was asked to develop a new module on intervention. The programme leader reviewed my content and liked everything except the session I intended to deliver on group work.

(Continued)

> She said that social workers just don't do group work any more, and suggested that I replace the session with a different intervention. When I was reviewing the module in preparation for the next academic year, the same programme leader asked me if I could include a session on group work as many students had fed back that they were convening groups during practice placements and did not feel prepared for this. Whilst there are undoubtedly 'trends' in social work practice, it is really important to think flexibly about what different approaches can offer and how they can be applied. "

Social work increasingly operates within schools and many social work students complete practice learning within school or college. It has been suggested that group work can help reinvigorate therapeutic social work, which has been in decline for some time through behavioural, relationship and support programmes delivered in schools (Sheppard & Clibbens, 2015). It seems that group work skills are important for contemporary practitioners though group work per se is less fashionable.

WHAT IS A GROUP?

At face value this question would seem to be pretty obvious, a group is more than two persons. The dictionary definition of a group is 'any collection or assemblage of persons or things; cluster; aggregation' and 'a number of persons or things ranged or considered together as being related in some way' (Dictionary.com). However, Lindsay and Orton suggest it may be difficult to arrive at a concrete definition of a group because 'groups do not exist necessarily as separate definable entities' (Lindsay & Orton, 2014: 3). Healy offers a more numerical approach by explaining that:

> [a] group refers to a collection of at least three people who identify as part of a group, share a common purpose or task related to that group, and who relate to each other to achieve this common purpose. (2012: 137)

Coulshed and Orme explain that:

> group membership extends beyond the time that the members spend together; it involves a commitment and loyalty which arises out of the individual's interaction with group members and the group leader(s)/group facilitator. (2012: 235)

This shared purpose is important. Groups are essentially a number of people with some shared sense of identity, whether formally or informally constituted.

AUTHOR'S EXPERIENCE (PHIL)

I facilitated a support group for parents and carers of children diagnosed on the autism spectrum. A man attending for the first time asked, 'Is this to do with how I manage my child's behaviour?' I advised him that this was not the primary purpose of the group, although we sometimes discussed behaviour and management techniques. He said, 'My social worker sent me – do I have to be here?' I told him it was entirely up to him, and I would not report back to children's social care services or any other body on whether he attended or not. This father did not see himself as part of this group and he left, exercising his right to decline membership.

AT NUMBER 6

Liam and Sally initially met through a small group for young people aged between 13 and 16 who were looked after by the local authority. The group met weekly for six weeks. The social workers facilitating the group, Lloyd and Bekki, prepared a programme focused on identity, health, relationships, sex education and finances. The first session concentrated on introductions and ground rules. Sally attended the group because she wanted to access information on sex and relationships. Liam attended the group because participants were paid £10 each session to produce training materials for future groups. After much debate and argument, the group agreed to make a video including raps. At first, Liam and Sally didn't get on, but as the weeks went by, they grew accustomed to each other. During the final session, the group agreed to carry on meeting every month as a support group.

EXERCISE 12.1

- What are three benefits/strengths of this type of group?
- What challenges/difficulties do you think Lloyd and Bekki might have experienced in attending the group?
- Can you identify the formal and informal elements to this group?

Knight and Gitterman (2017) suggest that group work practice in the community can present an opportunity to integrate micro (individual) and macro (community) interventions. Healy (2012) identifies the range of group types relating to social work practice as:

- *Group psychotherapy*, which often complements individual counselling and is based on a particular model such as Gestalt or Jungian therapy.
- *Group counselling* whereby members learn and explore shared experiences.
- *Behaviour change groups* focused on enabling members to explore and address certain behaviours, such as aggression.
- *Psychoeducational groups* to develop members' knowledge and skills to address a particular opportunity or challenge they may experience.
- *Support groups* to promote peer support through a group with members who share a common challenge.
- *Self-help groups* that seek to build on members' capacity to address a common challenge. This type of group is managed and facilitated by members and differs from a support group which is managed by a facilitator.
- *Social action groups* that seek to create change in the broader community or society.

An important aspect of working with groups in our practice is the opportunity to promote peer mentoring and learning opportunities. Reflecting on foster fathers, Heslop (2016) suggests that mentoring is a useful aspect of learning through peers. As Lindsay explains, 'a group provides opportunities for acquiring information about how one's behaviour is experienced and responded to by others' and 'offers opportunities for trying out new behaviours' (2013: 95).

The potential for group work to promote new behaviours is possibly never more challenging than when working with parents, particularly fathers of children within safeguarding. A review of a fathers' group called Mellow Dads recognised how group work can provide a source of advice on playing with children and parenting styles. However, the same review also recognised the real difficulties experienced by facilitators in forming and maintaining the group, particularly when some fathers lack practice in parenting skills and do not live with their children. They suggest that consideration is given to whether or not groups working with men should take a different approach from those working with women (Scourfield et al., 2016). Working in groups offers practitioners a useful way of working with people, particularly when seeking to promote user ownership and lasting change.

SOME THEORIES ABOUT WORKING WITH GROUPS

Groups do not stand still, they evolve and develop rapidly through various stages, and the group dynamics alter over their life course. The most frequently cited theory when reflecting on group work is Tuckman's *forming, storming, norming* and *performing* (Tuckman, 1965), later expanded to include *adjourning*, which is most commonly referred to as *mourning* (Tuckman & Jensen, 1977).

Tuckman's group stages

- Forming – the initial stage of any group. During this stage people come together to form the group due to shared aim(s) and experiences.
- Storming – following forming the group storm, pushing boundaries and questioning goals. Relationships may fray due to possible conflict over the group's direction. There may be

competition as roles are negotiated and individuals vie for leadership of the group. Many groups fail at this stage.
- Norming – having weathered the storm, the group sails into the norming stage. Group identity begins to mature as people get to know the limitations and strengths of the group and respective members.
- Performing – finally, the group begins to perform. At this stage, the group is stable and fluctuating membership should not affect the group's ability to perform.
- Adjourning (mourning) – included as a fifth stage, many groups adjourn once they have met their goals and ex-members can experience a sense of loss once the group ends.

Healy (2012) recognises that it is difficult to overstate the importance of Tuckman's stages in group work; they are almost immediately recognisable to anyone who has experienced being in a group. Lindsay and Orton (2014) generalise that there are two broad categories of group development, which are:

- *linear models*, which propose that groups follow a staged process, as if in a straight line progressing through the various stages, and suggest Tuckman's model is probably the best-known linear model of group development;
- *cyclical models*, which imply that groups follow a process of circling through the various stages, usually to progress towards a higher level of group development.

Social workers work with many different types of groups; those formally convened and identified as groups, as well as those groups we tend to find ourselves working in, e.g. social work teams, care teams and families. Brannan et al. (2018) consider leadership and team roles through reference to Belbin's nine team roles.

Belbin's nine team roles

Belbin (2010) identified nine behaviours and team roles displayed in the workplace. These are:

1. Resource investigator.
2. Team worker.
3. Coordinator.
4. Plant.
5. Monitor evaluator.
6. Specialist.
7. Shaper.
8. Implementer.
9. Completer finisher.

Working in teams is an integral part of social work practice (Brannan et al., 2018), and a team is a group with a shared purpose. Pullen-Sansfacon and Ward (2014) argue that social work management has tended to eschew knowledge from group work practice, preferring a top-down business model, which treats social work teams as business teams. They argue that this approach is restrictive because group work could help teams function more successfully and deliver improved services.

Planning

Anyone can convene a group. Or can they? Is our practice ever entirely random or spur of the moment? Hopefully not. Group work, if it is going to be successful, requires considerable planning on the part of the facilitator. Groups are often a source of support for people at times of vulnerability and crisis. A group may relate to shared challenges, such as health or relationship concerns, or be specific to roles, such as parents or carers. Whatever type of group you are considering setting up, think carefully and plan because 'Planning is the most important part of the groupwork task' (Lindsay & Orton, 2014: 23) and 'an essential communication skill without which no group work could succeed' (Rogers et al., 2017: 227). Coulshed and Orme (2012) identify five questions to consider when planning a group: Who? How many? How long? Which methods? What resources? Rogers et al. (2017) advise that the facilitator of the group must first clarify the identified need or aim of the group, and then identify aspects of priority coordination and decisions to be taken during this planning stage, which include:

- authority and permission to run the group;
- leadership (i.e. will the facilitator – you as the practitioner – run the group or will it be user-led?);
- membership of the group;
- planning and coordination of the group (most likely by you, the group convener);
- group contract and expectations;
- space and venue where the group will meet;
- days and times the group will meet;
- length and how long the group will run;
- economy and funding of the group.

AUTHOR'S EXPERIENCE (PHIL)

As a newly qualified social worker I joined a parents of looked after children group. My colleagues told me I was daft, but I enjoyed being a member of this group even though the parents tended to criticise me as a social worker. For me it was a humanising experience and one I have drawn on throughout the years in practice, teaching and when facilitating other groups.

When I couldn't access specialist autism awareness training for foster carers, my investigations determined that it simply did not exist. A colleague from the National Autistic Society (NAS) suggested we form a specialist foster carers' branch of the NAS, supported by the Fostering Network. We set up this branch, which supported any foster carer in north east England who looked after a child diagnosed on the autism spectrum. Buoyed by this success, I then set up a fathers' group through the National Autistic Society, and more recently, I have become a trustee with the

North East Young Dads and Lads project. I always learn a great deal from the support groups and self-help groups I am involved in, and value the opportunities they provide for knowledge exchange and collective social engagement. ”

Lindsay and Orton (2014) advise that practitioners obtain the support of colleagues and managers when intervening through group work. We are never blessed with too much time in social work and we don't want a good idea to become derailed because of workload commitments. This is all part of the planning process and it is important we get this stage as near to right as we can before moving on to the facilitating part of group work.

Facilitating

Thinking about setting up a group for the first time can be very daunting, even intimidating. Students who are placed in agencies applying group work models either relish the prospect of 'managing' a group or feel very unprepared and nervous. PCF 9 is concerned with professional leadership and we often find that students seek out some form of presentation to groups to evidence this particular domain (BASW, 2018). Confidence is an important part of facilitating groups, and for those without any group work experience, it is hard to know how to facilitate a group. Groups can flounder if the facilitator's personal style is overbearing or too withdrawn. Group work is not the same as presentation – although presentation may well be a part of it – it is a much more dynamic and interactive process. Lindsay and Orton adapted Heron's (1989) six categories to facilitating groups, which are being supportive, encouraging self-direction, valuing emotions, informing, seeking to direct behaviour and confronting unhelpful behaviour (Lindsay & Orton, 2014). Lindsay and Orton (2014) as well as Coulshed and Orme (2012) suggest that practitioners use the Johari Window model to explore personal awareness.

The Johari Window

The Johari Window is a tool that can help practitioners better understand their relationship with themselves and others (see Figure 12.1). It is primarily used in self-help groups and was created by two psychologists, Joseph Luft and Harrington Ingham.

A group of peers are given 55 adjectives and asked to work together to populate each person's Johari Window by selecting from these:

- Open – write an adjective about you known by both you and others.
- Hidden – write an adjective about you known to you but not others.
- Blind spot – adjectives not selected by you but only by your peers go here. These represent others' perceptions about you that you are unaware about.
- Unknown – these are adjectives that neither you nor your peers selected. This represents your unconscious or potential area (Luft & Ingham, 1955).

	Known by you	Unknown by you
Known to others	<u>Open</u> Known by both you and others	<u>Blind spot</u> Unknown to you but known by others
Unknown to others	<u>Hidden</u> Known to you but not by others	<u>Unknown</u> Unknown by both you and others

Figure 12.1 The Johari Window

Setting up the group, running the group and activities

Using Tuckman's stage group theory the initial sessions will be concerned with forming and then storming. This can be very daunting and challenging. As the facilitator, you will have planned the group and decided who you want to be involved in the group. The first meeting is really about setting the scene and agreeing the group's parameters. This is followed by the storming stage, which can be difficult and tiring as members seek to align themselves with a group identity and purpose, but it is crucial in enabling roles and function to be agreed. Group work facilitated by social workers does not have to be restricted to direct practice issues, e.g. groups have emerged to explore laughter therapy, dance, music and knitting. Indeed Kimmell and Gockel's (2017) exploration on the integration of group work into body-oriented psychotherapy, has led them to suggest that body-oriented psychotherapy appears to deepen the group process and enrich group work through facilitating working through and enhancing interpersonal connections, which they conclude is relevant for social work practice with groups.

AT NUMBER 1

Mary started to attend the reading group at her community centre. She quickly got into the swing of going to the meetings and discussing books: some she liked, others she didn't. In time she realised reading the books was much less important than socialising with the other members of the group. She made friends with people she felt comfortable talking to and they shared stories about their lives. Each had suffered and each had coped, but differently. She found the routine of the group, its activities, and above all the camaraderie she shared with other members to be very helpful.

EXERCISE 12.2

- How do you think this activity benefits Mary?
- Can this type of group support social work activities?
- What role, if any, does a facilitator have in such a group?

Power and group dynamics

Within any group, there will be some form of power dynamic. Think of the traditional phrase 'two is company, three's a crowd' – the more members, the more the risk of some form of disagreement emerging. It is worthwhile to think about where individuals fit within Tuckman's group stages. The five stages appear linear and sequential, but groups are prone to change and not everyone within a group experiences the stages concurrently. Successful groups require a mixture of personalities, but Coulshed and Orme (2012) identify three particularly problematic members as being the scapegoat, the monopoliser and the silent member. Rogers et al. (2017) emphasise the importance of self-awareness and sensitivity by the facilitator in managing group dynamics.

EXERCISE 12.3

First part – For this exercise we would like you to be honest (no one but you will know!) and consider two or three personal strengths that would help you to facilitate a group work intervention. Now try to identify two or three personal difficulties you might encounter when facilitating group work.

Second part – Identify two or three practice scenarios where group work would be helpful, and then consider two or three practice scenarios where it would be inappropriate.

Strengths and limitations of group work

Groups are a source of peer support and mentoring, and membership can be an empowering experience through which people share information, advice, stories and knowledge. A positive group can be a safe place to share and discuss deeply personal issues and behaviours. Connecting with people with shared experiences can provide insight and reduce feelings of isolation. Consider a group for men who have perpetrated domestic abuse. An individual who otherwise does not recognise the impact of his behaviour may well understand the upset caused through reflection with others who share such problematic behaviour. Reflecting on stories discussed and shared by others can lead to a better understanding of our own experience.

However, group work has limitations, and does not provide a solution to all the issues that we encounter as social workers. It is difficult to ensure confidentiality, as what one member may share in the safe place of the group may be taken outside by another. Some issues may well be too complex for group work, and groups may 'even be harmful as vulnerabilities are exposed, and stereotyping or discriminatory behaviour can take place' (Rogers et al., 2017: 231).

Scourfield et al. (2016) reviewed group work with fathers and identified some complex issues of group dynamics that require careful consideration, such as members who are self-obsessed and dominate at the expense of others.

SUMMARY

Group work has changed though it remains an integral part of our practice. Everything we do as social workers involves us being part of or interacting with groups, so even if we are not undertaking traditional group work, an underpinning knowledge of group theory is extremely beneficial. It seems that there is little attention afforded to teach group work skills to students, and we think this is unfortunate given the huge diversity and range of groups facilitated by contemporary practitioners. These range from formal training, such as parenting skills programmes, to self-help and support groups. We believe group work is an essential facet of our social work tool bag, and as group interventions are cost and resource efficient, there are indications that the current climate of austerity may prompt a resurgence of this approach.

SUMMARY AND FINAL THOUGHTS

We embarked on this book as two practitioners with nearly four decades' experience between us, reflecting on our transition to educators teaching social work in a university. We strongly believe our profession needs to hear the voices of practitioners, and in writing about our practice we underwent a further transition and became authors. We found this experience both challenging and extremely rewarding. We fundamentally believe that social work is about change. The people and relationships, knowledge and skills, systems and structures, context and policy of social work never stand still, and therefore nor must the practitioners who perform social work. As practitioners and educators, we have both been driven by our desire to work with people to secure change, at both an individual and a structural level.

Through this book, we set ourselves the task of following practice from assessment through to intervention. We are certainly not the first to write on this topic, and surely won't be the last. Rather naively, we initially thought that we could chart a linear progression. Of course, we recognised that assessments and interventions overlap, but as the book progressed we became increasingly aware that social work interventions are essentially assessments, and social work assessments are a form of intervention. We would encourage you to embrace the ambiguous and non-linear nature of working with people: actively intervening during assessments and assessing during interventions can only enhance your practice!

We have charted the historical development of social work, from charities and the welfare state to contemporary market-driven, safeguarding-based services: social work has evolved and will continue to do so. We have reflected on the purposes, processes and products of social work assessments, recognising the breadth of assessments and professional decision making social workers undertake. We recognise that contemporary social work practice – particularly in the statutory sector – often leaves practitioners feeling that they are tasked with impossible practice decisions where none of the available options are desirable. We have strongly advocated for defensible assessments, which are evidence based and accountable, but equally we have argued that the expectations placed on our practice must be bounded by an understanding that social workers are not infallible and we cannot see into the future. We work in unpredictable situations of conflict and risk, and sometimes outcomes are tragic. This is not easy. We have never said our job is easy. While our job is not easy we know it is possible to do a good job and social work is rewarding. Our focus on intervention models has highlighted the range of approaches available to social workers. We value social work's tendency to reject purist applications of models, and instead weave different theory, knowledge and skills into tapestries of intervention. Social work is skills based and whatever practice approach or model we adopt, our strength comes from the significance we place on working humanely and compassionately with people as fellow human beings, rather than as lofty and aloof professionals.

We are living through a time of austerity where budgetary restraints have reduced resources and raised thresholds. This is a very difficult climate in which to practise social work and our role is demanding and challenging. Nevertheless, it is a role we have chosen to undertake, whereas the people, families and communities we work with have rarely made an active choice. We enter the social work profession because we want to help people and make a difference. If our role becomes purely about gatekeeping resources by demonstrating that people do not meet the ever-escalating thresholds for involvement, we have lost our purpose and our unique offer. We conclude this book with a cautionary example of this from a recent group work session. One member asked, 'Do you feel like we only ever get assessed and no one goes on to actually work with us?' The others replied in unison, 'Yes!'

SUMMARIES OF LEARNING EXERCISES

No.	House	Learning
1.1	N/A	See the paragraph which follows the exercise.
1.2	5	Max may be finding it difficult to adjust and may be in denial. It might be difficult for Samantha to speak frankly in front of Max. The social worker could speak to her alone to explore her views and why she is reluctant to express them in front of Max. The social worker will need to be very honest with Max about the potential consequences of not accepting support.
1.3	1	The GP used the questioning model. The student social worker used the procedural model (form based). The community project worker used the exchange model (narrative). The exchange model finally gave Mary the opportunity to speak freely and feel listened to.
1.4	N/A	Many of our personal and professional values are complementary, others are not, e.g you may follow a religion that is of great personal importance, but you would not impose it on someone within your professional practice.
1.5	N/A	We can feel insulted when people use names/terms we don't like, and most of us prefer people to check with us how we would like to be referred to.
1.6	N/A	It is important to recognise how other people's experiences differ from our own and that this may the basis for discrimination. The Equalities Act 2010 provides legal protection for people experiencing discrimination on the basis of difference. This is congruent with social work values of anti-discriminatory and anti-oppressive practice. Experiencing multiple forms of discrimination concurrently is known as 'intersectionality'.
2.1	6	Your answers will be personal to you, but social workers often struggle in transitioning from one role to the other. Meeting the requirements of our role does not always make us feel good, and this may be something you need to explore with peers, colleagues or in supervision.
2.2	N/A	It is important to recognise that your beliefs will have an impact on your practice so you will need to identify and explore how you developed them.
2.3	1	Universal services provide support in common situations to prevent them from worsening. Contemporary services target those at the most risk or need. People may view contemporary service involvement as stigmatising rather than supportive, or worry their needs will not be significant enough to receive services. Older people can worry that services will reduce, rather than increase, their independence (see Chapter 5).

(Continued)

(Continued)

No.	House	Learning
2.4	N/A	Group theory (see Chapter 12) can be helpful in understanding how different social work teams and services behave. Adults and children constantly evolve and intersect with one another. We support a systemic approach (see Chapter 8) which understands people within the context of their relationships.
3.1	NA	We have a duty of care to work within our professional standards and ensure that our practice is considered, informed, safe and reasonable. This does not mean that we are responsible for eliminating every possible risk, and it does not mean that we can be successfully sued for any negative outcome. We must assess and identify risks and relate these to different perspectives as well as recognising that risks can have beneficial outcomes.
3.2	5	**Behaviour** – Samantha's increasing drinking and inability to manage the morning routine. **Hazards** – Tyra's age and vulnerability; Max's inability to get out of bed and respond to Tyra if needed; Max's condition and dependence on Samantha for support. **Motivation** – Samantha is lonely and does not know how to occupy her evenings. She may be struggling to cope with the changes in her relationship and lifestyle and may be depressed. **Danger** – Tyra and Max could come to harm because Samantha is unable to respond to their needs whilst intoxicated. Samantha's physical and mental health could suffer because of her alcohol dependence. Her employment may also be at risk if she is late/attends work hung over. The family stability is at risk.
3.3	6	Player, opponent and spectators are all at risk of injury. The player is at risk of being penalised/sent off, increasing her team's risk of losing. Liam's risky behaviour increases his vulnerability. He is at risk of exploitation and physical harm. He may influence other residents to partake in his risky behaviour, increasing risk to them. Whilst intoxicated, his behaviour may present risks to the organisation and jeopardize his placement. There is an element of choice and freedom as well as ability to understand risk. Risk is complex and never wholly one-dimensional.
3.4	N/A	See the paragraph which immediately follows the exercise.
3.5	4	Olivia might have felt angry with the police referring her when it was her partner who was abusive and not her. She might have felt pressure to minimise her true feelings and support needs and present an idealised version of her parenting, because she was scared and anxious the assessment would be critical of her parenting or result in the removal of her children. She might have felt powerless. The social worker might have felt pressure to make the 'right' professional judgement and move on. She might have felt empathy for Olivia or she might have felt that she had risked her children by being in a relationship with an abusive partner. The social worker's professional judgement was based on her underpinning knowledge of child development, attachment and relationships, information from the nursery, and her observation and interactions with Olivia and her children.
3.6	2	While the social worker is not autonomous, there is autonomy in the decision-making process and some flexibility in the methods/approaches used to inform decisions. The social worker is accountable to the fostering agency as well as the individuals being assessed, to children who may be placed with Alfie and Suzie in the future, and potentially the regulatory body. The consequences of making an incorrect assessment affect children who may be placed with Alfie and Suzie in the future, as well as the couple's own wellbeing.

No.	House	Learning
3.7	1	Acting on first instinct is not an accurate or defensible assessment. Developing and testing multiple hypotheses allows us to incorporate our theoretical knowledge and makes our professional decisions evidence based and accountable.
4.1	6	The assessment of Sally and her baby's situation and its outcome will have long-lasting effects on them both. The assessment must weigh up the baby's needs and welfare (paramount), Sally's parenting and capacity to develop, and family/environmental factors. Traditional social work responses have often been to look for a substitute family, most likely foster care initially with a view to adoption. However, *Friends and Family Care* (Department for Education, 2010) emphasises the potential of currently connected persons such as family and wider community members who may be available to look after children like Sally's baby.
4.2	N/A	Your answers will be unique to your situation, but thinking about your own experience of childhood will help you tune into the perspectives of the children you work with.
4.3	2	People applying to foster should receive training and be assessed as potential carers, which will give an indication to them and professionals of how prepared they are to foster. However, it is quite difficult to be fully prepared for fostering without direct experience, and of course, each child is different. Foster carers have to adjust to reduced privacy in their home as they open it up not only to children, but also to the professionals working alongside them. Supporting children who have experienced trauma, and learning to understand their behaviour and emotional needs is hard. Working with professionals, parents and childcare plans can be unfamiliar and demanding. Support is provided through home visits and helping carers to identify and access appropriate training and support groups. They may encounter a wide range of difficulties as carers, which include reduced privacy in their home as they open up not only to children but also to the professionals working with those children, to working with professionals (in their home), working within childcare plans, working with parents and understanding children's actions. Support is provided through training, support groups and home visits. However, the type of support is likely to vary from one social worker to another and from one service provider to another. The idea in this exercise is to consider how you would support and help a foster carer to look after a child.
4.4	N/A	It is all too easy to fall into a heroic narrative to social work and become consumed in rescue-based activities. However, we should not withdraw people's rights even when we feel morally justified. It is worth remembering that many looked after children go on to some form of family contact when they become adults. We should adopt practice that safeguards children but not at the expense of possible future relationships they may have with their parents. We feel it is socially just to promote family relationships that are as positive as they can possibly be and not seek to sever these. We suggest a compassionate and safeguarding perspective to practice that promotes positive childhood experiences that include honest and realistic parental participation in their lives. Furthermore, this approach is supported by legislation, policy and guidance.
5.1	5	The main barrier is likely to be the attitudes of potential employers, who tend to assume employees with disabilities will be more expensive as they may require adaptations and support, or may need time off for medical appointments.

(Continued)

(Continued)

No.	House	Learning
5.2	6	**Mental Capacity**: Liam's diagnosis may cause a lack of capacity; however, we must work from the presumption of capacity (MCA principle 1) unless there is *current* evidence that he may not be able to make his own decisions about his care and support. Liam should be given support to make decisions (MCA principle 2). If an assessment determines that he lacks capacity at that time, rather than making decisions in his best interests, decisions could be delayed until he has the capacity to make these as his condition is improving. **Advocacy & Participation Support**: Liam is entitled to an advocate and this may help to support his decision making. **Impact on Family & Carers**: Although we are not aware of any family members, we cannot presume that because Liam is a care leaver he does not have family relationships. His mental health has certainly had an impact on his housemates Sally and Adnan, and consideration should be given to whether they are acting as his carers. **Safeguarding**: There is no current suggestion of abuse or neglect, but this could change and must be considered throughout the assessment process. **Strengths-based Approach**: Liam has previously worked with a social worker very successfully to identify and achieve outcomes. Revisiting this positive experience may help him to recognise his strengths and capitalise on these now. **Proportionate & Appropriate:** The response to Liam's situation must recognise his identity. Young people take risks, and expectations should not be placed on Liam that would not be put on his peers. **Eligibility:** Liam is eligible to access social care services because his **needs** are related to a mental illness. Because of this, he was unable to meet **outcomes** related to his nutrition, hygiene, environment, safety, relationships, occupation or community participation, which had a significant impact on his **wellbeing**.
5.3	5	The financial advisor would be the person carrying out the transaction, so they must establish that Max has the capacity to do so. The relevant information would be the approximate amount of money that would be released and any charges associated with this, versus the likely continuing growth of the investments if left. Samantha's relationship and knowledge of Max's communication methods may help the financial advisor in establishing whether Max has capacity to make this decision.
6.1	4	Olivia may need to prepare food rather than buying it during the journey to ensure that Matty has something to eat which does not trigger his allergies. She will need to check with the train operator about the availability of disabled toilets and may also need to adjust travel times to access appropriate provision. It will be difficult to get on and off the train when travelling alone with two young children, one of whom uses a wheelchair, so Olivia may need to arrange support from station staff. Olivia may also need to spend time reassuring Georgia after her previous experience. This is a great deal of additional planning which can feel quite stressful and may actually discourage Olivia from making family trips.
6.2	4	Which element of your S.M.A.R.T. plan did you find most difficult to create?
6.3	4	Using the Skilled Helper Model can help elicit concerns and desired outcomes. S.M.A.R.T. planning can be incorporated during the action planning stage.

No.	House	Learning
6.4	2	While each agency will have its own 'paperwork' there is statutory guidance and all children should have placement agreements and care plans which detail and legalise the child's placement with the foster carer. Without a Court Order, David is placed through agreement with his parent(s) (those who have parental responsibility [PR]). In this situation, the local authority has no legal jurisdiction to supersede the parents' wishes concerning David. Where there is a Court Order such as an Emergency Protection, Interim or Care Order, then the local authority shares PR with the parent. In this situation, the local authority is deemed to hold the majority share of PR and to be required to consult with parents but can act without their consent.
6.5	6	Returning to college could work towards all of Adnan's longer-term desired outcomes. It could help him progress towards studying law, give him access to careers advice, give him access to library resources which may help him access useful data in his search for his family, and give him a routine which may be beneficial in structuring his meals (although clearly he will need ongoing specialist support with his eating disorder). Attending college will also build/rebuild social links. Working through the 8-stage process should suggest what could support Adnan to restart and maintain his college attendance.
6.6	N/A	See the paragraph that immediately follows the exercise.
7.1	6	The social worker is not communicating effectively with Adnan and is making assumptions, which are not based on his unique experience. Allowing him to tell his story and genuinely listening to him would build trust, which might help him to articulate his feelings. She should have checked with Adnan whether he wanted to have an interpreter. The interpreter is there to facilitate communication, not to exclude the person. Languages are not fully interchangeable, and it can be difficult to accurately translate abstract concepts such as emotions. Is an interpreter's role to merely translate the spoken word, or interpret cultural and contextual variables?
7.2	5	Self-assessment may be a barrier – while it can be empowering for some, it can make others feel dismissed. Sending out forms/information to a home address risks other people in the household seeing them. An appointment with an assessor outside of the family home might have helped Samantha consider her options before involving Max. Max's attitude is a further barrier, as whether intentional or not, his response to seeing the forms has made Samantha feel guilty for seeking support.
7.3	N/A	We have multiple, interconnected identities which are elements of our overall personal identity. Different identities recede or come to the fore depending on the situation we are in.
8.1	3	Each individual has a different perspective and focus of worry, but may not be aware of how others are feeling. Coming together to share this may help the family to understand what to prioritise and how to move forward.
8.2	N/A	Systems theories in general relate to those theories that recognise some form of relationship, interaction and connection between different component parts. Each of these theories represents an individual as part of an intrinsic system(s), for instance attachment reflects the adult–child bonding and inner working model. These theories help social workers assess individuals and their needs within their personal, social, biological and environmental networks. They each have distinct limitations. A general limitation for all of them is that they tend to dissociate individuals from their actions and seek to understand actions through some form of prior interaction. For instance, attachment theory implies a child experiencing disorganised parenting will become a

(Continued)

(Continued)

No.	House	Learning
		disorganised parent, and according to social learning theory a child observing success from violence will become a violent person. Humans are never fully conditioned by experiences and there is always an element of choice.
8.3	3	Stereotypical assumptions around traditional gendered parenting roles mean that Maureen is seen as selfish and unmaternal for working when her children are small, whilst Richie is seen as unusual and special for being a stay at home father. Harry has encountered a heteronormative assumption about his parents – although Maureen and Richie do not live together, they are still his mum and dad. Maureen and Claire live together, but this does not make Claire Harry's mum. The question 'which one's the dad?' is premised on a heteronormative stereotype, which assumes that when two women are in a relationship, one performs the role of a man and one the role of a woman.
8.4	N/A	These are features of *all* families. Often they are so ingrained that we are not aware of them, but if we look for them they are surprisingly easy to identify.
8.5	N/A	Completing a genogram can be a very powerful experience, which can reveal things we have not previously considered. Completing your own genogram can inform your future approach by giving you some insight into how people experience this process.
9.1	N/A	We each have our own personal thresholds, which determine what we do and do not consider a crisis. We cannot apply our own thresholds to other people's situations.
9.2	1, 2, 3	Mary, Alfie and Maureen's crises caused distress both to them and their families. Mary's sense of loss was actual, resulting from a bereavement. Alfie's sense of loss was anticipated, as he did not yet know whether he would lose his job. Maureen's sense of loss was both actual and anticipated, as her unexpected pregnancy changed her immediate situation and her imagined future. Mary, Alfie and Maureen's crises left them all feeling out of control due to unexpected events and disruption. They all faced uncertain futures and the potential for distress to continue over time.
9.3	6	Very different perspectives of crisis exist in this situation. Liam is unlikely to perceive his own behaviour as a crisis. His statement that no one cares is very significant and may be behaving in a risky way to test this out. Liam's foster carers are likely to perceive their current inability to maintain Liam's safety as a crisis. Liam's social worker may well view the potential for Liam's current placement to break down as the crisis.
9.4	3	Before any social needs can be considered, Maureen's physical health must be urgently assessed. She has abruptly stopping taking a substance to which she is physically dependent, which is extremely dangerous and in some cases fatal. Counterintuitive as it seems, Maureen may need to go restart the painkillers and withdraw slowly under supervision.
10.1	6	Sally appears to feel more confident that this social worker is listening to her. Through a well-crafted and co-produced contract, Sally will seek to meet her own goals rather than those imposed by others. The contract should include goals and tasks as well as identifying the roles and responsibilities of those involved. A good contract will include a mechanism of review and a planned ending.

No.	House	Learning
10.2	3	Maureen's situation is not resolved; it may never fully be. Some people who have had problems with substances consider themselves addicts for life, even though they have stopped using. However, recovery is a process, and Maureen working in a task-centred way has certainly helped her to make good progress against all three goals.
11.1	6	While Sally appears to have had a difficult childhood, the decisions about her care plan were based on a deficit model and the assumption that adoption would successfully provide her with a suitable family. The intended outcome was permanency through adoption; however, in reality she experienced an insecure and unstable childhood due to her frequent moves between placements. Sally has shown personal resilience and maintained a maternal relationship.
11.2	4	Knowing that the social worker was going to visit may have made Olivia feel that someone cared about her situation, and shifted her thinking from her problem to solutions, which she and the social worker may generate together. The phone call provided an exception, which seems to have been so effective that Olivia was actually able to feel more positive about investigating strategies herself, rather than needing the social worker's help to do this. Sometime we can feel frustrated when people cancel appointments, or when we attend a visit and find that we are not needed. It is important to recognise that this is not a waste of time but a great outcome.
11.3	2	A strength of applying SoS with this family is that it has identified the children's feelings, maternal warmth and family support. A general limitation is that the focus on strengths may not always fit with safeguarding, particularly in relation to emotional welfare. Another limitation is that the focus on strengths may inadvertently encourage parents to feel concerns are minimised. Possible outcomes for the children are that they are both or separately rehabilitated with their parent(s), placed together or separately with extended family (maternal or paternal) or connected persons (formally or informally), or placed longterm in local authority placements. The plan should address permanency, and therefore when placed in a long-term local placement, such as foster care, adoption should be considered. However, in reality, adoption is rarely an option for older children and most adopting families prefer preschool-aged children. Social work can promote outcomes through evidence-based, child-centred, relationship-based, robust and defensible assessments, which seek to address all concerns and strengths and consider all possible placement options.
11.4	1	Mary is not at risk, but is likely to have eligible needs, so conversations 1 and then 3 would be appropriate.
11.5	5	The solution-focused approach of the miracle question may *already* have helped Samantha. Although she has not shared her true answer, she has realised it herself and this might be a catalyst for change. As social workers, we see brief glimpses of people's lives, perhaps an hour or two a week, often less. Change my be stimulated during this contact, but will most probably occur outside of it.
12.1	6	This group benefits from being a self-help and support group as well as one that can facilitate training and recreational activities. The facilitators will have to plan this group well to ensure they do not lead to conflict and the possible victimisation of members. Confidentiality as well as participation are two other challenges they may encounter.

(Continued)

(Continued)

No.	House	Learning
		The formal is formal because it is facilitated by two professionals and seeks to provide training to young people. Informality is provided because attendance is voluntary; helpfully the facilitators will apply an informal style to the group and members will be more able to develop relationships away from the group.
12.2	1	The group – and the reading she undertakes in preparation for it – provides Mary with a purpose and occupation. She is connecting socially and making friendships, leading to further social opportunities. Such groups may be trivialised, but can be an excellent social work intervention. A facilitator could identify anyone who was anxious and make sure that they were included, or could notice changes in presentation and check with the member privately to see if they were okay.
12.3	N/A	Reflecting on the individual strengths and limitations you have identified will enable you to consider how you can utilise your existing skills and develop others. Group work can be a very appropriate format for providing mentoring, peer support, training, self-help and activities. Group work is not an appropriate alternative to case management, and will not be helpful if vulnerable persons interact with harming individuals, or confidentiality is an issue.

REFERENCES

Abbas, S. R. & Sulman, J. (2016) Nondeliberative crisis intervention in disaster zones: social group work using guided artwork with child survivors, *Social Work with Groups*, *39*(2–3):118–28.

Adams, J. (1995) *Risk*. London: UCL Press.

Adams, R. (2003) *Social Work and Empowerment*. Basingstoke: Palgrave.

Adams, R., Dominelli, L. & Payne, M. (2002) *Social Work: Themes, Issues and Critical Debates* (2nd edn). Basingstoke: Palgrave in association with the Open University.

Adams, R., Dominelli, L. and Payne, M. (2005) *Social Work Futures: Crossing Boundaries, Transforming Practice*. Basingstoke: Palgrave Macmillan.

Adams, R., Dominelli, L. & Payne, M. (2009) *Practising Social Work in a Complex World*. Basingstoke: Palgrave Macmillan.

ADASS (2011) *Safeguarding Adults Advice Note*, Association of Directors of Adult Social Services, London.

ADASS (2017) *Budget 2017 representation by the Association of Directors of Adult Social Services*. Available at www.adass.org.uk/budget-2017-representation-by-the-association-of-directors-of-adult-social-services (accessed 3 March 2018).

Ainsworth, M. & Marvin, R. (1995) On the shaping of attachment theory and research: An interview with Mary D. S. Ainsworth (Fall 1994), *Monographs of the Society for Research in Child Development*, 60(2–3, Serial No. 244), 3–21.

Andrews, J. (2001) Group work's place in social work: a historical analysis, *Journal of Sociology and Social Welfare*, *28*(4): 44–65.

Andrews, M., Squire, C. & Tamboukou, M. (2008) *Doing Narrative Research*. London: Sage Publications.

Ashley, C. & Nixon, P. (2007) *Family Group Conferences: Where Next? Policies and Practices for the Future*. London: Family Rights Group.

Association for Video Interaction Guidance UK (n.d.). *About VIG*. Available at www.videointeractionguidance.net/aboutvig (accessed 1 March 2018).

Ayers, S. (2017) 'Sharing mistakes in social work means you risk being blamed and shamed', *Community Care* online. Available at www.communitycare.co.uk/2017/01/25/sharing-mistakes-in-social-work-means-you-risk-being-blamed-disciplined-and-struck-off/ (accessed 1 February 2018).

Bailey, R. & Brake, M. (1980) *Radical Social Work and Practice*. London: Edward Arnold.

Baim, C. (2016) 'Guide to using attachment theory to work with adults'. Available at https://adults.ccinform.co.uk (accessed 1 December 2017).

Baginsky, M., Moriarty, J., Manthorpe, J., Beecham, J. & Hickman, B. (2017) *Evaluation of Signs of Safety in 10 pilots research report*. London: Department for Education.

Bamford, T. (2015) *A Contemporary History of Social Work*. Bristol: Policy.

Bandura, A. (1978) Social learning theory of aggression, *Journal of Communication*, *28*(3): 12–29.

Bandura, A. (1994) 'Self-efficacy'. In V. Ramachaudran (ed.), *Encyclopaedia of Human Behavior*, Vol. 4 (pp. 71–81). New York: Academic.

Banks, S. (2006) *Ethics and Values in Social Work* (3rd edn). Basingstoke: Palgrave Macmillan.

Barlow, J. & Scott, J. (2010) *Safeguarding in the 21st Century: Where to Now?* Dartington: Research in Practice.

Barnes, C. (1999) Disability studies: new or not-so-new directions, *Disability & Society*, *14*(4): 577–80.

BASW (2015) *PCF*. Available at www.basw.co.uk/pcf/capabilities/?level=10 (accessed 17 October 2017).

BASW (2017) *A Manifesto for Social Work*. Available at http://cdn.basw.co.uk/upload/basw_93101-7.pdf (accessed 3 March 2018).

BASW (2018) *The 2018 Refresh of the Professional Capabilities Framework*. Available at http://cdn.basw.co.uk/upload/basw_103714-5.pdf (accessed 3 March 2018).

BASW, Department for Education and Department of Health and Social Care (2018) *Joint Statement on the Relationship between the Professional Capabilities Framework (PCF) for Social Work and the Knowledge and Skills Statements for Children and Families and Adults*. Available at: http://cdn.basw.co.uk/upload/basw_101504-10.pd (accessed 3 March 2018).

Batty, D. (2004) 'Timeline: a history of child protection'. Available at www.theguardian.com/society/2005/may/18/childrensservices2 (accessed 26 June 2017).

Beck, U. (1992) *Risk Society: Towards a New Modernity*. London: Sage Publications.

Becker, G. (1993) *Human Capital: A Theoretical and Empirical Analysis with Special Reference to Education*. Chicago: University of Chicago Press.

Becker, G. & Tomes, N. (1986) Human capital and the rise and fall of families, *Journal of Labor Economics*, *4* (part 2) (3): 1–39.

Beesley, P., Watts, M. & Harrison, M. (2018) *Developing Your Communication Skills in Social Work*. London: Sage Publications.

Belbin, M. (2010) *Team Roles at Work* (2nd edn). London: Routledge.

Bellinger, A. & Elliott, T. (2011) What are you looking at? The potential of appreciative inquiry as a research approach for social work, *British Journal of Social Work*, *41*(4): 708–25.

Benall, R. (2010) *Doctoring the Mind: Why Psychiatric Treatments Fail*. London: Penguin Books.

Berger, P. and Luckmann, T. (1979) *The Social Construction of Reality: A Treatise in the Sociology of Knowledge*. London: Peregrine.

Berridge, D. & Cleaver, H. (1987) *Foster Home Breakdown*. Oxford: Blackwell.

Bogo, M. (2013) 'Understanding and Using Supervision'. In J. Parker & M. Doel (eds), *Professional Social Work*. London: Sage Publications.

Bogo, M., Rawlings, M., Katz, E. & Logie, C. (2014) *Using Simulation in Assessment and Teaching: OSCE Adapted for Social Work*. Alexandria: Council on Social Work Education.

Bola, M., Coldham, T. & Robinson, Z. (2014) 'A study of personalisation and the factors affecting the uptake of personal budgets by mental health service users in the UK', MIND. Available at http://clok.uclan.ac.uk/10755/> (accessed 1 December 2017).

Bolger, J. & Walker, P. (2018) 'Models of Assessment'. In J. Lishman, C. Yuill, J. Brannan & A. Gibson (eds), *Social Work: An Introduction* (2nd edn). London: Sage Publications.

Borg, M. & Davidson, L. (2008) The nature of recovery as lived in everyday experience, *Journal of Mental Health*, *17*(2): 129–40.

Bostock, L., Bairstow, S., Fish, S. & Macleod, F. (2005) 'Managing risk and minimising mistakes in services to children and families' (Vol. REPORT 6, pp. 97). Bristol: Social Care Institute for Excellence.

Boushel, M., Fawcett, M. & Selwyn, J. (2000) *Focus on Early Childhood: Principles and Realities*. Oxford: Blackwell Science.

Bowen, M. (1990) *Family Therapy in Clinical Practice*. Maryland: Rowman & Littlefield.

Bowlby, J. (1997) *Attachment and Loss: Vol. 1, Attachment*. London: Pimlico.

Brannan, J., Campbell, J. & Gibson, A. (2018) 'Teamwork'. In J. Lishman, C. Yuill, J. Brannan & A. Gibson (eds), *Social Work: An Introduction* (2nd edn) (pp. 237–50). London: Sage Publications.

Broad, B. (2007) Kinship care: What works? Who cares? *Social Work and Social Sciences Review*, *13*(1): 59–74.

Bronfenbrenner, U. (1977) Toward an experimental ecology of human development, *American Psychologist*, *32*(7): 513–31.

Bronfenbrenner, U. (1979) *The Ecology of Human Development*. Cambridge, MA: Harvard University Press.

Brown, H. (2011) The role of emotion in decision-making, *Journal of Adult Protection 13*(4): 194–202.

Brown, K. and Rutter, L. (2008) *Critical Thinking for Social Work*. Exeter: Learning Matters.

Brown, L., Callahan, M., Strega, S., Walmsley, C. & Dominelli, L. (2009) Manufacturing ghost fathers: the paradox of father presence and absence in child welfare, *Child & Family Social Work*, *14*(1): 25–34.

Brown, L., Moore, S. and Turney, D. (2012) *Analysis and Critical Thinking in Assessment* Dartington: Research in Practice.

Bushe, G. (2013) 'The Appreciative Inquiry Model'. In E. Kessler (ed.), *Encyclopaedia of Management Theory*, Vol. 1 (pp. 41–4). Los Angeles, CA: Sage Publications.

Butler, J. (1990) *Gender Trouble: Feminism and the Subversion of Identity*. New York: Routledge.

Butler, S. & Charles, M. (1999) The past, the present, but never the future: thematic representations of fostering disruption, *Child and Family Social Work*, *4*(1): 9–19.

Byng-Hall, J. (1985) The Family Script: a useful bridge between theory and practice, *Journal of Family Therapy*, 7: 301–5.

Calder, M. (2003) 'The Assessment Framework: A Critique and Reformation'. In M. Calder & S. Hackett (eds), *Assessment in Child Care: Using and Developing Frameworks for Practice* (pp. 3–60). Lyme Regis: Russell House.

Cameron, C. (ed.) (2014) *Disability Studies: A Student's Guide*. London: Sage Publications.

Cantor-Graae, E. & Selten, J. (2005) Schizophrenia and migration: a meta-analysis and review, *American Journal of Psychiatry*, *162*(1): 12–24.

Caplow, T. (1954) *The Sociology of Work*. Minneapolis: University of Minnesota Press.

Carpenter, J., Webb, C., Bostock, L. & Coomber, C. (2012) *Effective Supervision in Social Work and Social Care: Research Briefing 43*. London: Social Care Institute for Excellence.

Carr, S. (2010) *Personalisation: A Rough Guide* (revised edn). London: Social Care Institute for Excellence.

Carr-Saunders, A. (1928) *The Professions: Their Organisation and Place in Society*. Oxford: Clarendon.

Casey, L. (2012) *Listening to Troubled Families*. London: Department for Communities and Local Government.

Cass, E. (2011) How SCIE are guiding good practice on adult protection, *Journal of Adult Protection*, *13*(2): 87–8.

Centre for Policy on Ageing (2009) Ageism and Age Discrimination in Social Care in the United Kingdom: A Review from the Literature. Available at www.cpa.org.uk/information/reviews/CPA-%20ageism_and_age_discrimination_in_social_care-report.pdf (accessed 1 September 2017).

Chapman, M. & Field, J. (2007) Strengthening our engagement with families and understanding practice depth, *Social Work Now*, *38*: 21–8.

Chapman, R. (2016) *Undertaking Assessments in England*. London: CORAM/BAAF.

Child Migrant Trust (n.d.) *Child Migration History*. Available at www.childmigrantstrust.com/our-work/child-migration-history/ (accessed 23 February 2018).

Clarke, J., Newman, J. & Westmarland, L. (2007) The antagonisms of choice: New Labour and the reform of public services, *Social Policy and Society*, 7(2): 245–53.

Collentine, A. (2005) Respecting intellectually disabled parents: a call for change in state termination of parental rights statutes, *Hofstra Law Review*, *535*(2): 1–25.

Collins, A. (2014) 'Measuring what really matters'. Available at www.health.org.uk/publications/measuring-what-really-matters (accessed 3 March 2018).

Connell, R. (1995) *Masculinities*. Cambridge: Polity.

Connolly, M., Kiraly, M., McCrae, L. & Mitchell, G. (2017) A kinship care practice framework: using a life course approach, *British Journal of Social Work*, *47*(1): 87–105.

Cooperrider, D. & Srivastva, S. (1987) 'Appreciative Inquiry in Organizational Life'. In R. Woodman & W. Pasmore (eds), *Research in Organizational Change and Development*, Vol. 1 (pp. 129–69). Stamford, CT: JAI.

Cornell University (2005) 'Urie Bronfenbrenner, father of Head Start program and pre-eminent "human ecologist", dies at age 88'. Available at http://news.cornell.edu/stories/2005/09/head-start-founder-urie-bronfenbrenner-dies-88 (accessed 1 December 2017).

Cottrell, S. (2011) *Critical Thinking Skills: Developing Effective Analysis and Argument*, Basingstoke: Palgrave Macmillan.

Coulshed, V. & Orme, J. (2012) *Social Work Practice* (5th edn). Basingstoke: Palgrave Macmillan/BASW.

Crenshaw, K. (1989) Demarginalizing the intersection of race and sex: a black feminist critique of anti-discrimination doctrine, feminist theory and antiracist politics, *University of Chicago Legal Forum*: Vol. 1989, Article 8. Available at https://chicagounbound.uchicago.edu/uclf/vol1989/iss1/8 (accessed 1 December 2017).

Crowder, R. & Sears, A. (2017) Building resilience in social workers: an exploratory study on the impacts of a mindfulness-based intervention, *Australian Social Work*, *70*(1): 17–29.

Czarniawska, B. (2004) *Narratives in Social Science Research*. London: Sage Publications.

Dall, T. & Caswell, D. (2017) Expanding or postponing? Patterns of negotiation in multi-party interactions in social work. *Discourse and Communication*, *11*(5): 483–497.

Daly, J. (2016) Thinking about internal prejudice and anti-oppressive practice in child safeguarding social work with Irish Travellers in the UK, *Journal of Social Work Practice*, *30*(4): 335–47.

Davidson, L. (2005) Recovery, self management and the expert patient: changing the culture of mental health from a UK perspective, *Journal of Mental Health*, *14*(1): 25–35.

Dennis, S. (2018) 'Jeremy Hunt becomes secretary of state for health and social care', *Community Care*. Available at www.communitycare.co.uk/2018/01/08/jeremy-hunt-becomes-secretary-state-health-social-care/ (accessed 3 March 2018).

De Montigny, G. (2016) 'Social workers' peculiar contribution to ethnographic research. Qualitative Social Work'. Available at http://journals.sagepub.com/doi/pdf/10.1177/1473325016678310 (accessed 1 February 2018).

Department for Constitutional Affairs (2007) *Mental Capacity Act 2005 Code of Practice*. London: HMSO.

Department for Education (2010) *Family and Friends Care: Statutory Guidance for Local Authorities*. Available at www.gov.uk/government/uploads/system/uploads/attachment_data/file/288483/family-and-friends-care.pdf (accessed 3 March 2018).

Department for Education (2011) *Fostering Services: National Minimum Standards*. London: HMSO.

Department for Education (2014) *Knowledge and Skills for Child and Family Social Work*. Available at www.gov.uk/government/uploads/system/uploads/attachment_data/file/338718/140730_Knowledge_and_skills_statement_final_version_AS_RH_Checked.pdf (accessed 1 February 2018).

Department for Education (2015a) *Knowledge and Skills Statements for Practice Leaders and Practice Supervisors*. Available at http://cdn.basw.co.uk/upload/basw_105011-10.pdf (accessed 8 March 2018).

Department for Education (2015b) *The Children Act 1989 Guidance and Regulations, Volume 2: Care Planning, Placement and Case Review*. Available at www.gov.uk/government/uploads/system/uploads/attachment_data/file/441643/Children_Act_Guidance_2015.pdf (accessed 3 March 2018).

Department for Education (2016) *Knowledge and Skills Statement: Achieving Permanence*. Available at www.gov.uk/government/uploads/system/uploads/attachment_data/file/570659/Knowledge_and_skills_statement_for_achieving_permanence.pdf (accessed 3 March 2018).

Department for Education (2017) *Children Looked After in England (including Adoption and Care Leavers) Year Ending 31 March 2017*. Available at www.gov.uk/government/uploads/system/uploads/attachment_data/file/664995/SFR50_2017-Children_looked_after_in_England.pdf (accessed 3 March 2018).

Department for Education and Department of Health and Social Care (2018) *Social Work England Consultation on Secondary Legislative Framework*. Available at https://consult.education.gov.uk/social-work-england-implementation-team/social-work-england-consultation-on-secondary-legi/supporting_documents/Social%20Work%20EnglandConsultation.pdf (accessed 3 March 2018).

Department for Education and Skills (2006) *Working Together to Safeguard Children: A Guide to the Inter-agency Working to Safeguard and Promote the Welfare of Children*. London: TSO.

Department of Health (2007) *Independence, Choice and Risk*. London: HMSO.

Department of Health (2009) *Safeguarding Adults Report on the Consultation on the Review of 'No Secrets'*. London: Central Office of Information.

Department of Health (2015) *Knowledge and Skills Statement for Social Workers in Adult Services*. Available at www.gov.uk/government/uploads/system/uploads/attachment_data/file/411957/KSS.pdf (accessed 3 March 2018).

Department of Health (2017) *Strengths-based Social Work Practice with Adults*. Available at www.gov.uk/government/uploads/system/uploads/attachment_data/file/652773/Strengths-based_social_work_practice_with_adults.pdf (accessed 1 March 2018).

Department of Health, Department for Education and Employment and Home Office (2000) *Framework for the Assessment of Children and Their Families*. London: The Stationery Office.

Department of Health and Social Care (2018) *Care and Support Statutory Guidance*. Available at www.gov.uk/government/publications/care-act-statutory-guidance/care-and-support-statutory-guidance (accessed 16 April 2018).

Department of Health and Social Security (1969) 'Report of the committee of inquiry into allegations of ill-treatment of patients and other irregularities at the Ely Hospital, Cardiff'. London: HMSO.

Derrida, J. & Bass, A. (1995) *Writing and Difference*. London: Routledge.

de Jong, G. & Schout, G. (2011) Family group conferences in public mental health care: an exploration of opportunities, *International Journal of Mental Health Nursing*, *20*(1): 63–74.

de Shazer, S. (1982) *Patterns of Brief Therapy: An Ecosystem Approach*. New York: Guilford.

de Shazer, S. (1991) *Putting Difference to Work*. New York: Norton.

Dictionary.com (n.d.) Available at http://www.dictionary.com

Dix, H., Hollinrake, S. & Meade, J. (2018) *Relationship-based Social Work with Adults*. Northwich: Critical Publishing Ltd.

Dodds, C., Heslop, P. & Meredith, C. (2018) Using simulation-based education to help social work students prepare for practice, *Social Work Education: The International Journal*. Available at https://www.tandfonline.com/doi/abs/10.1080/02615479.2018.1433158

Doel, M. (2002) 'Task-centred Work'. In R. Adams, L. Dominelli & M. Payne (eds), *Social Work: Themes, Issues and Critical Debates* (pp. 191–196). Basingstoke: Palgrave Macmillan.

Doel, M. (2012) *Social Work: The Basics*. London: Routledge.

Dolan, G. (1981) There's a S.M.A.R.T. way to write management's goals and objectives, *Management Review*, *70*(11): 35–6.

Dominelli, L. (1996) Deprofessionalizing social work: anti-oppressive practice, competencies and post-modernism, *British Journal of Social Work*, *26*(2): 153–75.

Dominelli, L. (1997) *Sociology for Social Work*. Basingstoke: Palgrave Macmillan.

Dominelli, L. (1998) Feminist social work: an expression of universal human rights, *Indian Journal of Social Work*, *59*(4): 917–29.

Dominelli, L. (2002) *Anti-oppressive Social Work Theory and Practice*. Basingstoke: Palgrave Macmillan.

Drucker, P. (1954 (revised edn, 2007)) *The Practice of Management*. New York: Harper, revised edition Butterworth-Heinemann.

Duffy, S. (2006) *The Keys to Citizenship*. Sheffield: The Centre for Welfare Reform.

Dunne, J. (2011) 'Professional Wisdom in Practice'. In L. Bondi, D. Carr, C. Clark & C. Clegg (eds), *Towards Professional Wisdom: Practical Deliberation in the People Professions* (pp. 13–36). Farnham: Ashgate.

Dyke, C. (2016) *Writing Analytical Assessments in Social Work*. Northwich: Critical Publishing.

Egan, G. (2013) *Skilled Helper*. Available at www.myilibrary.com?ID=750220 (accessed 1 December 2017).

Elliott, J. (2005) *Using Narrative in Social Research: Qualitative and Quantitative Approaches*. London: Sage Publications.

Elliott, T. (2015) *Appreciative Inquiry in Adult Safeguarding: Practice Tool*. Totnes, Devon: Research in Practice.

Equality and Human Rights Commission (EHRC) (2017a) *Being Disabled in Britain: A Journey Less Equal*. Available at www.equalityhumanrights.com/sites/default/files/being-disabled-in-britain.pdf (accessed 3 March 2018).

Equality and Human Rights Commission (EHRC) (2017b) *How Is the UK Performing on Disability Rights? The UN's Recommendations for the UK*. Available at www.equalityhumanrights.com/sites/default/files/ehrc_un_crpd_report.pdf (accessed 3 March 2018).

Erikson, E. H. (1965) *Childhood and Society* (revised edn). Harmondsworth: Penguin Books in association with the Hogarth Press.

Erikson, E. H. (1968) *Identity: Youth and Crisis*. London: Faber.

Faulkner, A. (2012) 'The right to take risks: service users' views of risk in Adult Social care', JRF Programme Paper. Available at www.jrf.org.uk/publications/service-users-views-risk-adult-social-care (accessed 26 October 2017).

Fawcett, B. (1998) Disability and social work: applications from poststructuralism, postmodernism and feminism, *British Journal of Social Work*, *28*: 263–77.

Featherstone, B. (2003) Taking fathers seriously, *British Journal of Social Work*, *33*(2): 239–54.

Featherstone, B. (2014) 'Working with Fathers: Risk or Resource?'. In J. McCarthy, C. Hooper & V. Gillies (eds), *Family Troubles: Exploring Changes and Challenges in the Family Lives of Children and Young People* (pp. 315–26). Bristol: Policy.

Ferguson, H. (2003) Outline of a critical best practice approach to social work and social care, *British Journal of Social Work*, *33*: 1005–24.

Ferguson, H. (2011) *Child Protection Practice*. Basingstoke: Palgrave Macmillan.

Ferguson, I. (2007) Increasing user choice or privatising risk? The antinomies of personalisation, *British Journal of Social Work*, *37*: 387–403.

Ferguson, I. & Woodward, R. (2009) *Radical Social Work in Practice: Making a Difference*. Bristol: Policy.

Finch, J. (2007) Displaying families, *Sociology*, *41*(1): 65–81.

Finkelstein, V. (1980) *Attitudes and Disabled People*. New York: World Rehabilitation Fund.

Finkelstein, V. (1981) 'To Deny or Not to Deny Disability'. In A. Brechin et al. (eds), *Handicap in a Social World*. Sevenoaks: Hodder and Stoughton.

Flynn, M. (2007) 'The murder of Steven Hoskin: a Serious Case Review', Cornwall Adult Protection Committee. Available at www.cornwall.gov.uk/media/3633936/Steven-Hoskin-Serious-Case-Review-Exec-Summary.pdf (accessed 1 January 2018).

Fook, J. (2000) 'Deconstructing and Reconstructing Professional Expertise'. In B. Fawcett, B. Featherstone, J. Fook et al. (eds), *Practice and Research in Social Work: Postmodern Feminist Perspectives*. London: Routledge.

Fook, J. (2002) *Social Work: Critical Theory and Practice*. London: Sage Publications.

Fook, J. (2016) *Social Work: A Critical Approach to Practice* (3rd edn). London: Sage Publications.

Fook, J. & Gardner, F. (2007) *Practising Critical Reflection: A Handbook*. Berkshire: Open University Press.

Foucault, M. (1978) *The History of Sexuality, Vol. 1: An Introduction*, New York: Pantheon.

Foucault, M. & Gordon, C. (1980) *Power/Knowledge: Selected Interviews and Other Writings, 1972–1977*. Brighton: Harvester.

Freud, S. & Krug, S. (2002) Beyond the Code of Ethics, Part I: complexities of ethical decision making in social work practice, *Families in Society: The Journal of Contemporary Social Services*, *83*(5): 474–82.

Fulcher, L. (2009) 'Foreword'. In M. Smith, *Rethinking Residential Child Care: Positive Perspectives*. Bristol: Policy.

Furstenberg, F. & Kaplan, B. (2007) 'Social Capital and the Family'. In J. Scott, J. Treas & M. Richards (eds), *The Blackwell Companion to the Sociology of Families* (pp. 194–217). Oxford: Blackwell.

Galpin, D. (2016) *Safeguarding Adults at Risk of Harm* (2nd edn). Bournemouth: Learn to Care.

Gibbs, G. (1988) *Learning by Doing: A Guide to Teaching and Learning Methods*. Oxford: Further Education Unit, Oxford Polytechnic.

Giddens, A. (1992) *The Transformation of Intimacy: Sexuality, Love and Eroticism in Modern Societies*. Cambridge: Polity.

Giddens, A. & Pierson, C. (1998) *Making Sense of Modernity: Conversations with Anthony Giddens*. Stanford: Stanford University Press.

Gilbert, T. & Powell, J. (2010) Power and social work in the United Kingdom, *Journal of Social Work*, *10*: 3–22.

Gill, O. & Jack, G. (2007) *The Child and Family in Context: Developing Ecology Practice in Disadvantaged Communities*. Lyme Regis: Russell House.

Glasby, J. & Littlechild, R. (2009) *Direct Payments and Personal Budgets: Putting Personalisation in Practice* (2nd edn). Bristol: The Policy Press.

Goemans, R. (2012) A consideration of the nature and purpose of mental health social work, *Mental Health and Social Exclusion*, *12*(2): 90–6.

Goleman, D. (1998) *Working With Emotional Intelligence*. New York: Bantam.

Gollins, T., Fox, A., Walker, B., Romeo, L., Thomas, J. & Woodham, G. (2016) 'Think local, act personal: developing a wellbeing and strengths-based approach to social work practice: changing culture'. Available at www.thinklocalactpersonal.org.uk/Latest/Developing-a-Wellbeing-and-Strengths-based-Approach-to-Social-Work-Practice-Changing-Culture/ (accessed 22 April 2018).

Gómez, M., Bracho, C. & Hernández, M. (2014) Appreciative inquiry: a constant in social work, *Social Sciences*, *3*(4): 112–20.

Government of Western Australia (2011) *The Signs of Safety Child Protection Practice Framework* (2nd edn). Available at www.dcp.wa.gov.au/Resources/Documents/Policies%20and%20Frameworks/SignsOfSafetyFramework2011.pdf (accessed 1 March 2018).

Green, D. & McDermott, F. (2010) Social work from inside and between complex systems: perspectives on person-in-environment for today's social work, *British Journal of Social Work*, *40*: 2414–30.

Green, L. & Featherstone, B. (2014) 'Judith Butler, Power and Social Work'. In C. Cocker & T. Hafford-Letchfield (eds), *Rethinking Anti-discriminatory and Anti-oppressive Theories for Social Work*. Basingstoke: Palgrave Macmillan.

Greeno, E., Ting, L., Pecukonis, E., Hodorowicz, M. & Wade, K. (2017) The role of empathy in training social work students in motivational interviewing, *Social Work Education*, *36*(7): 794–808.

Griffiths, R. (1988) *Community Care: Agenda for Action*. London: HMSO.

Halford, S., Savage, M. & Witz, A. (1997) *Gender, Careers and Organisations*. London: Macmillan.

Hall, A., Finch, T., Kolehmainen, N. & James, D. (2016) Implementing a video-based intervention to empower staff members in an autism care organization: a qualitative study, *BMC Health Services Research*, *16*(1), open access.

Halmos, P. (1978) *The Personal and the Political: Social Work and Social Action*. London: Hutchinson.

Hancock, H. & Easen, P. (2004) Evidence-based practice: an incomplete model of the relationship between theory and professional work, *Journal of Evaluation in Clinical Practice* *10*(2): 187–96.

Hansan, J. (2011) 'Early history of social group work'. Available at https://socialwelfare.library.vcu.edu/social-work/social-work-early-history-of-group-work/ (accessed 1 March 2018).

Harris, J. & White, V. (eds) (2009) *Modernising Social Work: Critical Considerations*. Bristol: Policy.

Harris, J. & White, V. (2013) *A Dictionary of Social Work and Social Care*. Oxford: Oxford University Press.

Hart, A. (2018) 'Crisis Intervention'. In J. Lishman, C. Yuill, J. Brannan & A. Gibson (eds), *Social Work: An Introduction* (2nd edn) (pp. 280–95). London: Sage Publications.

Harvey, L. H. & Reed, M. (1996) 'Social Sciences as the Study of Complex Systems'. In D. Kiel & E. Elliott (eds), *Chaos Theory in the Social Sciences* (pp. 295–323). Ann Arbor: University of Michigan Press.

Hatton, K. (2015) *New Directions in Social Work Practice* (2nd edn). London: Learning Matters/Sage.

Hawkins, R. & Maurer, K. (2012) Unravelling social capital: disentangling a concept for social work, *British Journal of Social Work*, *42*: 353–70.

Health Committee (2012) *Fourteenth Report – Social Care*. House of Commons. Available at https://publications.parliament.uk/pa/cm201012/cmselect/cmhealth/1583/158301.htm

Healy, K. (2012) *Social Work Methods and Skills*. Basingstoke: Palgrave Macmillan.

Healy, K. (2014) *Social Work Theories in Context* (2nd edn). Basingstoke: Palgrave Macmillan.

Hearn, J., Edwards, J. & Popay, J. (1998) *Men, Gender Divisions and Welfare*. London: Routledge.

Hennessey, R. (2011) *Relationship Based Social Work*. London: Sage Publications.

Hepworth, D., Rooney, R., Rooney, G., Strom-Gottfried, K. & Larson, J. (2010) *Direct Social Work Practice: Theory and Skills*. Belmont, CA: Brooks/Cole.

Heslop, P. (2016) 'How I care': foster fathers recount their experiences of caring for children, *Adoption & Fostering*, *40*(1): 36–48.

Hills, J. (2013) *Introduction to Systemic and Family Therapy*. London: Palgrave Macmillan.

Hingley-Jones, H. & Ruch, G. (2016) 'Stumbling through'? Relationship-based social work practice in austere times, *Psychotherapeutic Approaches in Health, Welfare and the Community*, *30*(3): 235–48.

HM Government (2018) *Working Together to Safeguard Children: A Guide to Inter-agency Working to Safeguard and Promote the Welfare of Children*. Available at https://assets.publishing.service.gov.uk/government/uploads/system/uploads/attachment_data/file/722305/Working_Together_to_Safeguard_Children_-_Guide.pdf (accessed 7 July 2018).

Hobbs, A. & Alonzi, A. (2013) Mediation and family group conferences in adult safeguarding, *Journal of Adult Protection*, *15*(2): 69–84.

Hohman, M., Pierce, P. & Barnett, E. (2015) Motivational interviewing: an evidence-based practice for improving students' skills, *Journal of Social Work Education*, *51*(2): 287–97.

Hollomotz, A. (2009) Beyond vulnerability: an ecological model approach to conceptualising risk of sexual violence against people with learning difficulties, *British Journal of Social Work*, *39*(1): 99–112.

Holmes, M. (2007) *What is Gender? Sociological Approaches*. London: Sage Publications.

Home Office (1991) *Working Together under the Children Act 1989: A Guide to Arrangements for Inter-agency Co-operation for the Protection of Children from Abuse*. London: HMSO.

Hothersall, S. & Maas-Lowit, M. (2010) *Need, Risk and Protection in Social Work Practice*. Exeter: Learning Matters.

Hough, R. E. (2012) Adult protection and 'intimate citizenship' for people with learning difficulties: empowering and protecting in light of the No Secrets review, *Disability and Society*, *27*(1): 131–44.

Howe, D. (1999) *Attachment Theory, Child Maltreatment and Family Support: A Practice and Assessment Model*. Basingstoke: Macmillan.

Howe, D. (2009) *A Brief Introduction to Social Work Theory*. Basingstoke: Macmillan.

Hudson, C. (2000) At the edge of chaos: a new paradigm for social work, *Journal of Social Work Education*, *36*(2): 215–30.

Hudson, C. (2010) *Complex Systems and Human Behaviour*. Chicago, IL: Lyceum.

Hugman, R. (1991) Organization and professionalism: the social work agenda in the 1990s, *British Journal of Social Work*, *21*(3): 199–216.

Hugman, R. (2003) Professional values and ethics in social work: reconsidering postmodernism, *British Journal of Social Work*, *33*: 1025–41.

Humphrey, D. (2018) 'Task-centred Intervention'. In J. Lishman, C. Yuill, J. Brannan & A. Gibson (eds), *Social Work an Introduction* (second edn) (pp. 311–25). London: Sage Publications.

Ibarra, H. (1999) Provisional selves: experimenting with image and identity in professional adaptation, *Administrative Science Quarterly*, *44*(4): 764–91.

IFSW (2012) *Statement of Ethical Principles*. Available at http://ifsw.org/policies/statement-of-ethical-principles/ (accessed 1 March 2018).

IFSW (2017) *Global Definition of Social Work*. Available at www.ifsw.org/what-is-social-work/global-definition-of-social-work/ (accessed 1 February 2018).

Ingram, R. (2013) Locating emotional intelligence at the heart of social work practice, *British Journal of Social Work*, *43*(5): 987–1004.

Ipsos MORI (2015) 'Later life in 2015: an analysis of the views and experiences of people aged 50 and over'. London: Centre for Ageing Better. Available at www.ageing-better.org.uk (accessed 1 December 2017).

Jack, G. (1997) An ecological approach to social work with children and families, *Child & Family Social Work*, *2*:109–20.

Jack, G. (2000) Ecological influences on parenting and child development, *British Journal of Social Work*, *30*(6): 703–20.

Jewett, C. (1994) *Helping Children Cope with Separation and Loss*. Boston, MA: The Harvard Common Press.

Johnson, M. (2008) *Domestic Violence and Child Abuse: What is the Connection – Do We Know?* (pp. 10), National Council on Family Relations. Available at www.ncfr.org/ncfr-report/focus/child-abuse-neglect/domestic-violence-and-child-abuse-what-connection-do-we-know

Johnson, M. & Ferraro, K. (2000) Research on domestic violence in the 1990s: making distinctions, *Journal of Marriage and the Family*, *62*(4): 948–63.

Jones, C. & Hackett, S. (2011) The role of 'family practices' and 'displays of family' in the creation of adoptive kinship, *British Journal of Social Work*, *41*(1): 40–56.

Jones, O. (2016) *Chavs: The Demonization of the Working Class*. London: Verso.

Jordan, S. (2017) Relationship based social work practice: the case for considering the centrality of humour in creating and maintaining relationships, *Journal of Social Work Practice*, *31*(1): 95–110.

Kahneman, D. (2011) *Thinking, Fast and Slow*. London: Penguin.

Kemshall, H. (2013) *Working with Risk*. Cambridge: Polity.

Kerr, M. E. & Bowen, M. (1988) *Family Evaluation: An Approach based on Bowen Theory*. New York: Norton.

Kimmell, A. & Gockel, A. (2017) Embodied connections: engaging the body in group work, *Qualitative Social Work*, *17*(2): 268–85.

Kirin, C. (2016) How three conversations have changed the way we do social work, *Community Care* (3 May).

Klein, G. (1998) *Sources of Power: How People Make Decisions*. Cambridge, MA: MIT Press.

Klein, G. (2004) *The Power of Intuition*. New York: Doubleday.

Knight, C. & Gitterman, A. (2017) Merging micro and macro intervention: social work practice with groups in the community, *Journal of Social Work Education*, *54*(1): 3–17.

Kolb, D. (1984) *Experiential Learning as the Science of Learning and Development*. Englewood Cliffs, NJ: Prentice Hall.

Koprowska, J. (2014) *Communication & Interpersonal Skills in Social Work*. London: Sage Publications.

Lamb, M. and Tamis-Lemonda, C. (2004) 'The Role of the Father: An Introduction'. In M. Lamb (ed.), *The Role of the Father in Child Development* (4th edn). Chichester: Wiley.

Lambert, M. & Crossley, S. (2017) 'Getting with the (troubled families) programme': a review, *Social Policy & Society*, *16*(1): 87–97.

Lammy, D. (2017) 'Africa Deserves Better from Comic Relief', *Guardian*. Available at www.theguardian.com/commentisfree/2017/mar/24/africa-comic-relief (accessed 1 February 2017).

LaRocque, S. (2017) Group work education in social work: a review of the literature reveals possible solutions, *Journal of Social Work Education*, *53*(2): 276–85.

Larson, M. S. (1977) *The Rise of Professionalism: A Sociological Analysis*. Berkeley: University of California Press.

Law Commission (2011) *Adult Social Care*. Available at www.lawcom.gov.uk/app/uploads/2015/03/lc326_adult_social_care.pdf (accessed 1 February 2017).

Lee, C. (2014) Conservative comforts: some philosophical crumbs for social work, *British Journal of Social Work*, *44*: 2135–44.

Liberty (n.d.) *Human Rights*. Available at www.libertyhumanrights.org.uk/human-rights (accessed 1 February 2017).

Liebenberg, L., Ungar, M. and Ikeda, J. (2015) Neo-liberalism and responsibilisation in the discourse of social service workers, *British Journal of Social Work*, *45*(3): 1006–21.

Lightfoot, E., Hill, K. & LaLiberte, T. (2010) The inclusion of disability as a condition for termination of parental rights, *Child Abuse and Neglect*, *34*(12): 927–34.

Lindsay, T. (2013) 'Groupwork'. In T. Lindsay (ed.), *Social Work Intervention* (2nd edn) (pp. 91–108). London: Sage Publications.

Lindsay, T. & Orton, S. (2014) *Groupwork Practice in Social Work* (3rd edn). London: Sage.

Lishman, J. (2009) *Communication in Social Work*. Basingstoke: Palgrave.

Lishman, J. (2015) 'Research, Evaluation and Evidence Based Practice'. In J. Lishman (ed.), *Handbook for Practice Learning in Social Work and Social Care: Knowledge and Theory* (3rd edn) (pp. 455–77). London: Jessica Kingsley.

Lishman, J. (2018) 'Evaluation'. In J. Lishman, C. Yuill, J. Brannan & A. Gibson (eds), *Social Work: An Introduction* (2nd edn) (pp. 533–43). London: Sage Publications.

Luft, J. & Ingham, H. (1955) *The Johari Window, a Graphic Model of Interpersonal Awareness: Proceedings of the Western Training Laboratory in Group Development*. Los Angeles: University of California.

Luhmann, N. (1995) *Social Systems*. Stanford: Stanford University Press.

Lymbery, M. (2010) A new vision for adult social care? Continuities and change in the care of older people, *Critical Social Policy*, *30*(1): 5–25.

Macdonald, K. (1995) *The Sociology of Professions*. London: Sage Publications.

Main, M. & Solomon, J. (1990) 'Procedures for Identifying Infants as Disorganized-Disorientated during the Strange Situation'. In M. Greenberg, D. Cicchetti & E. M. Cummings (eds), *Attachment in the Pre-school Years: Theory Research and Intervention* (pp. 121–60). London: Guilford.

Mantell, A. & Scragg, T. (2011) *Safeguarding Adults in Social Work* (2nd edn). Exeter: Learning Matters.

Marsh, P. & Doel, M. (2005) *The Task-Centred Book*. Abingdon: Routledge.

Martin, R. (2010) *Social Work Assessment*. Exeter: Learning Matters.

Martins, C. (2014) *Appreciative Inquiry in Child Protection: Identifying and Promoting Good Practice and Creating a Learning Culture*. Totnes, Devon: Research in Practice.

Maslow, A. (1970 [1954]) *Motivation and Personality*. New York: Harper Collins.

Matthews, I. & Crawford, K. (2011) *Evidence-based Practice in Social Work*. Exeter: Learning Matters.

Mattsson, T. (2014) Intersectionality as a useful tool, *Affilia-Journal of Women and Social Work*, *29*(1): 8–17.

Mayer, J., Panter, A. & Caruso, D. (2012) Does personal intelligence exist? Evidence from a new ability-based measure, *Journal of Personality Assessment*, *94*(2): 124–40.

McColgan, M. (2013) 'Task-centred Work'. In T. Lindsay (ed.), *Social Work Intervention* (2nd edn). London: Sage Publications.

McFadden, E. J. (1998) Kinship care in the United States, *Adoption & Fostering*, *22*(3): 7–15.

McGinnis, E. (2013) 'Task-centred Work'. In T. Lindsay (ed.), *Social Work Intervention* (2nd edn) (pp. 35–51). London: Sage Publications.

McGoldrick, M., Gerson, R. & Petry, S. S. (2008) *Genograms: Assessment and Intervention* (3rd edn). New York: Norton.

McNicoll, A. (2016) '"Discredited" serious case review model to be scrapped community care'. Available at www.communitycare.co.uk/2016/05/31/discredited-serious-case-review-model-scrapped/ (accessed 3 March 2018).

Mental Health Foundation (2015) *Fundamental Facts about Mental Health 2015*. Available at www.mentalhealth.org.uk/sites/default/files/fundamental-facts-15.pdf (accessed 1 February 2017).

Miller, W. & Rollnick, S. (2013) *Motivational Interviewing: Helping People Change* (3rd edn). New York: Guilford.

Milner, J., Myers, S. & O'Byrne, P. (2015 [1998]) *Assessment in Social Work* (4th edn). Basingstoke: Palgrave Macmillan.

Morgan, D. H. J. (1996) *Family Connections*. Cambridge: Polity.

Munby, J. (2012) 'Safeguarding and Dignity: Protecting Liberties – When is Safeguarding Abuse?', *Brunswick Mental Health Care Review*, 7: 18, para 66.

Munro, E. (2011) *The Munro Review of Child Protection: A Child-centred System*. London: Department for Education.

Murphy-Jack, O. & Smethers, R. (2009) 'Recognition, respect, reward', *Grandparents Plus*. Available at www.grandparentsplus.org.uk/recognition-respect-reward (accessed 20 September 2017).

Naleppa, M. J. & Reid, W. J. (2003) *Gerontological Social Work: A Task-centered Approach*. New York: Columbia University Press.

Narey, M. (2014) *Making the Education of Social Workers Consistently Effective: Report of Sir Martin Narey's Independent Review of the Education of Children's Social Workers*. London: Department for Education, p. 45.

Neal, M. & Morgan, J. (2000) The professionalization of everyone? A comparative study of the development of the professions in the United Kingdom and Germany, *European Sociological Review*, *16*(1): 9–26.

Needham, C. (2014) Personalization: from day centres to community hubs? *Critical Social Policy*, *34* (1): 90–109.

NSPCC (2009a) *History of the NSPCC*. Available at www.nspcc.org.uk (accessed 21 July 2009).

NSPCC (2009b) Family Group Conferences in Child Protection. Available at www.nspcc.org.uk/globalassets/documents/information-service/factsheet-family-group-conferences-child-protection.pdf (accessed 1 March 2018).

Office for National Statistics (ONS) (2015) *Life Expectancy at Birth and at Age 65 by Local Areas in England and Wales: 2012 to 2014*. Available at www.ons.gov.uk/peoplepopulationandcommunity/birthsdeathsandmarriages/lifeexpectancies/bulletins/lifeexpectancyatbirthandatage65bylocalareasinenglandandwales/2015-11-04#national-life-expectancy-at-birth (accessed 20 September 2017).

Office for National Statistics (ONS) (2017) 'Domestic abuse, sexual assault and stalking: year ending March 2016'. Available at www.ons.gov.uk/peoplepopulationandcommunity/crimeandjustice/bulletins/domesticabuseinenglandandwales/yearendingmarch2016 (accessed 3 March 2018).

Oliver, M. (1990) *The Politics of Disablement*. Basingstoke: Macmillan.

Oliver, M. (1996) 'The Politics of Disablement'. In M. Oliver (ed.), *Understanding Disability: From Theory to Practice*. Basingstoke: Macmillan.

Olkin, R., Abrams, K., Preston, P. & Kirshbaum, M. (2006) Comparison of parents with and without disabilities raising teens: information from the NHS and two national surveys. *Rehabilitation Psychology*, *51*(1): 43–9.

Olsen, R. & Wates, M. (2003) *Disabled Parents: Examining Research Assumptions*. Dartington: Research in Practice.

O'Sullivan, T. (2011) *Decision Making in Social Work* (2nd edn). Basingstoke: Palgrave Macmillan.

Oxford English Dictionary (n.d.) Available at www.oxforddictionaries.com/

Parker, J. (2007) Crisis intervention: a practice model for people who have dementia and their carers, *Practice*, *19*(2): 115–26.

Parker, J. (2017) *Social Work Practice: Assessment, Planning, Intervention and Review* (5th edn). London: Learning Matters/Sage Publications.

Parker, J. & Bradley, G. (2014) *Social Work Practice* (4th edn). London: Sage Publications.

Parsons, T. (1951) *The Social System*. Glencoe, IL: Free Press.

Partners4Change (2016) Three conversations – multiple benefits. Available at http://partners4change.co.uk/three-conversations-multiple-benefits/ (accessed 1 March 2018).

Partners4Change (n.d.) Available at http://partners4change.co.uk/ (accessed 1 March 2018).

Parton, N. & O'Byrne, P. (2000) *Constructive Social Work: Towards a New Practice*. Basingstoke: Palgrave.

Payne, M. (2002) 'Social Work Theories and Reflective Practice'. In R. Adams, L. Dominelli and M. Payne (eds), *Social Work: Themes, Issues and Critical Debates*. Basingstoke: Palgrave.

Payne, M. (2005) *Modern Social Work Theory* (4th edn). Basingstoke: Macmillan.

Payne, M. (2006) *Narrative Therapy: An Introduction for Counsellors* (2nd edn). Thousand Oaks, CA: Sage Publications.

Payne, M. (2011) *Humanistic Social Work: Core Principles in Practice*. Basingstoke: Palgrave Macmillan.

Pennell, J. & Anderson, G. (2005) *Widening the Circle: The Practice and Evaluation of Family Group Conferencing with Children, Youths, and Their Families*. Washington DC: NASW.

Petrides, K. & Furnham, A. (2000) On the dimensional structure of emotional intelligence, *Personality and Individual Differences*, *29*: 313–20.

Pfau-Effinger, B. (2004) Socio-historical paths of the male breadwinner model: an explanation of cross-national differences, *British Journal of Sociology*, *55*: 377–99.

Phung, T. (2018) 'Relationship-based Social Work'. In J. Lishman, C. Yuill, J. Brannan & A. Gibson (eds), *Social Work: An Introduction* (2nd edn) (pp. 267–79). London: Sage Publications.

Piaget, J. (1955 [1976]) *The Child's Construction of Reality* (trans. M. Cook). London: Routledge and Kegan Paul.

Piaget, J. (2001) *The Psychology of Intelligence*. London: Routledge.

Piaget, J. & Gruber, H. E. (1977) *The Essential Piaget*. London: Routledge and Kegan Paul.

Piaget, J. & Inhelder, B. R. (2000) *The Psychology of the Child*. New York: Basic.

Poll, C., Duffy, S., Hatton, C., Sanderson, H. & Routledge, M. (2006) 'A report on In Control's first phase 2003–2005'. Available at www.in-control.org.uk/media/55724/in%20control%20first%20phase%20report%202003-2005.pdf (accessed 18 April 2018).

Postle, K. (2002) Working 'between the idea and the reality': ambiguities and tensions in care managers' work, *British Journal of Social Work*, *32*(3): 335–51.

Prochaska, J. & DiClemente, C. (1983) Stages and processes of self-change in smoking: toward an integrative model of change, *Journal of Consulting and Clinical Psychology*, *5*: 390–5.

Pullen-Sansfacon, A. & Ward, D. (2014) Making interprofessional working work: introducing a groupwork perspective, *British Journal of Social Work*, *44*(5): 1284–1300.

Putnam, R. (2000) *Bowling Alone: The Collapse and Revival of American Community*. New York: Simon and Schuster.

Ravenera, Z. (2007) Informal networks social capital of fathers: what does the engagement survey tell us? *Social Indicators Research*, *83*: 351–73.

Ray, M. & Phillips, J. (2012) *Social Work with Older People*. Basingstoke: Palgrave Macmillan.

Rees, A., Holland, S. & Pithouse, A. (2012) Food in foster families: care, communication and conflict, *Children and Society*, *26*(2): 100–111.

Reid, W. J. (1978) *The Task-Centred System*. New York: Columbia University Press.

Reid, W. J. & Epstein, L. (1972) *Task-Centred Casework*. New York: Columbia University Press.

Reid, W. J. & Shyne, A. (1969) *Brief and Extended Casework*. New York: Columbia University Press.

Ribbens, J., McCarthy, J. & Edwards, R. (2011) *Key Concepts in Family Studies*. London: Sage Publications.

Richmond, M. E. (1917) *Social Diagnosis*. New York: Russell Sage Foundation.

Richmond, M. E. (1922) *What is Social Case Work? An Introductory Description.* New York: Russell Sage Foundation.

Riessman, C. K. (1993) *Narrative Analysis.* London: Sage Publications.

Roberts, A. (1991) 'Conceptualizing Crisis Theory and the Crisis Intervention Model'. In A. Roberts (ed.), *Contemporary Perspectives on Crisis Intervention and Prevention* (pp. 3–17). Englewood Cliffs, NJ: Prentice-Hall.

Roberts, A. (2005) *Crisis Intervention Handbook: Assessment, Treatment and Research* (3rd edn). Oxford: Oxford University Press.

Rogers, C. (1961 [2004]) *On Becoming a Person: A Therapist's View of Psychotherapy.* London: Constable.

Rogers, M., Whitaker, D., Edmondson, D. & Peach, D. (2017) *Developing Skills for Social Work.* London: Sage.

Roulstone, A. & Morgan, H. (2009) 'Neo-liberal individualism or self-directed support: are we all speaking the same language on modernising adult social care?, *Social Policy and Society*, *8*(3): 333–45.

Ruch, G., Turney, D. & Ward, A. (2010) *Relationship-based Social Work: Getting to the Heart of Practice.* London: Jessica Kingsley.

Rutter, L. and Brown, K. (2015) *Critical Thinking & Professional Judgement in Social Work* (4th edn). London: Sage Publications.

Saleeby, D. (2013) *The Strengths Perspective in Social Work Practice* (6th edn). Boston, MA: Allyn & Bacon.

Salovey, P. & Grewal, D. (2005) The science of emotional intelligence, *Current Developments in Psychological Science*, *14*(6): 281–5.

Saltiel, D. (2013) Understanding complexity in families' lives: the usefulness of 'family practices' as an aid to decision-making, *Child and Family Social Work*, *18*(1): 15–24.

Schloendorff v. Society of New York Hospital, 211 N.Y. 125 (N.Y. 1914).

Schön, D. (1983) *The Reflective Practitioner: How Professionals Think in Action.* New York: Basic.

SCIE (2015a) Care Act 2014: Assessment and Eligibility Process Map. Available at www.scie.org.uk/care-act-2014/assessment-and-eligibility/process-map/ (accessed 1 February).

SCIE (2015b) *Care Act 2014: Strengths-based Approaches.* Available at www.scie.org.uk/care-act-2014/assessment-and-eligibility/strengths-based-approach/ (accessed 1 March 2018).

Scourfield, J. (2006) The challenge of engaging fathers in the child protection process, *Critical Social Policy*, *26*(2): 440–9.

Scourfield, J., Alley, C., Coffey, A. & Yates, P. (2016) Working with fathers of at-risk children: insights from a qualitative process evaluation of an intensive group-based intervention, *Children and Youth Services Review*, *69*: 259–67.

Scourfield, P. (2007) Social care and the modern citizen: client, consumer, service user, manager and entrepreneur, *British Journal of Social Work*, *37*: 107–22.

Serbati, S. (2017) 'You won't take away my children!': families' participation in child protection: lessons since a best practice, *Children and Youth Services Review*, *82*: 214–21.

Shakespeare, T. (2000) *Help: Imagining Welfare.* Birmingham: Venture.

Shakespeare, T. & Watson, N. (2002) The social model of disability: an outdated ideology? *Research in Social Science and Disability*, 2: 9–28.

Shell, R. (2006) *Bargaining for Advantage.* New York: Penguin.

Shennan, G. (2014) *Solution Focused Practice: Effective Communication to Facilitate Change.* Basingstoke: Palgrave Macmillan.

Sheppard, D. & Clibbens, J. (2015) Preventive therapy and resilience promotion: an evaluation of social work led skills development group work, *Child & Family Social Work*, *20*(3): 288–99.

Signs of Safety (n.d.) *Signs of Safety.* Available at www.signsofsafety.net/signs-of-safety/ (accessed 1 February 2018).

Skinner, B. F., Catania, A. C. & Harnad, S. (1988) *The Selection of Behavior: The Operant Behaviorism of B. F. Skinner: Comments and Consequences.* Cambridge: Cambridge University Press.

Sklare, G. (1997) *Brief Counseling That Works.* Thousand Oaks, CA: Corwin.

Slade, M. (2009) *Personal Recovery and Mental Illness: A Guide for Mental Health Professionals.* Cambridge: Cambridge University Press.

Slay, H. & Smith, D. (2011) Professional identity construction: using narrative to understand the negotiation of professional and stigmatized cultural identities, *Human Relation*, *64*(1): 85–107.

Smale, G. & Tuson, G. (1993) *Empowerment, Assessment, Care Management and the Skilled Worker.* London: National Institute for Social Work.

Smethurst, C. (2011) 'Working with Risk'. In T. Scragg and M. Mantell (eds), *Safeguarding Adults in Social Work*. Exeter: Learning Matters.

Smith, M. (2010) A brief history of (residential child care) ethics, *Scottish Journal of Residential Child Care*, *9*(2): 2–10.

Social Services Inspectorate (1995) *The Challenge of Partnership in Child Protection: Practice Guide.* London: HMSO.

The Social Work Reform Board (2012) *Building a safe and confident future: Maintaining momentum, progress report from the Social Work Reform Board*. Available at https://assets.publishing.service.gov.uk/government/uploads/system/uploads/attachment_data/file/175947/SWRB_progress_report_-_June_2012.pdf

Stevens, M., Woolham, J., Manthorpe, J., Aspinall, F., Hussein, S., Baxter, K., Samsi, K. & Ismail, M. (2018) Implementing safeguarding and personalisation in social work: findings from practice, *Journal of Social Work*, *18*(1): 3–22.

Stevenson, L. (2014) Sir James Munby: 'Re B-S ruling has not changed the law on adoption', *Community Care*. Available at www.communitycare.co.uk/2014/12/16/sir-james-munby-re-b-s-ruling-changed-law-adoption/ (accessed 1 February 2018).

Stevenson, O. (2005) Genericism and specialization: the story since 1970, *British Journal of Social Work*, *35*(5): 569–86.

Stevenson, O. (2007) *Neglected Children and Their Families* (2nd edn). Oxford: Blackwell.

Stewart, M. (2012) 'Understanding Learning: Theories and Critiques'. In L. Hunt & D. Charmers (eds), *University Teaching in Focus: A Learning-centred Approach* (pp. 3–20). Victoria, Australia: Acer.

Stickle, M. (2016) The expression of compassion in social work practice, *Journal of Religion & Spirituality in Social Work: Social Thought*, *35*(Issue 1–2: 'Mindfulness and Social Work'): 120–31.

Strauss, A. (1978) *Negotiations: Varieties, Contexts, Processes, and Social Order*. San Francisco, CA: Jossey-Bass.

Sutton, C. (1999) *Helping Families with Troubled Children*. Chichester: Wiley.

Swindell, M. (2014) 'Compassionate Competence: A New Model for Social Work Practice'. *The New Social Worker*, Spring. Available at www.socialworker.com/feature-articles/practice/compassionate-competence-a-new-model-for-social-work-practi/ (accessed 1 December 2017).

Taylor, B. (2013) *Professional Decision Making and Risk in Social Work*. London: Sage Publications.

Taylor, C. & White, S. (2000) *Practising Reflexivity in Health and Welfare: Making Knowledge.* Buckingham: Open University Press.

Tew, J. (2013) Recovery capital: what enables a sustainable recovery from mental health difficulties? *European Journal of Social Work*, *16*: 360–74.

The Bowen Center (n.d.) 'The eight concepts'. Available at https://thebowencenter.org/theory/eight-concepts/ (accessed 1 March 2018).

The Children's Society (2015) *Cuts that Cost: Trends in Funding for Early Intervention Services.* Available at www.childrenssociety.org.uk/what-we-do/resources-and-publications/cuts-that-cost-trends-in-funding-for-early-intervention (accessed 3 March 2018).

The College of Social Work (2013) *Advice Note: Roles and Tasks Requiring Social Workers Consultation Document*. Available at http://cdn.basw.co.uk/upload/basw_41135-9.pdf

The Spectator (1869) News of the week: 'Mr Goschen has published an able minute…'. Available at http://archive.spectator.co.uk/article/27th-november-1869/2/mr-goschen-has-published-an-able-minute-on-the-nec (accessed 6 November 2017).

Think Local, Act Personal (TLAP) (2014) *Delivering Care and Support Planning Supporting Implementation of the Care Act 2014*. Available at www.thinklocalactpersonal.org.uk/_assets/Resources/SDS/TLAPCareSupportPlanning.pdf (accessed 1 December 2017).

Think Local, Act Personal (TLAP) (2018) *Think Local, Act Personal*. Available at www.thinklocalactpersonal.org.uk/ (accessed 1 March 2018).

Thompson, N. (2002) *People Skills*. Basingstoke: Palgrave Macmillan.

Thompson, N. (2011) *Effective Communication: A Guide for the People Professions* (2nd edn). Basingstoke: Palgrave Macmillan.

Thompson, N. (2015) *Understanding Social Work* (4th edn). Basingstoke: Palgrave Macmillan.

Trevithick, P. (2014) *Social Work Skills and Knowledge: A Practice Handbook* (3rd edn). London: Open University Press.

Trussell Trust (2017) *The UK Foodbank Network*. Available at www.trusselltrust.org (accessed 3 March 2018).

Tuckman, B. (1965) Development sequence in small groups, *Psychological Bulletin*, *63*(6): 384–99.

Tuckman, B. & Jensen, M. (1977) Stages of small group development revisited. *Group Organization Management*, *2*(4): 419–27.

Tulle, E. & Lynch, E. (2011) 'Later Life'. In C. Yuill and A. Gibson (eds), *Sociology for Social Work: An Introduction*. London: Sage Publications.

Turbett, C. (2014) *Doing Radical Social Work*. Basingstoke: Palgrave Macmillan.

Turnell, A. (2012) *The Signs of Safety: Comprehensive Briefing Paper*. Perth, Australia: Resolutions Consultancy Pty Ltd.

Turnell, A. & Edwards, S. (1999) *Signs of Safety: A Safety and Solution Orientated Approach to Child Protection Casework*. New York: Norton.

United Nations (1989) Convention on the Rights of the Child. Available at www.unicef.org.uk/what-we-do/un-convention-child-rights (accessed 1 September 2017).

United Nations Committee on the Rights of Persons with Disabilities (2016) *Inquiry concerning the United Kingdom of Great Britain and Northern Ireland carried out by the Committee under article 6 of the Optional Protocol to the Convention Report of the Committee*. Available at https://digitallibrary.un.org/record/1310721?ln=en (accessed 3 March 2018).

Van der Gaag, A., Gallagher, A., Zasada, M., Lucas, G., Jago, R., Banks, S. and Austin, Z. (2017) People like us? Understanding complaints about paramedics and social workers: Final report to the HCPC'. Available at www.hcpc-uk.org/assets/documents/1000558EPeoplelikeusFinalReport.pdf (accessed 10 October 2017).

Van Dijk, T. (2011) 'Introduction: The Study of Discourse'. In T. Van Dijk (ed.), *Discourse Studies: A Multidisciplinary Introduction*. London: Sage Publications.

Varese, F., Smeets, F., Drukker, M., Lieverse, R., Lataster, T., Viechtbauer, W., Read. J., van Os, J. & Bentall, R. P. (2012) Childhood adversities increase the risk of psychosis: a meta-analysis of patient-control, prospective- and cross-sectional cohort studies, *Schizophrenia Bulletin*, *38*(4): 661–71.

Vassos, E., Pedersen, C. B., Murray, R. M., Collier, D. A. & Lewis, C. M. (2012) Meta-analysis of the association of urbanicity with schizophrenia, *Schizophrenia Bulletin*, *38*(6): 1118–23.

Veling, W., Susser, E., van Os, J. Mackenbach, J. P., Selten, J. P. & Hoek, H. W. (2008) Ethnic density of neighborhoods and incidence of psychotic disorders among immigrants, *American Journal of Psychiatry*, *165*(1): 66–73.

Vygotsky, L.S. (2016 [1966]) Play and its role in the mental development of the child, *International Research in Early Childhood Education, 7*, 2. [See pp. 6–20]. Original article translated from Russian by Nikolai Veresov and Myra Barrs. Available at https://files.eric.ed.gov/fulltext/EJ1138861.pdf (accessed 4 September 2018).

Vygotsky, L. (1978) *Mind in Society*. Cambridge, MA: Harvard University Press.

Watkins, C. (2017) 'What works (and what doesn't) when celebrating social workers' successes'. Available at www.communitycare.co.uk/2017/11/06/works-doesnt-celebrating-social-workers-successes/ (accessed 1 March 2018).

Watson, J. (2011) Resistance is futile? Exploring the potential of motivational interviewing, *Journal of Social Work Practice*, *25*(4): 465–79.

Webb, S. (2006) *Social Work in a Risk Society*. Basingstoke: Palgrave Macmillan.

Webber, M. and Joubert, L. (2015) Social work and recovery, *British Journal of Social Work*, *45* (1): i1–i8.

Weeks, J., Heapy, B. & Donovan, C. (2007) 'The Lesbian and Gay Family'. In J. Scott, J. Treas & M. Richards (eds), *The Blackwell Companion to the Sociology of Families*. Oxford: Blackwell.

Weld, N. (2008) 'The Three Houses Tool: Building Safety and Positive Change'. In M. Calder (ed.), *Contemporary Risk Assessment in Safeguarding Children*. Lyme Regis: Russell House.

West, C. & Zimmerman, D. (1987) Doing gender, *Gender and Society*, *1* (2): 125–51.

Weston, K. (1991) *We Choose: Lesbians, Gays, Kinship*. New York: Columbia University Press.

Whalley, P. & Williams, M. (2015) *Child Neglect and Video Interaction Guidance: An Evaluation of an NSPCC Service Offered to Parents Where Initial Concerns of Neglect Have Been Noted*. London: NSPCC.

Wicks, S., Hjern, A. & Dalman, C. (2010) Social risk or genetic liability for psychosis? A study of children born in Sweden and reared by adoptive parents, *American Journal of Psychiatry*, *167*(10): 1240–6.

Wijedasa, D. (2015) 'The prevalence and characteristics of children growing up with relatives in the UK: Briefing paper 001'. Bristol: Hadley Research Centre for Adoption and Foster Studies.

Wiles, F. (2013) Not easily put into a box: constructing professional identity, *Social Work Education: The International Journal*, *32*(7): 854–66.

Williams, S. and Rutter, L. (2015) *The Practice Educator's Handbook (Post-Qualifying Social Work Practice Series*. Exeter: Learning Matters.

Wilson, K., Ruch, G., Lymbery, M. and Cooper, A. (2011) *Social Work: An Introduction to Contemporary Practice*. Harlow: Pearson Education.

Winter, K., Cree, V., Hallett, S., Hadfield, M., Ruch, G., Morrison, F. & Holland, S. (2017) Exploring communication between social workers, children and young people, *British Journal of Social Work*, *47* (5): 1427–44.

Women's Aid (2017) 'How common is domestic abuse?' Available at www.womensaid.org.uk/information-support/what-is-domestic-abuse/how-common-is-domestic-abuse/ (accessed 13 December 2017).

Wood, L. and Kroger, R. (2000) *Doing Discourse Analysis: Methods for Studying Action in Talk and Text*. London: Sage Publications.

World Health Organization (2016) *Disabilities*. Available at www.who.int/topics/disabilities/en/ (accessed 3 January 2018).

Wyke, J. (2013) 'Support Groups: What They Do and How They Help'. In D. Pitcher (ed.), *Inside Kinship-care: Understanding Family Dynamics and Providing Effective Support*. London: Jessica Kingsley.

Yuval-Davis, N. (2006) Intersectionality and feminist politics, *European Journal of Women's Studies*, *13*(3): 193–209.

INDEX

Note: tables and figures are indicated by page numbers in bold print.